RAHEL KERN was born in Germany in 1978 but moved to England after completing school education. She studied for a BA and MA in Philosophy at the University of Reading with a particular focus on modern European Philosophy. She has been an avid student of anthroposophy since her teens, with a particular interest in Steiner's contributions to philosophy and the evolution of consciousness, as reflected in the development of thought throughout the centuries. She currently lives in London and works in international marketing. Her work takes her on frequent travels around the globe.

 BRIEN MASTERS' career has included two professions, in music and education, the latter the focus of his PhD. In addition, he has pursued a decades-long interest in the anthroposophical approach to karma and reincarnation, which has resulted in lectures and workshops on Schubert, Wagner, Böcklin and Garibaldi, and published articles on Emerson and Oliphant. After various appointments, which included lengthy periods serving as Choirmaster and Organist in the Anglican Church, Chair of the Steiner Schools Fellowship, Editor of *Child and Man/Steiner Education* and Director of the London Waldorf Teacher Training Seminar, Brien Masters is now largely retired, though still lecturing and writing.

Kindling the Word

The Karmic Background of Marie Steiner-von Sivers

RAHEL KERN
and
BRIEN MASTERS

TEMPLE LODGE

To our friend Lenka

Temple Lodge Publishing
Hillside House, The Square
Forest Row, RH18 5ES

www.templelodge.com

Published by Temple Lodge in association with Perevale Publications 2012

© Rahel Kern and Brien Masters 2012

The moral rights of the authors have been asserted under the Copyright, Designs and Patents Act, 1988

All rights reserved. No part of this publication may be reproduced, stored in a retrieval system, or transmitted, in any form or by any means, electronic, mechanical, photocopying or otherwise, without the prior permission of the publishers

A catalogue record for this book is available from the British Library

ISBN 978 1 906999 42 1

Cover by Andrew Morgan Design
Typeset by DP Photosetting, Neath, West Glamorgan
Printed and bound in the UK by 4edge Limited, Essex

Contents

1	**Proem** A Karmic Door Opens *Brien Masters*	1
2	**Introduction** The Grounding of Anthroposophy *Rahel Kern & Brien Masters*	7
	Orpheus with his Lute *William Shakespeare*	11
3	**Marie Steiner-von Sivers I** Following in the Footsteps of Her Childhood *Brien Masters*	13
4	**Marie Steiner-von Sivers II** The Confluence of Two Wellsprings of the Spirit *Brien Masters*	19
	Hypatie *Leconte de Lisle*	37
5	**Marie Steiner-von Sivers III** By Word of Mouth *Brien Masters*	39
6	**Orpheus** His Song and the River of Time *Brien Masters*	51
	Metamorphoses *Ovid*	59
7	**Pherecydes of Syros** Bifocal Vision Emerging in Greek Consciousness *Rahel Kern*	61
8	**Hypatia of Alexandria** New Perspectives on her Personality *Rahel Kern*	67
	Epigram *Palladas*	85
9	**Albertus Magnus I** The Cultural Hinterland of Scholasticism *Rahel Kern*	87

10	**Albertus Magnus II** His Life's Path and Meeting with Thomas Aquinas *Rahel Kern*	93
	Theology as a Science *Albertus Magnus*	105
11	**Albertus Magnus III** Scholasticism and its Resurgence in Anthroposophy *Rahel Kern*	107
12	**What was the Point of Gothic?** Architecture and the Development of Human Consciousness *Brien Masters*	125
13	**The Mission of Drama** And its Alignment with Music Drama and Mystery Drama *Brien Masters*	131
	Dialogue at the Sepulchre on Easter Morning	139
14	**Heads and Tales** Being Aware of Both Sides of the Steiners' Spiritual Coin *Brien Masters*	141
15	**Redemption of the Senses** Fading 'Into the Light of Common Day' and Beyond *Rahel Kern*	147
16	**The Karmic Background of Marie Steiner-von Sivers** Tracing How Awareness Filtered Through *Brien Masters*	159
17	**Summary and Conclusion** Libretto for the West *Rahel Kern & Brien Masters*	167
	The Stars Spake Once to Man *Rudolf Steiner*	181
	Sequence of Events	182
	Notes	187
	Bibliography	199

1
Proem

A Karmic Door Opens

Brien Masters

The connection between the two co-authors of this karmic study began, broadly and externally speaking, within the context of the London Waldorf Teacher Training Seminar: Rahel as one of the students, Brien as one of the tutors. After Rahel's 'graduation', her destiny drew her back to England where her unusually strong roots became known to her former tutor. Through a mutual acquaintance (a fellow student), she had already once been to visit the historic garden that was in the possession of the erstwhile tutor's family. The visit chimed in with her enjoyment of a breath of country air (out of London) and her love of Englishness, here in the longstanding traditional form, yet at the same time a highly unusual and exceptionally beautiful garden.[1]

Slowly a connection emerged which superseded that of tutor and student: a search for what could be done to strengthen anthroposophy which, judging by the very modest number of those involved in anthroposophical events and the increasing difficulty of attracting modern people to undertake formal training for anthroposophical activities,[2] was navigating through a phase of severe doldrums after the fair winds that had filled its many sails in the 1980s/90s. Whatever *outer* attempts might be made to solve (or at least address) this problem, it became abundantly clear, during conversations that the two new friends had on subsequent visits to the garden, that little real progress would be likely to be made unless there was a deepening of inner anthroposophical work from which the focus, drive, inner fire and commitment would then be forthcoming to support, either directly or indirectly, whatever outer measures.

On one such visit there was time enough to explore this phenomenon at greater length than had been hitherto possible, which led to the ensuing questions: (a) What was Rudolf Steiner's core mission? (b) Had the direction in which anthroposophy had gone taken this core mission sufficiently into account? (c) What had the two of them done in their past anthroposophical work which touched on this? (d) What were their current interests? and (e) Might there be some room and reason for joining forces in some manner *along these lines*? Outwardly, circumstances did not look conducive to two people joining forces for a common study:

more than a train journey separated their two homes; and while Brien's schedule was fairly accommodating, Rahel's was anything but, with little free time on English soil and an itinerary that involved her in long flights to other parts of the world in order to carry out her daily work. Not only that, there seemed no obvious overlap at first of topics towards which their minds had been drawn, and in which their mutual concern could take root. Although the study of karmic relationships was a common interest, the two were looking at different human destinies; but there gleamed momentarily a look in Rahel's eye, when she expressed an interest that she had been nurturing for some time in Hypatia. This seemed worth noting as a valuable pointer, and led to the tentative decision being reached to go down that avenue of enquiry together.

The decision's tentativeness, however, was not long-lived. Imagine the uncanny feeling which followed the next day when Brien received an invitation from the organizer of the Friday lecture series in Rudolf Steiner House, London to 'speak about ...' and then followed a list of names, lifted out of the first lecture which Steiner gave in the Christmas days of 1910, on the theme of Occult History. David Lowe, the organizer, included *all* the individualities mentioned in the lecture (27 December) but then went on to say that other people who had been invited to contribute to the series had already chosen most of them. There was, however, one left lying on the shelf: Hypatia!

I am allowing myself a little 'artistic licence' in describing the course of events, as above, not because I wish to be sensational—the juxtaposition of the friends' research choice and the lecture organizer's email carries enough impact of its own—but because, as is so frequently the case, the study of karma can often be traced to some twist of destiny (let's call it), some seemingly external and unconnected incident—even another person's isolated remark can trigger it—which then ushers the karmic reality into the individual's life, while awakening awareness of that reality at some level or other. Several times Rudolf Steiner recounted some incident in his own life that pointed directly to such a twist of destiny, nudging him spiritually towards his own karmic research. Indeed, it would not be going too far to infer that he implied that *such research has in it of necessity a gift of grace coming from that spiritual being who presides over human karma*. In this case, the London invitation to lecture on Hypatia and her extraordinary destiny and karmic background left the two researchers in no doubt as to their being on the right track, and work began in earnest.

In the event, the Friday lecture (which took place in Rudolf Steiner House on 4 February 2011) became a team effort,[3] with both researchers—who had meanwhile been coordinating their work through meetings and correspondence—making contributions to the evening. Moreover, it was as if what came their way, by way of research through this sharing, did so with an unusual readiness. Within two months it was as if the reverse of a domino effect sprang into view, the first awareness of mutually discovered interest being the 'last' domino of a lengthy line to flip from the unseen horizontal into the visible vertical, with the penultimate domino following suit, until even on the eve of the lecture the last of a host of 'resources' hove into their shared view. With a vital difference! In this case, instead of the dominoes having shiny black blanks and up to twelve white blobs on their revealed surfaces, they 'popped up' with insights and mutually fructifying ideas—as one might expect in harmoniously motivated research, even though the research cluster consisted of only two people who were far too seldom geographically clustered.

Furthermore, and inevitably, in approximately the second half of the period to which attention is here being drawn, the investigation led from Rudolf Steiner's two or three brief but salient indications to those of his followers who had pursued a similar route and—inevitably again, since several key publications were written in German, which happily was Rahel's mother tongue—disclosed findings that had become part of the public domain only in recent years. This brought with it on the one hand feelings of immense thankfulness to those who had 'gone before'—duly acknowledged when their findings are referred to in the text—but on the other hand the need to question and make more precise our aim in the light of such a volume of painstaking material. Regarding the latter, it is a self-evident and therefore an unsurprising phase that every researcher faces in theory, and knows she will face. But when it happens in practice, it is a wonderful wit-awakener. In our case, it was little less than a driving force which clarified and affirmed still further the shared direction on which we had resolved.

That direction will probably be clearest by the time one has reached the end of the book. Suffice it to say here that (i) it confirmed us in our approach to make Hypatia the starting point of our research, which contrasted sharply with the approach that the other half dozen German writers had taken: making Marie Steiner-von Sivers their starting point, and in two notable cases, confining their biographical remarks to that one (albeit all-important) incarnation; and (ii) it imbued our aim not only to make the wealth of facts available to English readers but to try and achieve a book whose character reflected as far as possible that of the individual being portrayed, not only—I am tempted to say 'not merely' but would not want to be misunderstood—because the whole focus of the *content* of the book reveals more and more of that individual, but also because the book's style and structure reflect the individual's inner stance and impulse, seen against her karmic background. So what alternatives were there to a straightforward biography?

When Owen Barfield wrote his 'Afterword' to Thomas Meyer's biography of *D.N. Dunlop*,[4] he expressed his confirmed opinion that Meyer had placed biography on a footing that had not been achieved before. It came as a great delight, vaguely in the same vein, when the first biography of Barfield himself appeared in 2006, with Simon Blaxland-de Lange as its author, that the very structure of his biography revealed an exceptional quality of his 'subject'.[5] It would be over-pretentious to claim here to follow in these outstanding footsteps, and in any case, for a deeper reason which will become apparent, the present work is best regarded *not as a biography but as a study of an individuality*. Nevertheless, the co-authors have felt encouraged by the examples, and by other considerations, to give the study its present form. This resulted in the structure of the book, starting with the life of Marie Steiner-von Sivers even though our research had been prompted by Hypatia.

A core part of that study strives to identify, reveal and assess—or at least outline the significance of—the most recent incarnation of that individuality for her time. Not only to identify her significance, but to present it in such a way that may prompt or even inspire those of us who follow in her wake to enhance their realization of that significance and possibly identify that which is within their means and capabilities which might make a contribution to that impulse in her life, which itself was a contribution of the highest value to contemporary culture—contemporary in a sense that extends into an evolutionary epoch. For it is certain that her impulse does not confine itself to those decades which saw it coming to amazing fruition, though one must admit that the echoes of her impulse, so essential for Western humanity, were tragically muffled both by difficulties in the Anthroposophical Society which manifested in the 1930s[6] and in which Marie Steiner-von Sivers was herself a key player, and by the catastrophic intrusion into world evolution caused by the Second World War.

It is a major part of the aim of the present work, though in all modesty, to help the muffled echoes re-resonate. To help achieve that but without attempting to précis the content of this non-door-stopper-sized book here, or present its content in the style of a formal *abstract* of a thesis, it will perhaps be a useful guide to the reader if it is stated that the authors see that impulse as a major contribution to the importance that *art* played, as described by Rudolf Steiner in Torquay[7] in the spiritual development of Western civilization and thence in the next stage of world evolution.

Finally, it may be of technical interest to the reader to know how we parcelled out the extensive task of putting pen to paper, or tapping fingertips on computer keyboards—that the authors were not just one, but *two* generations removed, was beautifully reflected in the way their thoughts arrived (often tentative or hesitant, frequently rambling, on occasion heart-searching, sometimes ineffable, now and then astonishingly blunt) from unseen distances to become black, squiggly symbols on white paper! Thus, as it panned out, certain chapters were written by Rahel and others by Brien, each chapter after the first draft being shared, discussed, enhanced, clarified, pruned, grafted or otherwise edited together, albeit retaining the distinctive style of the two authors. But this is not quite all.

It was one of the Renaissance lutenists who conceived and composed a remarkable duet for two people but only one lute. Recently this was performed by man and wife, with the latter sitting on her partner's lap—though no doubt Renaissance 'man' would not have been queasy about such delicate gender issues that this raised! Fortunately *thoughts* can be co-marshalled without having to string oneself to the other person in such an intimate way. This good fortune resulted in the introductory and concluding chapters being co-authored. We hope that the reader will find the co-authorship, not only of these two chapters but of the study as a whole, a harmonious experience of this colleague and companion of Rudolf Steiner's, one that does justice to the Orphic dimension of her karmic background as well as an inspiration for restoring to the life of anthroposophy that which, inspired by Rudolf Steiner *as well as inspiring him*, was the mission to which she dedicated herself unreservedly, poignantly and with every fibre of her fiery being.

2

Introduction

The Grounding of Anthroposophy

Rahel Kern and Brien Masters

Rudolf Steiner's reply, written from his sick bed, to Walter Johannes Stein's letter (November 1924), not two months after *the last address*, presents a problem. It had become clear during the revelatory lectures in which Steiner presented his long-awaited research into karmic relationships—long awaited at least by himself and the Michaëlic powers in the spiritual world and equally long-resisted by the powers of opposition—that his core mission was the teaching of karma and reincarnation. To say simply that the abundant outpouring of this mission had been heartily welcomed by those who had attended the lectures would be an understatement. There were those, admittedly few, who immediately and strenuously put Steiner's recommended exercises for karmic research into practice—not without result. In his letter, Walter Johannes Stein, writing of insight he had gained into the karmic background of Alexander the Great, said how he planned to speak of this in a lecture he was to give shortly in Vienna. And now the problem: Steiner's reply was to applaud his plans *except for* the Alexander point.

There were no explanations, but we may take it that the question of exercising the utmost spiritual tact over the delicate matter of repeated earth lives was what hung in the balance—in this case, balanced against Stein's proposal. And Stein had probably got further in his research in this respect than almost all others. However, Steiner's warning, without being severe, was nevertheless clear and concurred with his often expressed view on the subject:

> [...A] contemplation [of karma and repeated earth life] requires the very greatest earnestness, for it may indeed be said that the temptation is very great for man to spin out all manner of ideas for karmic connections and repeated earth lives. The temptation is great; the source of illusion is exceedingly great.[1]

Bearing Steiner's reservations in mind, the present study has come about through the conviction of its two authors that in the case of Marie Steiner-von Sivers her karma and her mission holds something of vital importance for the spiritual and cultural development of the West. We arrived at this conviction by considering the work in which Marie Steiner-von Sivers was involved through her life partnership with Rudolf Steiner and in the light of three of her previous incarnations, in the Ancient Orphic Mysteries, as Hypatia in the fourth/fifth centuries AD, and as Albertus Magnus—as related in the following pages—not to mention her own exceptional, inherent talents.

All through our research, however, like a string of pearls, we were confronted with a number of recurring, penetrating questions:

- In view of her immense contribution to the development of anthroposophy from the moment that she and Rudolf Steiner began their collaboration, under the auspices of the Theosophical Society in 1902, throughout the next 23 years and beyond his death, why has she been seemingly so neglected? This neglect includes an appreciation of all that she undertook, achieved and developed, the conscious attribution of the part that she played, and the meticulous devotion with which she fulfilled her responsibility for the publication of Rudolf Steiner's literary estate.
- Compared with Rudolf Steiner himself and several others in his circle, why did studies concerning her life and work take so long before they were published?
- In spite of being the wife and tirelessly active partner of Rudolf Steiner in so many fields, was it inevitable that her life's work should be overshadowed by his incomparable achievements and his ability to turn his consummate skills in so many directions that life called for?
- Was it, in fact, an integral part of her very being that her personality should be veiled behind the zealous dedication and highly professional attitude with which she fulfilled her outer tasks?
- Was this facet of her life, moreover, a hallmark which can be traced through previous incarnations? Albertus Magnus, though the teacher of Aquinas, is generally acknowledged to have been superseded by his pupil; Hypatia, though hugely influential through attracting to Alexandria the illuminati of her day, has been far from adequately acknowledged in philosophical, historical, mathematical and astronomical areas (all those disciplines in which she excelled) by mainstream research; and in her incarnation within the Ancient Orphic Mysteries, though the teacher of the acclaimed Pherecydes of Syros, Steiner only refers to her as *die Namenlose* (the one who is nameless).[2]
- Considering that it has now come to light that Rudolf Steiner had arrived at the karmic connection between Hypatia and Albertus

through his spiritual research, why did he stop short and only 'intimate' that Hypatia's subsequent incarnation was at the turn of the twelfth and thirteenth century, and not go further and divulge who that was, either on that day or, if he only made the connection some time later, when he returned to the subject of occult history on another occasion?[3] He did return to this substantively, of course, on the occasion of the Christmas conference 1923/24.
- Given that Rudolf Steiner makes so much of the 'paradoxical grandeur' of Hypatia's violent death, and emphasizes that it was no mere act of petty jealousy on behalf of the Church officials in Alexandria but was symbolic of the part played by the human senses in the development of human consciousness, which was connected with the Orphic Mysteries, why does he make no reference to the second part of the 'myth' of Orpheus in relation to this?[4]
- Amidst the welter of all the above, how does Marie Steiner-von Sivers' mission in life come to be linked to Steiner's assertion in August 1924 that it is through art that the West will come closer to a reinstatement of the spirit in its world outlook?[5]
- How can Steiner's direct remark to Emil Molt be understood that it would not be appropriate to write a *biography* of Marie Steiner-von Sivers because 'sie ist ein kosmisches Wesen' (literally: 'she is a cosmic being'; or as one might interpret it: 'in her there dwells a cosmic being')? And has this remark, which filtered incisively into the canon of anthroposophical anecdote, had an inhibiting effect on the full appreciation of Marie Steiner-von Sivers' karmic stature?[6]

It was these questions which urged us forwards, caused us to reflect, confronted us with the occasional impasse and enthused and motivated us to continue, and made us realize that, while the subject we had aimed to address was seminal, it was not something to be nailed down in the manner of a painstakingly documented biography but in some other form. We looked for a form that embraced the unmistakable fact that the artistic nature of her incarnation as Marie Steiner-von Sivers together with the symptomatic nature of her mission as seen resounding in all her incarnations could be adequately acknowledged, artistically yet clearly presented, and experienced as a source of inspiration.

The structure that resulted from this consists of a number of essays in which the lives, deeds, cultural legacies and thought of the individuals concerned is addressed. These are interspersed with further essays in which themes are taken up which have bearing on the missions of both Rudolf Steiner and Marie Steiner; and with short extracts from literature which reverberate with *the word* in the sense in which Marie Steiner-von Sivers' karmic mission was so intimately intertwined with that of her lifelong work-companion and soul-partner, Rudolf Steiner.

Orpheus with his Lute[1]

William Shakespeare

Orpheus with his lute made trees,
And the mountain-tops that freeze,
Bow themselves when he did sing;
To his music plants and flowers
Ever sprung; as sun and showers
There had made a lasting spring.

Everything that heard him play,
Even the billows of the sea,
Hung their heads and then lay by.
In sweet music is such art;
Killing care and grief of heart
Fall asleep, or, hearing, die.

3
Marie Steiner-von Sivers I

Following in the Footsteps of her Childhood

Brien Masters

The special quality of the Baltic States, Estonia, Latvia and Lithuania, becomes transparent almost on first landfall. I am particularly thinking of midsummer time. Though not as competitive on the clock as in Finland and the vast spaces that lie within the Arctic circle, the lingering light at the end of each day, caressing the half darkness of the nights and the soft call of dawn to return from dreamland and take up again the day's work, wraps both nature and the social landscape in some sort of gentle spiritual ecstasy. The crowds—not that they are Paris-dense—appear more colourful. Their great folk festivals of song, dance, folk costume and instrumental music create an atmosphere of unifying joy, lifting performers and audience in their thousands into a colossal spiritual cloud that arches over land and lakes, like the mighty canopy of their festival aulas. The flames of St John's fires and the echo of music fill the night air with magic; the floral flames of a million petals dance around the posies of cornflowers, roses, moon daisies, cosmos and other flowers which young and old hold in hand—an image of the soul's life blessing, blossoming in the land and in the tongue in which they have incarnated.

Where or exactly when is not recorded, but what has come down as Marie von Sivers' first memory is standing beside the sea, perhaps where the Gulf of Riga merges majestically into the Baltic, wondering at the play of wave on shore and the liberating, uninterrupted expanse of sky, stretching as far as the child's waking senses could see. Though apparently not outwardly exaggerated as in storm, or grandeur of sky-flushed sunsets, the elemental power of nature seems in such moments—and they continued through her childhood—to have entered her whole being, thrilling every fibre of her soul with the cosmic voice of creation. It is in his lectures *Background to the Gospel of St Mark*,[1] where Rudolf Steiner points out that, whilst it is the ranks of the Third Hierarchy (Angels, Archangels and Archai) who influence we humans from within, it is from the Second Hierarchy, from the Exusiae—designated as Elohim in the opening chapter of Genesis—that we experience the 'forces of outer nature; they are the "directors" as it were of air and light, of the different ways in which foodstuffs are produced in the kingdoms of nature [...] the phenomena of thunder and lightning, rain and sunshine [...] the whole ordering of earthly conditions we ascribe to spiritual beings of the hierarchies higher than the Angeloi, Archangeloi and Archai. We see [their effects]; for example, in *the light that works upon us* ...' The sensitivity of the child, in whose entelechy lived the intensely lyric (sounding from the strings of Orpheus' lyre), the oft-outpoured admiration of those throngs who had listened spellbound as Hypatia expounded the wonders of the world, the myriad of fine observations that Albertus' nature-penetrating eye had beheld during the thousands of miles he had walked from place to place in his extended See centred on Cologne as he carried out his ecclesiastical offices, all this, in the sensitivity of the child, imbibed in that light-filled coastal atmosphere the 'elemental power' which, Logos-like, was the prime mover of all that her von Sivers, fifth post-Atlantean incarnation stood for.

Furthermore this place on earth, was where the spiritual forming of Europe itself had been instigated, emerging from the depth of the ocean in ancient times as a great primeval prologue, so to speak, to the awakening of the West. Steiner identified

> a formative agent working on [the] countenance [of Europe as] an ancient and powerful spiritual force, surging from the ocean depths and extending its tentacles, so to speak, via the Gulfs of Riga, Finland and Bothnia into Europe from the north. It conveyed etheric formative forces onto the land and into the people's constitution. It formed an ancient, albeit post-Atlanean race. [... T]he inner linguistic connection between Finnish, Estonian and Hungarian[2] might find an explanation here, a facet of evolution which seems to have escaped orthodox scholarship.[3]

Be that as it may, it is noteworthy that the von Sivers family moved from Marie's place of birth to St Petersburg, located absolutely centrally in the path of the ancient European formative influence—wrested, moreover, by Peter the Great from humanly inhospitable marshland, as if the watery-etheric origin of the post-Atlantean continent was reluctant to let go. Here the linguistically gifted child, Marie, picked up an accent pervaded by an O-quality, milder than the Muscovite Russian. And here, too, amongst the affluent social life and the ostentatiousness of its architecture and the opulence of its well-appointed interiors she suffered the oppressiveness of being imprisoned, it seemed,

> between the stark walls of over-large rooms [...] in a town where for months on end the dank mist lay thick upon everything; where the

sparse sun never emerged and artificial light was burning the whole day long [...]. So dark was it, so damp, that the sun was forgotten [...] added to this, there often soughed over the town the sharp west wind, blowing the mist-waves in restless tatters still further...[4]

Out of this dismal antithesis to her first childhood memory of light, open skies and clear atmosphere irradiated with sunshine emerged something from within her childlike, yet remarkably rich and pre-natally directing soul: a yearning for Greece—the sun-drenched atmosphere of the Greece she 'imagined', the beauty it personified which welled up from within, the presence of its Mediterranean-encircling blue, its (as yet unconceptualized) mission of art, though it is not recorded whether the family was high enough in the social echelons of St Petersburg for them to get a taste of the artistic wealth in the Hermitage. Even if they did, it is surely unlikely that younger members of the family would have got a share of that taste and its language—that Greek which she had spoken as she, Hypatia, had attracted scholars and other eminences from all over the (still Classical) world. Here the family's prejudices stone-walled the child's yearning to learn Greek. To give them their due, she did receive a 'good' schooling which, together with tuition in languages—one of her greatest gifts—stood her in good stead for all that life held in store, but Greek was beyond the pale. And in any case, looked at karmically, her pre-natal 'choice' of incarnating into a German-speaking family meant that her mother tongue was the language most suited to the resurgence of the spirit in European culture which anthroposophy was able to bring about, and in which she was to play such a vibrant part.

As far as we can judge it was during Marie's second septennial phase that her deep connection with poetry came to the surface, seemingly untutored, from within. She relished the sounds and rhythms manifest in poetry, the imagery it evoked and its throb of *life* that was absent from the prosaic use of language which was the normal experience of everyday usage in her social environment, in those years which followed the etheric birth. One envisages that it was the otherwise concealed connection between spirit and nature, and human experience and the spirit world itself, which is the very stuff of poetry and which nourished her hungry soul when she spoke it aloud—as she did—which drew her.

The second seed which germinated in connection with language, and with her innate talents, albeit more slowly with the astral birth, was drama. The family, being German expats, must have participated in the social life which their friends enjoyed, which included productions of classical German plays. Whether Marie and her brothers tagged along to such performances has not yet been recorded, but theatre must have been a vital part of the social ethos of the German enclave of which the audiences must have consisted. We know that it was during the Jubilee celebrations of her old school that she acted the title role of Schiller's *Maria Stuart*—more of which later. There must have been some build-up to this—at least, inwardly. We know from the lecture that Rudolf Steiner gave on Shakespeare's birthday, 1922 in Stratford on Avon during the conference 'New Ideals in Education', that the characters in Shakespeare's plays are to be found as spiritual archetypes on the astral plane. Repercussions of this visit find themselves in a meeting that Steiner had with the teachers in the Waldorf School in Stuttgart, shortly after his return from England. After commenting on the plays that he and Marie Steiner-von Sivers had seen performed in Stratford, he goes on to comment, '... [D]o not take anything dramatic before the age of eleven or twelve.'[5] Later, warning the same group of teachers about the maleffect on the ego that a prematurely developed astral body can bring about, he returns to the subject of school plays: '... [I]t is impossible to do dramatic work with children before the age of ten, whereas it is quite good to do it after that.'[6] It is fascinating to think that the visit to Stratford was instrumental in precipitating this insight of Steiner's into drama and education and that Marie Steiner-von Sivers was present on that occasion, meeting in the literary world such leading poets in their day as John Masefield and John Drinkwater in Shakespeare's birthplace, and that she was, by then, to have made a name for herself as having an outstanding ability on the stage—culminating in the performance of Steiner's Mystery Dramas.

If the notion of a girl in the 1870s learning Greek had been absurd to her very formal, steeped-in-etiquette, fashion-following family, the wish that the adolescent expressed to follow a career in drama must have been verging on the repugnant, certainly totally out of the question. For all their enthusiastic support of the German theatre in St Petersburg, the social gulf between her family's standing in society and the actors and actresses they admired in the context of drama was utterly unbridgeable. The idealism of youth, no doubt aflame within its burgeoning astrality, could not identify with such prejudiced aversion, of course, and Marie persisted to whatever extent was within her means. She was to find, however, when later it came to the crunch in Berlin, that her hoped-for career was blocked—not by family but by her own finer feelings—by the seamier side of all that went with a career on the stage. Her family's prejudices stemming from their moral expectations of ordinary human decency, proved to be not unfounded. Karmically, when the crunch crunched, it proved to be a godsend, but we are not there yet. Despite all their concern, and no doubt as a result of relentless teenage resistance to being overruled by the older generation, her Schillerian success and the obvious innate talent which she displayed (which from their frequent theatre-going they clearly recognized when they saw it), affirmed by popular acclaim moreover, wore down the family objection. In principle at any rate. But in practice her career would have to be beyond the ken of St Petersburg's society. Out of sight, out of mind. Berlin or Riga, for instance.

At this point, when some sort of a future seemed to be opening up, and after the girl's confirmation, Frau von Sivers decided on a tour abroad—whether to clear the air, or to find some workable way of bonding with her single-mindedly independent daughter, or possibly to ease her own conscience that life in St Petersburg had been too culturally claustrophobic and that she needed to rectify that, or simply on a whim ... who is to say? But significantly for Marie it was approaching the threshold of her first moon node; it gave her a taste of other European cultures (though ironically not Greek!) and direct and welcome exposure to their languages—which she was to master with extraordinary aplomb—and whether the bonding happened with the mother, on whatever new plane or not, gave her the feeling of future independence and somewhere deep down renewed aim in life, which is what the moon nodes are about. For in her case, it was powerfully self-evident that her aim in life ran contrary to the average 'society' girl's lot: to be married off in well-to-do circumstances and become, to all intents and purposes, buried in female domesticity, however grandiose on the social surface the eulogy happened to sound, or the burial and the gravestone happened to look.

4
Marie Steiner-von Sivers II

The Confluence of Two Wellsprings of the Spirit

Brien Masters

It was only in the last century that the mineral known as spectralite was discovered. It was identified in Finland on the southern part of the country's border with Russia. Shard and rugged lumps of it can be purchased usually on a stall in the colourful market situated at the ferry end of Helsinki's harbour. There are few colour experiences like that which can be obtained from a piece of spectralite. At most angles it presents itself as being somewhere between a dark clerical grey and rich, anthracite black; but tilt it this way or that way and the remarkable colours that have inspired its name reveal themselves. One piece, depending on the lapidarist's cut, will have a sheen of divine blue across its entire face; another piece as if sunken in slate, will glint with rainbow-like streaks of orange or gamboge; yet another will present a see-saw of spectral polarities as you rock it to and fro.

Though Marie von Sivers' eyes were reported by all who met her as sapphire blue, the inner shades of her being shone out from her outer-contained, high-society poise with colour after colour of exceptional talent. To follow the footsteps of her life from the first moon node to the second is to discover the essence of those talent-shades in what might be called a karmic spectrum. The *Weltmensch*-breadth of her nature began to burgeon from waiting bud to opening blossom with the tours referred to above, the languages, the people, the landscapes and the folk souls of Europe, ushering in, as it were, the fourth septennial phase of the sentient soul.

If we regard age 21 as the incisive moment when the ego—having been held at bay to one extent or another during adolescence by the swings and sways of astral awakening—steps authoritatively into the arena, symptoms of this, in the case of Marie von Sivers, might be seen in two facets of her relationship with her brother. As a highly inwardly-sensitive teenager she suffered intensely from the popular 'music' that her brother favoured. Yet far from causing a lasting rift between them, at age 21 she followed him into social work in the region of Novgorod. One might interpret what took place as the ego, discovering in the astral the ideals of youth, stirring *in youth* yet outwardly dormant in any practical sense, rising up in the Russian soul as 'compassion for the needy; respect for those lower than oneself in the social scale: a feeling of guilt that poorer brothers and sisters had fewer material possessions [...]; disdain for certain lies of civilized life; a searching after truth'; many Russian youths were moved to 'forsake everything, to serve in reverence ...' Caught up in this spiritual wave, the two of them set off to work in one such impoverished area amongst the peasants. The above quotes came from Savitch's account of the time spent there.[1] However, through a series of misfortunes, including her brother's death, this episode came to a conclusive end as far as her life as a whole is concerned.

There followed a prolonged and karmically crucial stay in Paris, starting when she was age 28. Here we find a triple confluence: firstly, in her own phase of life, the mission of the French in the consciousness-soul age inserts itself and that unique quality in France which affected even that archetypal-forming spirit, described in the previous chapter, as rising up from the ocean's depths and forming the ancient Finnish race, circling clockwise from the three Gulfs of Riga, Finland and Bothnia, turning south this side of the Urals (the German for 'archetypal' is *Ur*, though this may be a coincidence), entering the south of Europe via the Black Sea and then expanding across what is now France and Spain. And the effect? 'Steiner sees what he calls the (French) Romance Impulse as superseding [the faculty of clairvoyance, which trailed on for centuries amongst the Celtic pockets of western Europe, Brittany included]. What existed in the spiritual heyday of Carnutum (the present-day Chartres) as vision on the etheric plane discontinued.'[2] Chartres was where Gothic had been born in all its fulness as an immediate antidote to the fading faculty, and the spread of its architectural style across to Amiens (1220–70), Reims (finally roofed in 1299), Bayeux (consecrated in 1077 with its present Gothic dating from thirteenth century) and Paris (its west façade 1200–50), etc.—whose cathedrals were some of several built in the region and dedicated to 'Notre Dame'[3]—coincided with the spiritual activity the Scholastic stream of thought of which Albertus Magnus and Thomas Aquinas were in the vanguard. In his booklet *The Education of the Child in the Light of Anthroposophy* (1907), Rudolf Steiner, anticipating the lectures of November 1914, seven years later, refers to the mission of the French in our present, consciousness-soul age: this was to recapitulate, and take further, what had been established in Greece as the member of the human being designated the intellectual soul. This French mission is clearly epitomized in the reign of Louis XIV and the Age of Enlightenment which followed. Indeed, this stirring stream in the development of human consciousness, whose tidal flow moved from enlightenment to (French) revolution, has been connected directly with what took place, as described above, amongst the Russian youth in the last third of the nineteenth century, with what flourished in the plays of Chekhov and then sparked the tinder which ultimately brought about the Bolshevik revolution.

Here we are concerned with its Parisian focus and the fact that it was as Marie von Sivers was entering her own phase of intellectual soul development in 1895 that she was drawn to the French capital. Monet at that time had moved on from the exhibitions of 1872–86 to his series of Haystacks, and Rouen Cathedral, in which sense Impressionism was crossing new thresholds. Debussy's *Pelléas et Mélisande* was being composed. Diaghilev, Stravinsky and Isadora Duncan were beginning to spread their wings as they formed the styles with which they became so influential. Amongst all this, and particularity amongst what was happening in the field of literature, both in poetry and drama, Marie von Sivers, found a teacher, Mme Favart, who was to give her the foundations upon which she built what could have amounted to an outstanding career on the stage, and retained a discernment for what was true art, singling out, for instance, a preference for a poet whose work had attracted only marginalizing reviews from the critics.

Her years in Paris, however, not only demonstrated her artistic discernment; they revealed the spiritual rock upon which her whole being was built. Amongst the Parisian banquet of toothsome attractions in all the arts, her gaze fell upon the work of Eduard Schuré. His esoteric work, in itself constituting the refutation of Anatole France's popular ridiculing of the occult, and in spiritual substance containing the very treasure for which Marie von Sivers was seeking, had been steadily infiltrating into the public domain. Before she had arrived in Paris he had published his mystery play *The Sacred Drama of Eleusis* (1890) in the wake (the previous year) of his magnum opus *The Great Initiates*; and in 1900 his second mystery play, *The Children of Lucifer*, appeared.

It was a year which was to prove a guiding star in Marie von Sivers' life. Her star shone with four main rays. Firstly, Schuré's *The Children of Lucifer* inspired her to want to translate it. Secondly, correspondence between author and would-be translator prompted the former to make known to her the existence of the Theosophical Society. Thirdly, her outstanding talent as an actress drew forth an invitation to take the title role in Schiller's *Maid of Orleans*, which would undoubtedly lead to public acclaim and, given a successful performance, a wide open road to a career on the stage. And fourthly, she heard Rudolf Steiner lecture for the first time—of what must have been hundreds and hundreds of similar occasions. One could hold that all of these four were gifts strewn by a favourable karma in her life's path. They were: but they were connected with an event which came from the inner core of her own being, as the following account demonstrates.

She was on her way to a meeting in connection with her anticipated role in the Schiller production. It was in Berlin—more than comfortably far away from the family's social squeamishness over being labelled as stepping seriously across the boundary of propriety through having one of its daughters enter the theatre. Yet the *reality* of their reservations (which, after all, only existed in principle) was catching up with her. She could not stomach the thought of being expected to 'make visits which would require soul make-up', as Marie Savitch[4] delicately puts the accepted practice, in which young talent entering the profession was virtually required to curry the favour of theatre newspaper critics by paying them unchaperoned visits. This, moreover, which went against the grain of her own moral principles, was compounded by two more technical worries. She discovered what almost amounted to an allergy, as far as her sensitive skin and eyes were concerned, to wearing stage make-up; and she was directed to take elocution lessons in order to make her German accent in keeping with the taste of Berliners. A small matter, one might dismiss: don't theatre schools have their dialect/accent coaches? Yet so deep in her soul was the feeling for language—the garment of the Logos, could one say?—that she found the lessons unusually grating.

As it happened, the time of the meeting clashed with another visit she had planned. The picture that has come down to posterity is that while she was en route to the former, while waiting at a tram junction, 'she felt as if all the forces of her soul rose to an overwhelming tension, as if her whole life-experience gathered itself up and stood before her bound up with the urge of a mighty impulse'.[5] In the event, she decided not to keep the career appointment and consequently met Rudolf Steiner. Savitch doesn't go into the exact details, but it seems clear that, with the awareness of the Theosophical Society which Schuré had awoken in her, she saw a notice in the library of a lecture that Steiner was giving, which she attended. There was no turning back. She was 33 years old. Eventually, conversations between 1900 and 1902 led to a lifelong cooperation between her and Rudolf Steiner which had the deepest significance for the way in which Anthroposophia was able to incarnate into the stream of Western spiritual life.

The extent of that cooperation is virtually inestimable. Here, we shall look at it from seven perspectives in the hopes that these will give the reader an impression of the contribution of Marie von Sivers (from 1914

Marie Steiner-von Sivers) to the work of Rudolf Steiner in introducing spiritual science into the culture of modern life. The following perspectives are connected with influences in human life and thought to which Steiner drew attention, for it was during the last year of his lecturing life that Rudolf Steiner came to emphasize the significance of the great archangelic forces streaming into evolution, epoch by epoch. These are not zodiacal epochs but planetary. Michaël (to use the archangel's Hebrew name) radiates Sun Intelligence; Oriphiel, after approximately 350 years, brings Saturn Intelligence; Anael pours down the blessing of Venus Intelligence; Zachariel is regent of Jupiter Intelligence; Raphael emanates the healing power of Mercury Intelligence; Samael inserts Mars Intelligence into earthly life; and finally Gabriel imbues inner and outer life, through influencing human consciousness, with the material-anchoring orderliness of Lunar Intelligence.[6]

As with manifestations of spiritual beings in evolution, such Intelligences are to be traced in several realms of earthly and human life. It is thus illuminating to see how the relationship between Marie von Sivers and her teacher developed from the beginning of their 'practical' cooperation (in 1902) during the years which saw the turning point around Marie von Sivers' third moon node by looking at this in the order Oriphiel, Gabriel, Raphael, Anael, Michaël, Samael, Zachariel, though this is not to suggest that the respective planetary spiritual qualities that flowed into their relationship did so in sealed compartments. Life in its reality is full of inter-flow.

An occult law that we see hallmarked very clearly in Rudolf Steiner's biography and therefore in his life's work is that a new spiritual impulse shall be connected with, and linked onto, one that already exists. There are several ways we could view this. In the present context it is the connection with the Theosophical Society that we take as our starting point. This connection dates from the turn of the century and led to Steiner's first visit to London (1 July 1902) for the Twelfth Annual Convention of the Theosophical Society, European Section, where he and Marie von Sivers met Annie Besant and other prominent members of the society. It was at this Convention that Steiner made the statement that the newly formed German Section of the society, of which he was appointed General Secretary, would work as a place of *independent spiritual research*. Fräulein von Sivers translated contributions to the Convention. In fact, Steiner had only accepted the appointment as General Secretary on condition that she would also accept the official position of Secretary.

Similar visits took place the following two years. From the 1904 occasion there are records of the artistic activities/performances which formed part of the proceedings. In view of the importance which Rudolf Steiner attached to art—an importance to which he later drew attention, ironically emphasizing the difference between the direction in which the Theosophical Society eventually went and that in which the newly formed Anthroposophical Society was heading—the rich array of artistic items which formed part of this Convention seems particularly pertinent in the present context, in which we are considering the relationship between Marie von Sivers (who was to become so central in the anthroposophical impulse in the performing arts) and her teacher. Although Mrs Besant does make reference to the importance of art, quoted below, she rightly does not claim that all the items included in the programme have arisen from the Theosophical Society's impulse. Nevertheless, these items in total are impressive and formidable—especially as the event took place all within the space of three days (8–10 July). Some of the known particulars of these are as follows.

Plays (at the Royal Court Theatre): *The Shrine of the Golden Hawk* by Florence Farr; and *The Shadowy Waters* by W.B. Yeats.
Exhibition of Arts and Crafts in Kensington
    Paintings by A.E. (George Russell) from the Guild of Mahel
Organ Recital in the Queen's Hall
Choral work by L. Nightingale Duddington, *Hail to the Day-star*
Choral work by William Sterndale Bennett 'God is a Spirit' from the Oratorio *The Woman of Samaria*
Music by Handel, Dolmetsch, Rameau, Boccherini, Tchaikovsky and Grieg for string orchestra
A setting of Shelley's 'Music when soft voices die', and 'The Silver Swan'
Solo songs by Brahms and Hugo Becker
Piano solo: Prelude to Grieg's *Holberg Suite*
Poetry: Three stanzas from Tennyson's *In Memoriam*; Shakespeare's *Orpheus and his Lute*; and
12 poems from Blake's *Songs of Innocence* (set to music)
Solo violin: Chaconne from J.S. Bach's *Suite in D minor*
Songs by Gluck, Spohr and others
String Quartet by Brahms.

Two speeches made by Annie Besant, referred to by Crispian Villeneuve in his *Rudolf Steiner in Britain: A Documentation of his Ten Visits*,[7] are revealing in that they must have made some impression on both Rudolf Steiner and Marie von Sivers, which, while taken a step further through spiritual science, could be seen as prompting a place for art in such gatherings as the Theosophical Conventions in London and then later the

Theosophical Congress of 1909 in Munich, more of which later. On the 7 July it was reported that, in her address 'The work of the Theosophical Society in the world', she said that Theosophy declared that art ought not to be the mere presentment of what is called the real, the objective, but the representation to us of the unseen, the ideal. 'Surely the artist, the man of genius, should make real to us the unseen behind the veil [...] I see in art the ideal is being searched for more than it has been since religion dropped the pencil and the brush ...' The next time she gave a presidential address, it contained, Villeneuve notes, a passage that particularly caught the attention of Steiner. After praising the paintings of A.E., on show in the arts and crafts exhibition mentioned above, she continues by referring to a Roman sculptor whose carving of 'The Dead Christ' obtains a 'face which he has presented in a dream or vision [...] the noteworthy fact [being] that this face is the face of the being Christ and not the face of Christ symbolized in ordinary art [... Theosophy] may bring to the world fresh forms of truth and beauty which the artist without that inspiration will be unable to achieve.' Leaving aside the question of which (theosophical) artist had developed, or was to develop, these inner faculties and the outer capability that Mrs Besant's remarks imply, it is surely of great significance that attending the convention, when these remarks were made were Rudolf Steiner and Marie von Sivers as part of the very first phase of their long collaboration precisely in the realm of the arts, so central to Marie's impulse and to anthroposophy itself.

Looking for the quality of human influence in the relationship between the two individualities with whom we are now mainly concerned, we could not do better than picture the situation in Motzstraße from where their activities radiated into the world. Moon periods in evolution introduce a closer relationship between spirit and matter.[8] This we can see in three respects in the work of Marie von Sivers. Firstly in her administrative capacity in the German Section of the Theosophical Society, she acted as hostess on countless occasions to those who were attending functions of the society: this entailed attending to the minutiae of many people's well-being. Secondly, the organization of Rudolf Steiner's lectures in Berlin and his lecture tours further afield fell to her. Just the travel arrangements by train and other means of transport, with an itinerary such as his, were a formidable task on their own, let alone all the other practical details. Thirdly, there was her position in the production of the journal *Luzifer* (a little later re-entitled *Luzifer-Gnosis*), which Steiner and she considered necessary now that Germany had its own branch of the Theosophical Society, dedicated—as Steiner was careful people should not lose sight of—to 'independent spiritual research'.

This journal took on an extraordinary life of its own. The first number came out in June 1903.[9] Frequently Steiner as editor wrote most or all of the contents himself. In other respects:

> Marie von Sivers made the production [of the journal] possible; not only did she make all the material sacrifices within her power, but she devoted all her working capacity to anthroposophy. To begin with, we could really only work in the most primitive conditions [...] Marie von Sivers looked after the correspondence. When an issue was ready, we did all the wrapping, addressing and stamping, and we personally carried the copies to the post office in a laundry basket.[10]

The seven issues of *Luzifer* came out June–December 1903 and, after 27 issues, *Luzifer-Gnosis*, ceased in 1908.

This impulse, to make available in printed form the result of Rudolf Steiner's spiritual research, took a further step in 1908. Again, Marie von Sivers was absolutely central in the practical side of this, founding the first anthroposophic publishing company and using her own means to do so.[11] Not only that, she made it a life task, editing the transcripts of Steiner's lectures, correcting all proofs and writing 'Forewords' to each publication, which provided a bridge for the reader who was embarking on the journey which leads to spiritual science, as well as a context for those who were already some distance along the way. Rudolf Steiner stated clearly in his several-times written will that she should have the sole responsibility of handling his literary estate. It is, one might say, the most important aspect of their outer collaboration, which remained with her actively until her last days.

We step now from Moon influences to those connected with Mercury. Earlier we saw how the yearning for beauty, which the young Marie von Sivers identified in her imagination with Greece, transferred itself into a love of art. This, in turn, played an important part, not only in the relationship between her and Rudolf Steiner but also in the way that anthroposophy was formulated in the early years of the century. It is as well to recall that the plethora of first-class reproductions that are now available in book form or through the media did not exist at that time. The slides that Steiner used in his course on the history of art[12] were in monochrome. As far as we know, the art books that are available in the average home today even if they are few and modest productions, did not exist in Steiner's home next to the station in Neudorf. Indeed, one wonders to what extent he may or may not have visited the museums in Vienna during his student days.

All this changed radically when Marie von Sivers began her work for the Theosophical Society by his side. A world opened up for him that had seemingly hitherto been closed when, on lecture tours, it became invaluable to Steiner that not only did they visit art galleries, museums and other art treasures, in the various places in which lecture engagements had been arranged, but that as they did so she gave verbal expression to her perceptions of the greatness of art, of that which expressed the beautiful in art, and of the subtle nuances in the art works they visited.

For all the richness of artistic contributions which we saw were part of the programme of the Theosophical Congress in London in 1904, at the end of his life Steiner reflected that what dawned in his mind at that time, and in Marie von Sivers, was the realization that the *styles* of the various arts needed cultivating within the Theosophical—and, soon after, Anthroposophical Society—'Artistic interests were barely cultivated *within* the Theosophical Society.'[13] Anthroposophically inspired painting and sculpture was still some way off, of course; nevertheless one senses its seed in such statements as the following, a statement that must have had behind it a good deal of searching conversation between the two of them. 'Because we could develop art through spiritual knowledge, we increasingly penetrated the truth of modern spiritual experience. Art originally grew out of dreamy, pictorial experiences of spirit. As this spirit experience receded in the course of human evolution, art had to find its way alone.' The editor of Steiner's autobiographical account of the years 1861–1907, Paul Allen, helpfully draws attention to an experience as early as 1888 (an exhibition in Vienna) when Steiner first saw some paintings by Arnold Böcklin: 'These paintings induced [Steiner] to occupy [himself] incessantly with the art of painting.'[14] This is some 14 years before what we are right now considering took place, so the ground in Steiner's soul, 'incessantly' occupied with painting, must have been considerably fertile when he and Marie von Sivers stood before the great works of the Renaissance and other periods which they sought out on their journeys.

Having said that, it was not in the realm of the *visual* arts that Marie's personal talents lay—and here we pass from the Mercury quality in the relationship between teacher and pupil to that of Venus. Her profound connection was, to begin with, with poetry. In fact, we have already touched on two of the poetry stepping-stones that led to the unique flowering of the art of recitation which together they evolved (quite quickly, it would seem). It is fair to assume that that one-time initiate in the Orphic Mysteries achieved a use of language that spoke with *mantric force*. Similarly, the scholars who thronged around Hypatia were moved by the *beauty* as well as by the content of her speech, as she held forth day by day—as if an instrument such as an Aeolian harp on whose strings the wisdom of past ages breathed its magic. In Albertus, the word achieved *philosophical-religious heights* that towered in the still-blue sky of Christian thought. And now in her von Sivers' incarnation it was the language of the poet, the spirit in the Logos elevated by poetry, that was to sound as the heart-centred mission of her life. Hammacher dates this collaborative work as beginning in 1903, with the first showing occurring three years later when, accompanying a lecture that Steiner gave on the poem *Eleusis* that Hegel dedicated to Hölderlin, Marie von Sivers recited the poem.

We are fortunate that Steiner was able to reach this point in his life (1907) before he had to discontinue writing his autobiography (70 weekly instalments were completed). It becomes clear that through the art of speech, inner life can be reawakened, an inner awareness of the spirit working in all things—the antithesis, one might say, to that use of speech which expresses (both in sound and in content) a form of thought which, however exact in the mineral or mechanical or rational realms, is essentially void of life.

> [The] conscious thought element that has dominated culture since the beginning of the consciousness soul [...] has a deadening effect on art.
>
> Just the opposite occurs, however, when *directly perceived* spiritual meaning fills the imagination with life. All the powers that have ever led to art among humanity are resurrected in this way. [And *immediately*, in this very context:] Marie von Sivers was truly accomplished in the art of speech formation and greatly gifted in dramatic art. A sphere of art was then present within the anthroposophical activity, and based on this we could test the fertility of spiritual perception for art.[15]

No more than a hint can be given of the creative power of speech that such a perception of, and practice of, speech unlocks, but it is hopefully enough to highlight the vitally important part that Marie von Sivers' personal talent had to play in the outpouring of Anthroposophia.

> ... true spiritual experience enters the 'experience of the word' as if by instinct. It learns to feel its way into the vowel's reverberation sustained by the soul and into the consonant's painting energized by spirit [...] One needs enthusiasm kindled by *spiritual insight* to lead the word back to its own sphere. Marie von Sivers developed such enthusiasm.[16]

The next planetary port of call is that of Michaël: the Sun sphere. In the early days, when this work for the development of speech formation was under way, a passage in a letter from Rudolf Steiner to Marie von Sivers sheds light on the matter of 'spiritual insight' that kindles enthusiasm. The letter is dated 8 April 1904. It would appear that the inner work undertaken by von Sivers as Steiner's by now esoteric pupil had arrived at a point (or was going through a patch) where she felt inwardly uncertain. Steiner reassures her: 'Believe me, my dear Marie, you are making faster progress than you might notice yourself.'[17] Presumably, then, not only was she developing such enthusiasm as was needed for the development for the art of speech formation, but also the 'spiritual insight' without which the enthusiasm would be less likely to be 'kindled'.

But why is the connection between esoteric teacher and pupil the first thing that comes to mind when considering the relationship between Rudolf Steiner and Marie von Sivers in the light of the Sun sphere, Michaël's domain? It has been pointed out that Steiner, both frequently referring to the spiritual hierarchies throughout his life and, therefore, of the Archangeloi, only drew pointed attention to the cycle of archangelic regencies (c. 350 years) towards the last years of his teaching. With this came the call to which of the archangels was regent at the present time (leaving aside for now Michaël's advance to Time Spirit) and what that meant for present-day consciousness and culture. Rudolf Steiner himself had arrived at his first moon node when Michaël's regency superseded that of his archangelic predecessor, Gabriel, in 1879. Marie von Sivers was at the cusp of what is considered usual in child development, when the child's inherently imaginative consciousness and the beginning of rationality are at home, side by side. Steiner was seemingly never in any doubt that the worlds to which his fast-advancing clairvoyance gave him access needed to be presented to the modern world not in a mystical way, but via a consciousness that was as disciplined in spiritual matters as was the scientist's vis-à-vis the manifestation of the material world that he was investigating. When the two of them met 21 years after the Michaël Age had been running, in the winter of 1900/1901, the road to anthroposophy as we have come to know it still stretched into the future.

Indeed, it would be fair to say that, while the direction of that road was clear to Steiner, the *way* in which he should make its whereabouts, its character, the implications that its 'gradient' and 'surface' would mean for the soul who wished to travel along it, and similar features, known to contemporary society, was not yet fully evident. Furthermore, the door to the storehouse of initiate knowledge required a key, not in the initiate's possession before it could be unlocked. Marie von Sivers provided that key through the question she put in one of the conversations they had prior to their collaboration:[18] Was there not a specific form of esotericism which would be right for the Christian West? Also, as we have seen, her several-sided connection with the arts influenced greatly the way in which Steiner formulated spiritual-scientific knowledge. The Mystery Dramas are clearly in the forefront of that; but we could also trace the influence in a dozen and one other ways.[19]

Centrally important in this, too, is the transition from the ancient world to the Christian and with it the confluence of the stream of what early Christianity referred to as paganism with the stream whose spring, welling from the bedrock of the whole of evolution, was the Mystery of Golgotha. Though no writer makes a great thing of it—perhaps because of the comparative uncertainty surrounding it—it has been said that Marie von Sivers was herself fascinated by this confluence right from her early days. The fact that she received an orthodox Christian confirmation suggests that there was at least some conventional religious observation in the family, a streak perhaps in her childhood experience alongside all that her intense connection with nature and her own inner yearning for the arts—pre-eminently at that stage, her love of poetry—that prompted her to feel the need to come to terms with a world in which Christianity, though qualitatively 'here to stay', quantitatively was less in evidence than other influences. All this must surely have stirred the Hypatia soul-wealth that resided deep down in her being.

Before leaving this Michaëlic quality in the Steiner-von Sivers relationship, it is worth noting that, as far as we know, the von Sivers incarnation is the first that occurs in either a major or a minor Archangel Michaël regency. Although this by no means implies that she was not party to the School of Michaël, which Rudolf Steiner describes as taking place in the spiritual world between the present and the previous Michaël age,[20] she does not have this particular feature in her curriculum vitae, so to speak, as does Steiner. Yet the cosmopolitanism of her life's path, the radiance of her nature as seen in her role as hostess in the Brockdorff days, the light in her eyes, and the warmth that untold numbers experienced in her voice as she recited for eurythmy performances all point to Sun-majesty as something uppermost, innermost and outermost in her whole deportment and attitude to life. The connection with her incarnation prior to Hypatia is surely surfacing here: in the Orphic Mysteries. Whilst we have noted that for Steiner it was significant that Orpheus' mother Calliope, one of the divine Muses, was seen by that elevated consciousness which the Greeks still enjoyed as endowing Orpheus with his *spiritual* capacities, it was equally significant that that same imaginative consciousness gave him Oeagrus, the Thracian river-god, as his father, and thereby his *connection to the earth*. At the same time, there is in ancient

Greek mythological lore the tradition that Orpheus is the son of Apollo, the sun god, the spiritual/macrocosmic aspect of the sun (as distinct from Helios, the object which rose in the east each morning bringing light, life and warmth to the day).

Be that as it may, there remains the fact that, as each archangel assumes regency, the planetary Intelligence, the emanation of the archangel's being, rains down upon all facets of life on earth and in every one of its 'four corners'. This is richly demonstrated in Páleš' research, in which he discovers the drops of that spiritual rain falling everywhere without exception. There remains, however, the question: Might that Intelligence flow into earthly human life not simply from *above*, bringing its influence to bear irrespective of the degree of people's awareness of what is happening, but from *within*? That is to say, influencing the course of events and their consequences through someone (or through more than one) *cultivating an inner soul life that is consciously receptive to what is raining down archangelically?* From this perspective it is clear that such individuals become the proactive, conscious instruments of the spiritual world, and it is in this light that Rudolf Steiner's—and his exceptionally gifted pupil Marie von Sivers'—contribution to the Michaël Age can be placed. Whilst their meeting and recognizing one another was an endowment of karma, their collaborative work in the fields we are considering was not merely fortuitous; rather it was a constantly cultivated endeavour which, in von Sivers' case, in certain respects she adhered to unfailingly for her whole life.

Apart from other attributes, Mars Intelligence is that cosmic force which lifts things onto a new plane. We saw, as regards Saturn, that the initiate, in what he or she has to bring, follows the occult law of linking appropriately onto the spiritual past. Steiner made us aware that his professor of German literature had had the karmic potential of 'lifting' Goetheanism onto a plane suitable for and vitally applicable to the modern age, as a counterforce to the necessary materialism that humanity needed as a challenge to its further development in evolution. Schröer the professor, it transpired, could only take his karmic potential so far.[21] We might therefore conclude that within the archangelically blessed work which Steiner and von Sivers undertook, described above, a Samael-Mars-uplift was also at work.

We also know—and the paramount importance of this has emerged more and more in the last three or four decades—that it was Rudolf Steiner's *core mission* to introduce the knowledge of repeated earth lives and the karmically rich interweaving between those lives and between individuals connected with one another. The resistance he encountered in doing this, as well as fulfilling Schröer's potential on his behalf, has been well documented.[22] In our present study, it will be fitting to try and ascertain how Marie von Sivers related to the core mission of her teacher, her indefatigable co-worker and (from December 1914) her husband and their deeply founded life-partnership. While doing so it will be well to bear in mind the necessity of exercising spiritual tact, in general, but especially in this field—which may appear somewhat paradoxical at first sight, since Steiner set such great store on it. In this respect, perhaps it is because of this that the karmic connections of Marie Steiner-von Sivers took the half century that they did after her death to come fully to light. Looking at a remark Steiner made in a letter he wrote to her on 9 January 1905, we might well conclude that the seeming slowness of the relevant facts to enter the public domain might well have been occasioned by her taking to heart what he had to say: 'Not a day passes when the Masters do not give a clear warning: "Be careful, think of the unpreparedness of your time [...] it is your destiny to reveal elevated secret teachings to children." '[23] Though 1908 is early compared with the year 1924 when it became possible for Steiner to start to fully disclose the content of his core mission, most of what we now know concerning von Sivers' early experiences in this domain had been revealed. (The lectures on *Occult History* followed only a few years later in 1910.)

Rudolf Steiner, it seems, though not able for most of his life to break through the resistance *amongst his followers* (!) to the importance of lifting the veil regarding reincarnation as part of (let us call it) the School of Michaël, was nevertheless mindful of opportunities that occurred, provided they would be karmically amenable to the other individual, of 'awakening a vision of karma'. This can sound sensationally dramatic. Just the opposite comes across as the *way* in which Steiner recognized the opportunities and acted accordingly. First of all the inner disposition had to be there in the other one, and secondly Steiner needed to find— sometimes, or even mostly, instantaneously—a right way of doing this. Good examples are coming to light which, whilst not lying within the scope of the present work, encourage one to feel that 'we are in good company'.

In the case of Marie von Sivers, certain experiences have become known which give us an inkling of how she stood inwardly in this respect. As far as English readers are concerned, Marie Savitch's *Marie Steiner von Sivers: Fellow Worker with Rudolf Steiner* (to give it its full title) which was published in English translation in 1967, tells of how, in struggling to find the inner essence of Novalis' *Hymns to the Night* for her recitation, it was her own realization that the poet's former incarnation was Raphael the

Renaissance painter that gave her the clue. When describing this to Rudolf Steiner, who frequently selected such texts for her to work at, the mild expression on his countenance became suffused with 'a smile'. Shortly afterwards (6 January 1909 in Munich) he spoke for the first time of the other connections that stretched back over millennia into the karmic history of the poet. This experience of hers, corroborated by Steiner, is the most explicit indication we have into the apparently thin veil that Marie von Sivers' consciousness had to draw aside in order to gain access to that stream of spiritual life that was her teacher's core mission.

It will be for the reader to assess how explicitly genuine the other two experiences appear to be. According to a letter written to Eduard Schuré in August 1907, 'It was as early as 1902, the year when their collaboration began, when she had a decisive reincarnation experience in relationship to her friend and teacher.' The experience which she underwent 'so intimately' was of his former incarnation which 'was confirmed both by Herr Steiner, who was greatly alarmed [...] and also by a thousand small details...'[24] How one wishes she had gone on, at some point, to express what those small details were—which would tell us considerably more about her. At the same time, Steiner's *alarm* seems to be calling for interpretation: (1) He was himself, comparatively speaking, near the beginning of the signs—which have to come as grace from without—that revealed to him what that incarnation was. (2) He makes it clear that it could be offensive to another person's privacy if one deliberately set out, with whatever clairvoyant insight, to investigate the karmic background of that other person—unless they have made a specific request in that direction. Similarly, one might conclude, to investigate their own faculty in this respect. The 'alarm' suggests that neither of these circumstances was in place. Steiner must have had the self-control to keep hidden alarming reactions to all sorts of things that came his way. This incident, however, if the interpretation is correct, found its way even past his guard. (3) It could also be that it was early days in the esoteric 'tutoring' of his pupil, and that divulging this insight which had occurred to her 'so intimately' yet leaving no 'shadow of doubt'[25] she jumped the gun—her rapid inner progress outran the wisdom that ideally should attend it, which would bring spiritual tact to bear. She was, of course, on safe ground with Steiner and, if a lesson had needed to be learnt, by the time she wrote to Schuré of the experience five years later in 1907 it most certainly *had been* learnt. Despite this, Meyer identifies and highlights her lingering doubt (regarding the lesson learnt or not) by quoting very poignantly that now to reveal Steiner's previous incarnation—and it took her a week before she did this by adding to what she had first written on 18 August—was 'what [she] ought to tell [Schuré]. But really it is like *pulling out a limb*'. There cannot have been anyone on the face of the earth more qualified to use the metaphor (which is my emphasis and not hers) than the reincarnated Hypatia.[26]

Finally there is the question of the perception of her own karmic past. In this respect, Schuré himself seems to have tumbled to something. Earlier in the letter he had received than the passage just quoted comes a reference to something Mrs Besant had communicated to her, that when she had been 'born into Christianity it was only to fight against it ... and to be killed'.[27] This passage is open to a variety of interpretations, none of which we need necessarily rehearse here. What *is* of interest is that, in the left-hand margin at this point in the letter he had received, Schuré writes (spelling the name in French) *Hypatie?* (his question mark). Some spark of karmic import clearly leapt in his consciousness. Exactly what it was is admittedly open to conjecture. Nevertheless it seems very clear that in the triangle Rudolf Steiner, Marie von Sivers, Eduard Schuré there lives a karmic vibrancy, the reverberations of which can be heard in these events and experiences now being considered a) in relation to this moment in the inner development of Marie von Sivers; b) in relation to Steiner becoming aware of her karmic past; and c) in relation to the initiative he is known to have taken in order to properly awaken in her a 'vision' of that karma. Above we looked at this remarkable process from a somewhat historical perspective, which we may now allow to echo on in this karmic content before passing onto the third and final stage in our considerations.

Turning finally to the seventh archangel, Zachariel is the Hebrew name for the archangelic Intelligence of the Jupiter sphere. Here it will be possible to leave this sevenfold journey in the relationship between Marie von Sivers and Rudolf Steiner in, so to speak, a poised position. Jupiter is associated with the next embodiment of the Earth, the sixth (post-Atlantean) epoch. I am aware that we have stepped a few years beyond the moment when Marie von Sivers passed her second moon node, justified I trust by the facts surrounding her sequence of earth lives and the way these surfaced at the time and have since—only very recently—come to light. Did this surfacing have to wait for the Zachariel sub-regency, one wonders, which began in 1989? Be that as it may, it is salutary, to say the least, that Steiner emphasizes the evolutionary importance of 'awakening a vision of karma': for it is those in whom this awakening has begun who will *become leaders of the next epoch.*

This concludes what we may think of imaginatively as the dance of the planets, as they paeoned the symphony of collaboration between Rudolf

Steiner and Marie von Sivers up until around the time of her second moon node. In what follows, the third section of this part of our study, which focuses on her third moon node, we shall look at some of the implications and ramifications of those arts in which Marie Steiner-von Sivers excelled; this presents us with an unshakable rock amongst the ocean of karmic storms which have been written about almost ad nauseam, certainly to the extent that prompted the present authors to attempt to redress the balance by looking at that within her nature, whose stature has been somewhat eclipsed, which carries untold significance and potential for the West.

Hypatie

Leconte de Lisle

Je ne puis oublier, en un silence lâche,
Le soin de mon honneur et ma suprême tâche,
Celle de confesser librement sous les cieux
Le beau, le vrai, le bien, qu'ont révélés les Dieux.
Depuis deux jours déjà, comme une écume vile,
Les moines du désert abondent dans la ville,
Pieds nus, la barbe inculte et les cheveux souillés,
Tout maigris par le jeûne, et du soleil brûlés.
On prétend qu'un projet sinistre et fanatique
Amène parmi nous cette horde extatique.
C'est bien. Je sais mourir, et suis fière du choix
Dont m'honorent les Dieux une dernière fois.
Cependant je rends grâce â ta sollicitude.
Et n'attends plus de toi qu'un peu de solitude.

In coward silence can I not forget
What to myself is due, my task supreme—
Beneath the heavens what the Gods reveal
Of beauty, truth and goodness to confess.
For two long days, like to a scum impure,
The desert monks have swarmed into the town;
Bare-footed, beards unkempt and hair unclean,
Burnt by the sun, wasted by constant fast.
Men say a plan fanatical and dread
Brings this ecstatic horde into our midst.
Tis well—for instant death I am prepared,
Proud that for this last time the puissant Gods
Have deemed me worthy to endure that fate.
Yet your concern fills me with gratitude;
Now, solitude is all I beg of you.[1]

5
Marie Steiner-von Sivers III

By Word of Mouth

Brien Masters

Much has been made, quite rightly, of the outstanding contribution that Marie Steiner-von Sivers made to a renewal of the arts of recitation and drama and the founding and early development of the 'new' art of eurythmy. Here, I would like to look at this contribution from the standpoint that Rudolf Steiner presents in Dornach on 29 December 1914,[1] where he describes the arts in relation to the human being's sevenfold membering: physical, etheric, astral, ego, Spirit Self, Life Spirit, Spirit Man, and which, significantly, was the first of two related lectures given on the two days prior to his marriage to Marie von Sivers. There, as a result of his spiritual research, we are presented with the engaging fact that whilst we imbibe the *laws* connected to each of the seven members we do so not through the *organ of perception* that that same member exercises but through the organ of perception of the member that belongs immediately 'below' that region from which the laws flow. For example music embodies the laws of the ego in which the ego is the youngest (most infant) of our four lower members and is at home in (and is therefore the citizen of) two worlds, the spiritual and the earthly; the ego is prone to attack from spiritual powers opposed to the progressive evolution of humanity etc.[2] and, whilst it cargoes these laws on its tidal flow of sound to the listener, the receptive organ of perception of them is the listener's soul—whether in thinking, feeling or willing. The thinking listener might attend a pre-concert talk or immerse himself in programme notes, and sit there consciously waiting for the return of a rondo theme or the first sounding of a Wagnerian motif, and may well scrutinize the critics' views in the press on the following day. The feeling listener is the one who is probably most inwardly moved by the music, leaving the recital with a lightness of step, the elation of being hoisted into another world, and an effusion of emotion—none of which can be put into coherent sentences other than nebulously euphoric praise. The will-accentuated listener might wag a toe whilst listening, or (thinking in historic terms, of the Court of Louis XIV) might get up and dance movements of a suite, or, re-energized by the music, will double his output for days after the experience—whether his tool for doing so be paintbrush or chain-saw.

Where do Marie Steiner-von Sivers' three 'professions' of recitation, drama and eurythmy stand in relation to this complex culture-guiding and life-enriching process?[3]

We may recall that from the outset she had a strong inner connection to poetry, which would seem to have been independent of family surroundings. Had the family been Grecophiles they surely wouldn't have adopted such an out and out objection to their daughter's learning some Greek, giving her the inner access to the *Iliad*, for example, which the yearning in her young soul longed for. Not that this dampened her childlike ardour or deprived her of poetry in either the short or the long term. In fact, with that childlike ardour, she spoke it aloud; something in her dictated that the word had to live *in the air*, and what a lifelong, ground-breaking motif this proved to be. Like bringing a child up on good food and avoiding junk food, it would seem that speaking poetry aloud affected her very soul digestion of the art, beginning already with the 'mouthwatering' taste of the word to such an extent that when years later she arrived in Paris, as we have seen, she discerned who the *real* poet was amongst all the scintillatingly fashionable 'departures' of the day.

We can only, at this distance in time, surmise how the collaborative work between Marie von Sivers and Rudolf Steiner made progress from this innately gifted speech that she had acquired of herself—and through the teaching of Mme Favart in Paris (whom Steiner mentions in his autobiography), who it would appear had developed the art of speech to a high degree based on all that had come down in classical French culture—to what they developed over time, he through indication and guidance, she through indefatigable practice, as speech formation (*Sprachgestaltung*). Favart's achievement, in the event, was to be tragically swept away by the champions of theatrical naturalism, which was in such vogue at the time, spurred on by Emil Zola and his associates. Nevertheless, it was a stroke of good fortune that von Sivers arrived in Paris in the nick of time and—maybe like a blessing in disguise, albeit heavy disguise—that she experienced the demise of the fine classical art of speech in so far as it was instrumental in bringing about the fairly fierce antipathetic recoil that led her eventually to her next significant step. For just as speech formation lived on and in the outer air, so also, borne upward by the spiritual air, one might say, was the creative response that Rudolf Steiner brought in his choice of texts for her to work with, and the outpouring of verses, meditations, dramas and mantra that began at this time, in which language becomes an elevating factor in the life of the soul—a timely and drastically needed counterforce to what was seeping from Parisian naturalism into contemporary culture.[4] All of which culminated—if we glance well ahead—on the one hand in the lectures Rudolf Steiner gave on speech in 1921–3[5] and September 1924, and on the other hand in the unceasing effort that Marie Steiner-von Sivers put into her *teaching* of the new art of speech.

Although giving it here little more than *en passant* status in her personal development, it is perhaps as good a place as any to draw attention again to the fact that her having to work at Novalis' *Hymn to the Night*—and this was already in autumn 1908 when the work with Rudolf Steiner was taking its very first steps—led her to the inner certainty that the poet's previous incarnation had been the Renaissance painter Raphael.[6] For this surely implies that the speaking of language in which the Logos has breathed the spirit of truth can bring about incisive transformations in the soul. This is something for which any number of examples could be cited in a whole range of contexts: parliament, courts of law, the pulpit, the lecture theatre and the broadcasting media, at the high profile end of the spectrum; Speaker's Corner, the humble classroom, the pub and suchlike at its other end. In her case the transformational power of language worked on the plane of repeated earth lives—seemingly quite quickly and despite an inner opaqueness which she had to work through. One wonders, therefore, what inner release the working with other texts that Steiner selected for her might have brought about. Savitch lifts the veil on this process, though only slightly, when referring to how she received a text from her teacher together with his suggestion to work at it: '[She] experienced these poetical works as deeply moving, indeed tremendous events in her destiny. Because of this, the spiritual background of the poems she was studying became perceptible to her.'[7] The expression 'tremendous events in her destiny' suggests infinitely more than the average reciter's relationship to the *beauty* of poetry. Might it not be that the examples of poetry she worked at, which are frequently cited— especially Hegel's *Eleusis,* Goethe's *Orphsiche* and Leconte de Lisle's *Hypatie*[8]—made transparent for her whatever 'destiny' Savitch had in mind in using such exceptional language to describe an artist merely (!) practising her art? One wishes Savitch had said more. Why was she reticent about this *destiny*? The inescapable fact, however, is that she did not, at least not in published form; and we shall move on from poetry to the next profession.

Although drama (as far as Marie von Sivers' artistic collaboration with Rudolf Steiner is concerned) followed chronologically on the heels of recitation—and in her own life, indeed, had been the springboard to her meeting her teacher—here we shall next turn to eurythmy. In what came through, uncannily it could seem at first hearing, in her practising the recitation of certain poetic masterpieces (masterpieces being those works in which existed spiritual reality) we get an inkling of the process described above: *in poetry live the laws of the Spirit Self, which are perceived by the ego.* The next step upwards takes us beyond the newly inspired art of speech formation to the newly created art of eurythmy.

For an insight into how this entirely new art emerged from its chrysalis, we are inexpressibly indebted to eurythmists, such as Marie Savitch, who worked with Marie von Sivers in order to present items of eurythmy in the weekly performances which took place at the Goetheanum in Dornach, or when the eurythmists accompanied Rudolf Steiner to places beyond Dornach where he was lecturing in order to present the art to other audiences, or when eurythmy was an integral part of drama productions on stage. At the same time, uniquely deep and fundamental though it is, Marie Steiner-von Sivers' connection with the new art cannot strictly be described as that of a performer. In order to come close to comprehending this, let us consider a parallel by way of contrast.

In order to acquire the virtuosity that she needs to perform her art, the violinist goes along to the regular lessons that she receives from her teacher, occasionally attends a master-class conducted by an acknowledged virtuoso on the instrument, and listens to the performances of those world-class violinists who have gone before and on some aspects of whose style of playing she may be modelling her own. Peer into the Renaissance, however, and there will be no violin or violinist anywhere to be seen. The instrument first had to be invented and constructed, its sound potential discovered and the caterwauling demons (that lurk in it defying the ungifted or the wavering-in-determination to make headway) conquered before the sublime gates of heaven, to which a Beethoven or a Brahms possessed the key, can be entered and the devachanic sounds that orbit on the other side of that threshold be coaxed into filling the air in the concert hall, thereby lifting the soul of the listener into realms hardly otherwise accessible. With eurythmy, we are concerned with the equivalent crucible in which the art fermented during its creation. Going a step further with our violin metaphor, there are the Stradivarius-calibre craftsmen who evolved the proportions of the instrument and selected the materials which would give the optimum resonance and timbre; there are the Paganini virtuosi who, as well as displaying the acrobatics of head-and-shoulders-above technique, brought a sufficiently cultured soul life to bear which conveyed the lofty aesthetic qualities of which the instrument was capable; and there are the Beethovens. The *instrument for the art of eurythmy is the human body* (physical and etheric); the choreographic creator is the one who translates the spirit of the spoken language (poetry etc.), or of the musical composition, into forms and gestures made visible in space. The Paganini is the eurythmist. She does not need to purchase two air tickets when flying from A to B (as does the cellist) one for herself and one for her instrument! Her 'instrument' is her own body. In this respect, Marie von Sivers holds a somewhat unique place in the 'original' constellation of people who inaugurated the art.

Due to personal life circumstances, she was severely limited in being able to demonstrate the art, being more and more confined to a wheelchair as the years went on. However, as we have seen, because of her uniquely outstanding connection with 'the word'—that is the *spoken* word—she was able (a) to recognize whether the eurythmic gestures that she beheld the eurythmist making in rehearsals expressed the spiritual nuance in the language *or not*; and (b) in the latter case (the eradication or correction of which is what rehearsals are partly about) chose her words so exactly that they directed the eurythmist's perception of her own inner experience in such a way that the resultant physical movement of the body—and, even more importantly, the etheric movement which prompted it—became a truer visible manifestation of what was otherwise invisible. This entailed a highly advanced degree of perception combined with an acutely developed awareness of the Logos that lives in speech.

Thus we are concerned with a threefold process. The choreographic form was drawn on paper by Rudolf Steiner, in accord with his spiritual vision. (There were also indications for costume and lighting which need not concern us right now.) The choreography was then put into practice by the eurythmists with Marie Steiner as director, and with rehearsals continuing for hours and hours on end, mostly in two sessions per day. And one further comment which reveals another facet of this individual's nature: from all descriptions it seems as though her acute perception of what impression the eurythmist made while she (Marie Steiner) spoke the poem built up into a sort of tension. And, like the tension that increases as the archer draws back the bowstring, at a certain point when the moment was right she released the tension by making her direct comment. Arrows fly straight to the target. Those who were 'professionally' involved in these rehearsals were the recipients of such comments—experiencing their director's remarks and observations like arrows flying and unequivocally hitting the target. It would be inexact to say that 'Frau Doktor's' comments were tactless, and yet the (tact-free) arrow seems to be the right image. When Rudolf Steiner himself was at rehearsal, he 'often [made] his indications more precise by the movement of his hand. There arose, as it were, a harmonious concordance between the indications he gave and the criticisms [*sic*] of Marie Steiner. He addressed himself directly to the human being in the artist, so that the essentially human could find expression in movement and gesture.'[9] Perhaps one could summarize the situation in the following way. When two musicians play together—and we can now bring our violinist and cellist onto the same concert platform—not only do they tune up, the *intonation* of each note has to be exactly in tune so that there is nothing discordant between the two of them. Likewise with Marie Steiner as director of eurythmy. Through her developing higher faculties—the Spirit Self connected with poetry and the Life Spirit connected with eurythmy—she was able to determine whether the eurythmist's movements and gestures were concordant or discordant with the tone, rhythm, sound and 'inner breathing' of the speaker's voice (usually *her* voice), and via that with what lived in the heart of the poem.

On 29 December 1914, a lecture that Steiner gave in Dornach included his by now well-known research into the relation of the arts to the seven members of the human being. On the one hand, this opens up vistas of understanding for and appreciation of the respective arts: architecture, sculpture, painting, and so on. On the other hand, we are left in no uncertainty as to the seedlike nature of those steps that were being taken in anthroposophy towards establishing a new impulse in the arts. Steiner couches the modest claims of spiritual science in the most humble of terms, as can be gleaned from the following:

> Round about us, in the environment of soul and spirit which we shall absorb at a later stage, the Life Spirit is also present. Therefore one day the Life Spirit may come to be lowered into the Spirit Self. But of course at the moment this is something that will only reach a certain degree of perfection in the very distant future. For when he tries to lower the Life Spirit into the Spirit Self man will have to be living entirely in an element which is as yet absolutely strange to him. So what we can say in this domain is like the babbling of a child compared with the later perfection of speech.[10]

This gives us, perhaps, a deeper understanding of the way—*method* is already too formulated an expression—in which we have glimpsed Marie Steiner directing eurythmy rehearsals than merely letting our gaze rest on the veneer of what it must have been like for someone who had next to no possibility of movement in the lower limbs having to carry the responsibility of being the co-inaugurator of a new art of movement. Even if Rudolf Steiner *was* at her side, this appears in no way to have detracted from a clear understanding of who held the director's reins. Far from interpreting his use of the expression 'like the babbling of a child' however as a disclaimer—certainly not as derogatory—it may point us in the right direction as to what was going on if we consider the expression in some depth. It has often been observed that the physical body is the most perfected of the human being's four members (physical, etheric, astral and ego) and that in fact in the very broadest scheme of things, since we are only just past the halfway mark of Earth evolution—following Ancient Saturn, Ancient Sun and Ancient Moon—it would be premature to expect anything else. The ego, on this count, is consequently the *infant* member of our constitution. How are we then to view those higher members whose present seedlike condition will blossom in the far future: Spirit Self, Life Spirit and Spirit Man? View them, that is on a 'scale' of maturity (physical) or infancy (ego)? Whatever answer to the question we might favour, it makes one thing clear: Steiner's 'like the babbling of a child' is quite a generous estimation of the situation, if we take into consideration the fact that *in* the babbling of a human child there lives a higher spiritual 'voice'.[11] It was surely that voice speaking Logos-like in spiritual heights that Marie Steiner-von Sivers had developed an inner ear for, had acquired and developed a gift for making it audible in her own recitation and, in tandem with this, had developed a remarkably honed intuitive perspicacity for identifying its presence or absence in the movements and gestures of those whom she was directing at rehearsals.

Furthermore, the child (still a babbler) expresses itself through the *will*. Its soul activity lives in the limbs. Indeed as parents we often experience the child's wilfulness as superior to our own command of our will! Thus it becomes less surprising that this new art, eurythmy, itself coming to expression through the will—movement and gesture—was coaxed into being (if that is the right expression) not at all primarily through the director's verbal directions, directed with minutely prescriptive detail *at* the forms of movements and gesture, but through constant repetition and the continuous process thereby of putting the eurythmist in touch with her own higher nature, the seed member whose germination, let alone blossoming, was still part of future evolution. That Steiner himself, when at rehearsal, 'made his indications more precise by the movement of his hand', supports this view. Choreographer, performer and rehearsal-coach all worked, in their own way, in the realm of the will, that realm which hierarchically is the most sublime of all in human nature. They all listened to the 'babbling' as to the voice of the Highest, echoing, so to speak through the glades which all three had discovered and entered, just as Parzival did in the domain of the Grail Castle.

Moving upward now from eurythmy, that art which Steiner places sixth in the sequence *architecture, sculpture, painting, music, poetry, eurythmy,* but without claiming that Marie Steiner's connection with drama pointed directly to the so-called 'seventh art'—that art which Rudolf Steiner pointed out will be added in the distant future to the other six—it seems, nevertheless, that it is right to place it here in this present sequence of enquiry because of its profound implication for society. (The seventh art has been referred to as the *social art*.)[12] To do justice to this view, it will be necessary to recapitulate some of the karmically eventful phenomena in her biography that have drama connotations or implications; but since we are nearing the end of tracing and following in the more factual footsteps of the individual's incarnation as Marie Steiner-von Sivers, the recapitulation 'exercise' may prove an enrichment of our study, at least in a similar vein to that in which we find Richard Wagner embarking on lengthy—sometimes epic—recapitulations in his music dramas. He did not do this as in the form of a classically musical da capo but in a zoom-lensing fashion, by overhauling psychologically and otherwise what has been referred to in the 'narrative', frequently incidents that have taken place before we have even heard the prelude to the first act. For the Wagnerian music drama, such flashbacks—not that they flashed by in the blink of a musical eye!—had significance for the tonal *structure* of the piece. Here, in the present context of looking at phenomena in the life of Marie Steiner-von Sivers, a similar process might give a valuable perspective on this particular strand of her life, that of drama, so intricately interwoven with the other strands being considered. Following the route card—with its straight stretches, its surprise bends, its grand vistas, and its climacteric crossroads—that such a recapitulation entails, thus gives an overview which hearkens back to the moment of birth and includes each symptomatic-symbolic signpost that marks her life's journey.

Being born into a German-speaking family is the first signpost, standing as it were at the crossroads between the present life and the previous death. Linguistically, to be part of an influential enclave amongst a population speaking a 'foreign tongue' and, *at the same time*, having a powerfully karmic connection with the Logos at so many levels must have created within the child's ever-changing consciousness—widening as the sense-world environment loomed, and simultaneously shrinking as the hitherto spirit-world environment receded—a tension, like the strings on a lyre that were to twang in the manner of a rising scale as the signposts hove into sight at the crossroads we are reviewing.

Through most of her childhood, the incisive part that drama was to play in her destiny had to wait until she performed on the stage in the Jubilee celebrations of her 'old' school in St Petersburg—a performance which could manifestly be seen as her theatrical début. Both on this occasion and on that of her next big breakthrough, it is fascinating to realize that the two roles in question, Maria Stuart and Joan of Arc, were the central figures in two of Friedrich Schiller's greatest works. Fascinating (a) because, being German classics, the experience launched her into the theatre on the great tide of past achievement, just at the time when, as we have seen, this tide was to ebb before the flow of theatrical naturalism; (b) because of all German playwrights Schiller championed the cause of humanity as a whole through his profound realization of the significance of *aesthetics* in human evolution and the part it had to play for the individual called upon to take his—or in this case, her—own destiny in hand; (c) because, with Schiller being the undisputed Matterhorn amongst the lofty mountain range of German playwrights—*Faust* had yet to step out of the wings of obscurity (the baffling second part) into the spotlight of full recognition—the family *with their resistance* could do no other than change their opinion (being swept along by the popular acclaim with which Marie's performance was greeted, they had little choice but to veer away from what they had considered to be a misguided whim, detrimental to the respect due to the name of von Sivers, to a recognition and acceptance, at some level, at any rate, of their wilful daughter's talent and artistic integrity); and (d) (though I do not intend to pursue the point) because the Schiller route seems to be the perfect complement to what we might call Rudolf Steiner's Goethean route.[13] Not that this was the only complementary factor in their life partnership, which led to the four Mystery Plays and, beyond Rudolf Steiner's death, to the enormously long build-up to the first *Faust* production at the Goetheanum in 1938.

The next crossroads, proving to be a cross in more than one metaphorical sense, was in Paris. On the one hand it was the breeding ground of what von Sivers sought at that point in her life: the theatre per se seemed to hold a commanding place in her soul's landscape as well as an ongoing magnetic attraction. This is evidenced by her sussing out what theatrical performances to go to, already it seems when she and Steiner were travelling on the boat train from the port of entry into England, to London, on one of the first visits in which she officially accompanied him in 1904, and the relish with which she attended the Shakespeare plays which they saw in Stratford on Avon—a moon cycle later!—on the high profile occasion of the conference for 'New Ideals in Education'. It was in Paris that fortuitously she found her first significant teacher in Mme Favart whose guidance must have been the reason for von Sivers' unprecedentedly rapid ascendancy—the Berlin offer of the title role in *The Maid of Orleans*, which we will meet again presently. It is necessary also to acknowledge at this stage that the tragedy in Mme Favart's life—the demise of her justly won fame—was essentially at the hands of the latest popular celebrity of the hour who epitomized the direction in which theatre in general was to go, which, from the classical viewpoint, embodied and spawned in speech, in gesture, in stage sets and in the substance of the dramas' plots, all that was becoming decadent and corrupt at the hand of naturalism. In the case of the life-mature Mme Favart, the new tendency essentially spelt the end of her life's work. In the case of the younger, drama-adventurer Fräulein von Sivers, it clearly conjured up the antipathy which was strong enough to lead to her seeking an alternative way forward.

This alternative (crossroads again) led to the deep appreciation she had for the work of Eduard Schuré. Apart from his books, he was the author of the two plays (*The Sacred Drama of Eleusis* and *The Children of Lucifer*) that made apparent for the modern audience (1890–1900) not what was going on in the morality-atrophying, tobacco-smoke-drenched, absinthe-driven depravities into which large pockets of contemporary society in Paris were sliding, but what had been vital pillars in the spiritually ennobling achievements of humanity's distant history. Amongst all the artistic jostling and spiritual dilettantism that was going on, Marie von Sivers appears immediately to have recognized Schuré's spiritual supremacy. We have seen the karmic significance of the triangle Schuré, Steiner and von Sivers; here we are simply acknowledging the touchstone part that drama played in their mutual connections.

Finally, the most inwardly dramatic moment of all the crossroads in her life was, as we have seen, when she was 33 years of age, in Berlin, the moment when the 'alternative' became a never-to-look-back imperative for her—a *coming home* (not that this implies any personal prodigality). Thinking over her own estimation of the moment, she communicated it to Savitch who reports: 'Suddenly in a flash of realization she knew: here and now falls the final decision.'[14] Poised at the junction of the two tramlines—and could there be a more Open-Sesame-like image?—it appears as a destiny moment, paralleled by those arresting experiences that many recall as the saving call of Christian Rosenkreutz, when the individual who hears *and recognizes* the call stands blindly before an outer or inner precipice. The image is used only as a simile, but perhaps one may be permitted to suggest that whereas Hypatia's life, when literally torn apart limb by limb, was also *symbolic* of that central experience in the Orphic Mysteries described earlier, here is a karmically connected turning point. Circumstances—the draw of life fulfilment and possibly even the glitter of outer fame in her pursuing a path that defied family prejudices and standing in society as a woman of independence, with the lure of the sensual world exuding right, left and centre in the life of the big, increasingly sprawling cities and so on—such circumstances could easily have torn her away from the unimaginably rich destiny-potential that lay in her future at that moment.

But she took the right turning at the crossroads—'she', that is, that within her nature that karmically-instinctively beckoned towards the future, progressive evolution of humanity, i.e. all that resides latently within the higher members of the human being. That final crossroads (final in the sense of the present route we are following and reviewing in her life) led to the central part she played, both on the stage and karmically, in the coming into being of Steiner's four Mystery Dramas, and the social dimension that they represented in the stream of anthroposophy—social enough, surely, to weave them, however tenuously, into the as-yet-in-the-future fabric of the *seventh art*.

6
Orpheus

His Song and the River of Time

Brien Masters

On one of the rare occasions when Rudolf Steiner spoke of Orpheus, we have what appears to be an unusually careful choice of words. This is not to suggest that Steiner was ever anything other than careful in the way his clear thinking was expressed with equal clarity in the way he spoke. In this instance, however, it is as if Steiner is acutely aware of treading on ground that might prove controversial to his audience—or some of them. For it would appear that the being of Orpheus is being presented, not as tradition would have it—part of Greek mythology (the general assumption being that mythological characters have no connection with earthly reality)—but as one who could be found on the earthly plane. The reference occurs in the sixth lecture of a cycle that Rudolf Steiner gave in Berlin in 1910/1911, entitled *Background to the Gospel of St Mark*.[1] Let us cite the passage.

> Interpretations of ancient legends do not convey their real meaning [since scholars and researchers today are unaware that former forms of thought were different, resulting in a different use of words as regards content and implication]. We are told, for instance, of Orpheus a Greek singer. I refer to him because he belongs to the period several centuries before Christianity. We may think of him as the one responsible for the organization of the Greek mysteries. This fourth post-Atlantean epoch,[2] of which he was an important figure in the opening stage, was a preparation for the Christ event[3] and what humanity was to receive through it. Thus in Greece Orpheus was the great preparer.
>
> If a man of the present age were to encounter a figure such as Orpheus, he would simply say: he is the son of such and such a father and such and such a mother—and science might possibly look for inherited characteristics [...] That is not how people thought in the days of Orpheus. The man of flesh and his physical attributes were not what really mattered to them. The essential qualities were those that enabled Orpheus to be the leader and organizer of pre-Christian Greek culture—certainly not the physical brain or nervous system.

> The essential thing was that he had within him—in his own field of experience—a quality derived from the spiritual world and united with the material-physical element provided by his parentage. The eyes of the Greeks were directed not to the physical figure of Orpheus, descending from father and mother [...] the figure was [...] merely the outer sheath [...] a physical-material element [that had been] able to unite with the supersensible in his personality.

Here we have Steiner being crystal clear about the limitations of that kind of thinking that is the outcome of the consciousness of 'scholars and researchers today'—with their limited ability to enter into 'how people thought' some three millennia previously in the evolution of human consciousness. Having prepared his audience somewhat circumspectly, Steiner then presents Orpheus in a way that seems to leave little room for placing the 'Greek singer' in the category of orthodox Greek myth. There are more than half a dozen expressions in the lecture which leave us in no doubt as to where Steiner is coming from.

Orpheus *belongs to* a particular period: this expression is not deliberately vague—the 'once upon a time', say, of the fairy tale. He was 'an important figure' connected with the beginning of the fourth post-Atlantean epoch, a figure 'responsible for the organization of the Greek mysteries'. So far, one would not need to be a cynic to argue that the use of these expressions could be equally valid if the figure of Orpheus was only that of a spiritual being. However, take these alongside what follows in the next paragraph. Encountering such a figure, someone today would 'simply say'—this doesn't sound like an unexpected vision or the like—that 'he is the son of such and such [parents]' (even grandparents are mentioned in the lecture!). Steiner then takes the stance—and thereby helps his listeners do the same—of Orpheus' contemporaries, looking at the attributes, the *spiritual* attributes, of the bard, which were 'what really mattered'. But he does this by highlighting what did *not* matter: 'the man of flesh and his physical attributes', driving the point home in the next sentence, even more clinically, might one say, with 'certainly not the physical brain and nervous system'. Nor has Steiner finished making his point. Maybe at the risk of repetition, he extols Orpheus' spiritually derived qualities which unite 'with the material-physical element', and returns to the 'outer sheath', the 'physical figure' of Orpheus, which has *descended* from the physical progenitors of his 'father and mother', a 'physical-material' element with which the supersensible being of Orpheus was 'able to unite'.

Would it, perhaps, be an admissible interpretation of what almost borders on persuasive rhetoric to think that Steiner perceived amongst his audience of Berliners—most of whom were probably born in the Gabriel age (which ended in 1879), and who therefore probably had a more Gabrielic way of thinking—a strong element of incredulity, or at least that element of mental inertia which either lacked imagination or was slow to leap across the gulf from rationality (be it humdrum or cuttingly active) to a different, in this case innovative mode of thought? And faced with this acutely fine perception—whether from the audience's facial expressions or via his advanced clairvoyance, we can leave on one side—he needed to get his point across to each and every laggardly thinker, as well as to the audience as a whole, through reiterating it in the way that the stenographer's report of the lecture richly demonstrates?

Be that as it may, the end result surely more than strongly suggests that Orpheus had a physical body, the result of the fusion of two genetic streams, that he lived at a certain place (Thrace), and at a certain time, and that he incarnated in order to fulfil a vital task in the cultural development that ancient Greece manifests in all that emanated from its age-old mystery centres—indeed, inaugurated. In the Orphic Mysteries, a mystery stream flowed which had the stamp of his spiritual status and impulse at its heart. We will come to what is implied by that, but first let us look more closely at the story we associate with Orpheus. This, unavoidably, must at first seem paradoxical for, having built up a considerable edifice, to convince his audience of the earthly existence of Orpheus—it could, of course, have been an *embodiment*, as was so often the case with the leaders of humanity in those far-off times—Steiner then makes no further reference to this personal aspect of Orpheus, rather adhering to his main purpose which is to ensure that the bard's significance in evolution is adequately represented and far-reachingly interpreted. With the former of these in mind notwithstanding, it will be good for our present purposes, as I say, to take as our point of departure the story's main components.

Orpheus was the son of Calliope—one of the nine Muses, she was associated with epic poetry, her sisters with other arts (these 'arts' included Urania with her *astronomy!*)—and Oeagrus the Thracian river god. (Steiner does not refer to other accounts in which, for instance, Apollo is deemed to have fathered Orpheus, and I am not sure that it would be fruitful here to meander into such anomalies.) From the Muses, he has inherited spiritually the gift of music. Steiner does subscribe to this, calling Orpheus the 'Greek singer', though it has been pointed out that the term *muse* ... has a wider interpretation[4] which is in accord with the traditional connections of each of the nine sisters and her art: Melpomene with tragedy, Euterpe with lyric poetry, and so on. In fact, the nearest we get to music per se amongst these nine arts is dancing, the artistic domain of Terpsichore, and sacred song the artistic domain of Polyhymnia. That singing as such is central to the story of Orpheus is, however, certainly not in doubt. Virgil and Ovid amongst the Roman poets emphasize this attribute: and our own English bard Shakespeare, well versed in the Classics, concentrates exclusively on his music. The song in *Henry VIII* begins 'Orpheus with his lute'; in *The Two Gentlemen of Verona* it is the power of his music that comes across, in inimically Shakespearean language, with 'could soften steel and stones, / Make tigers tame and huge Leviathans / Forsake unsounded deeps to dance on sands.' Perhaps most significant of all, it is in *The Merchant of Venice* that Shakespeare comes closest to the Orphic spiritual stream, for he refers to him between two of the most famous of all 'Shakespeare' passages, the first macrocosmic ('Sit Jessica: look how the floor of heaven / Is thick inlaid with patines of bright gold'); and the second microcosmic ('The man that hath no music in himself...'), which leads us—here, not in Shakespeare—to the tragedy of Orpheus, the epic element which Ovid brings out so poignantly in Book XI of his *Metamorphoses*.

Already before the wedding of Orpheus and Euridice had got fully under way, Hymen's smouldering torch proved to be an ill omen. Eurydice, with her naiads was pursued by Aristaeus, an unwanted guest (the shepherd who 'lost his bees through wound and sickness', as Virgil describes him). In order to avoid his advances, she runs off and in doing so treads on a snake that is lurking in the grass, the poison from whose fangs, biting into her ankle, causes her death. Orpheus, inconsolable, resolves to enter the world of shades and implore Pluto, who reigns there amongst the dead, to restore Euridice to him, and permit him to take her back to earth. This was allowed on condition that Orpheus not look at his bride before they were once more in daylight, a condition which, he failing to keep, results in her loss for ever. Although many operatic versions of the story go no further—an art form in which it proved popular amongst both composers and librettists—in fact the tragedy by no means ends here. More disconsolate than ever, Orpheus mourns his loss with laments so powerful that the whole of nature is affected in like manner. *With the exception*, that is, of the Ciconian women who are enraged to such an extent that they drown his music with their din: the 'huge uproar of the Berecynthian flutes, mixed with discordant horns, drums and the breast-beating of the Bacchanals' as Ovid puts it.[5] Without the sound of his lyre nature cannot save him and he is rendered defenceless and slain. Their 'mad fury' knowing no bounds, they tear him apart, *leaving his limbs scattered around*. Only his head and lyre were, so to speak, saved from their terrifyingly destructive atrocities, and were borne by the Hebrus river out to sea. The tale ends with an apotheosis: his lyre is placed by the gods in the heavens—the constellation we know as Lyra.

Having gone out of his way, as we have seen, to emphasize the 'physical-material' reality of Orpheus, Rudolf Steiner nevertheless pays close attention to the main elements of the story (though only somewhat tangentially to the second part, i.e. not referring to the wild Bacchanalian women by name). The first reference rather confirms the impression that, while Orpheus lived on earth in a human body with ordinary earthly ancestors, he had that spiritual attribute of a leader of humanity in ancient times—a connection with the gods. From the lecture it is not clear whether this is an embodiment. Steiner speaks of how those early leaders of humanity received messages of guidance from the divine world through the etheric body. In this we have the source of old clairvoyance described, and in the case of Orpheus depicted as Eurydice. The loss of clairvoyance takes place by degrees: the snake bite, his failing to honour the condition he has accepted in being allowed to return to earth with Euridice from Pluto's realm, and his own death—slaughter would describe it in accord with the dramatic imagery in the story. In essence, all three stages are the result of his becoming more and more at home in his earthly environment. The snake, confined to an existence *on the surface of the earth*, strikes the first blow; the yearning in his own soul for the past as, *at the same time he enters the realm of earthly daylight*, strikes the second blow; and the third decisive blow is given by those who, using tools of farm labourers and *digging into the earth itself* as they are wont with hoe, plough and mattock, cannot bear the cosmic quality that emanates from his clairvoyant consciousness.

Returning to the lecture once more, it comes as a surprise—often the case with Steiner—that the exploration of this (one of the most prominent) Greek stories is sandwiched between a theme that is normally associated with Christianity. Hence, perhaps, it sheds some light on the explanation behind Steiner's referring to Orpheus as part of the 'preparation' at the beginning of the fourth post-Atlantean epoch 'for the Christ event'. Orpheus, uniting in his 'outer sheath' that which is 'supersensible in his personality', represents a certain stage in the development of human consciousness. On the one hand, we may take it that behind the *imagination* of all that is depicted in the well-known story, traditionally assigned to mythology, is an actual person alive on earth who goes through a significant transition from an original clairvoyant state of consciousness (supersensible) to a state in which the clairvoyance has given way to a consciousness which is informed by *earthly senses*. On the other hand, we may take it that Orpheus symbolizes that which humanity as a whole experiences, pinpointed in the fourth post-Atlantean epoch, but as a centre point for a much wider spectrum of time.[6]

Viewing this condition of consciousness from the perspective of ontogeny, Steiner relates this to the young child's experience at the point where memory starts to dawn, usually associated with the child's saying 'I' to itself (and of its own accord). Before the 'I' dips into the physical-material sheath to the extent that it does for this fulcrum-of-consciousness moment to come about, it is the spiritual that prevails. Thereafter, the spiritual is gradually superseded by earthly impressions that are *conveyed via the senses*. The sense world, which informs our modern thinking and does indeed tend (very successfully!) to displace any other informant, tears to pieces, so to say—*dismembers*, in terms of the Orphic imagery—the earlier, supersensible form of consciousness.

In the *motif* of Orpheus being torn apart limb by limb we have not only a dramatically powerful pointer towards what was to become of humanity—a key element in the divine plan of inserting the quality of freedom into an otherwise ordained universe of stars and planets and all that dwells therein and thereon—but an indelible image that can be a signpost for anyone seeking to move forward through the ages karmically. In this respect, Steiner explains why he favours Oeagrus as Orpheus' father rather than Apollo: 'as the son of Calliope and nothing more than that, Orpheus could have given expression only to manifestations of the supersensible world [...] It was also his mission to give expression to what would be of service to physical life in that epoch [...] his own life gave expression to the supersensible in such a way that the physical world was also important to his life. [To reflect this in the imagery which the people of that time could access] Orpheus was made the son of Oeagrus, the Thracian river god.'[7]

We thus have a world-karmic sequence, following the second and third post-Atlantean epochs in which the leaders of culture perceived in their etheric bodies what the divine world would have them communicate to their contemporaries (this included the Celts). Orpheus symbolizes the sequel to this. As was the case generally in ancient Greece, in him (to begin with) there existed a balance—spiritual and earthly. His destiny—a tragedy if one only takes the spiritual perspective—was to tilt the fulcrum implicit in this balance towards the earthly. In subsequent chapters we shall see how this is followed with further steps: in Greek *philosophy*; in the realm of the *personality* (in post-Christian Alexandria), which in turn leads us to the Middle Ages; and finally to the West in the fifth post-Atlantean epoch. In following this sequence, we shall not only come face to face with that world-karma here expounded in imaginative terms, but through the Orphic motif become aware of a sequence of repeated earth lives that finally arrive at Marie Steiner-von Sivers, and in particular—as if listening to the melodic cadences in the song of Orpheus as his head and lyre float onward down the river of time—what this may imply for the life of anthroposophy in the West.

Metamorphoses

Ovid

Te maestae volucres, Orpheu, te turba ferarum,
te rigidi silices, te carmina saepe secutae
fleverunt silvae, positis te frondibus arbor
tonsa comas luxit; lacrimis quoque flumina dicunt
increvisse suis, obstrusaque carbasa pullo
naides et dryades passosque habuere capillos.
membra iacent diversa locis, caput, Hebre, lyramque
excipis; et (mirum!) medio dum labitur amne,
flebile nescio quid queritur lyra, flebile lingua
murmurat exanimis, repondent flebile ripae.

The mourning birds wept for thee, Orpheus,
the throng of beasts, the flinty rocks, and the trees
which had so often gathered to thy songs;
yes, the trees shed their leaves as if so tearing their hair in grief for thee.
They say that the rivers also were swollen with their own tears, and that naiads and dryads alike mourned with dishevelled hair and clad in garb of sombre hue.
The poet's limbs lay scattered all around;
but his head and lyre, O Hebrus, thou didst receive and (a marvel!) while they floated around mid-stream the lyre gave forth some mournful notes, mournfully the lifeless tongue murmured, mournfully the banks replied.[1]

7
Pherecydes of Syros

Bifocal Vision Emerging in Greek Consciousness

Rahel Kern

The history of man shows tremendous soul metamorphoses and changes of consciousness. When looking at the evolution of human consciousness and our experience of the world, it becomes apparent how awareness, cognition and insight show very different characteristics when comparing consecutive periods of humanity. While true insight always keeps something identical, insight is an element of human life and as such is not inanimate but alive. In other words, the notion of insight constantly transforms and metamorphoses. While its content may stay the same—truth is always identical with itself—knowledge can be presented in very different forms; it can be depicted in symbolic, imaginative or conceptual form, and it can be given or independently arrived at. Each age develops different ways of gaining insight and its own specific notion of what constitutes insight.

One of the most striking turning points in the earth's history was towards the end of the Atlantean times. Up till then, man had lived closely connected with the life forms around him and under the guidance of the group soul. Man was primarily determined by the lower forces of nature, ruled by emotions and living by instincts, desire and lust. When in the macrocosm, the world slowly started to appear through the lifting of the watery, nebulous hazes covering the concrete shapes; from a microcosmic point of view, that is within the inner human being, there lit up a consciousness of the individual's own being. Out of a clairvoyantly enlightened state, the veils were lifted and self-awareness shone through for the first time: the old imagination (*Bilderleben*) makes way for a more conceptual thought life (*Gedankenerleben*). Over long periods of time and in rhythmical cycles, the being of man unfolds. The development of the ego consciousness and the increasingly ego-bound human being began—an evolution that led up to today's conscious man who is determined by his intellect and own judgement.

The Greek thinker Pherecydes from the island of Syros in the sixth century BC is a personality that allows us to retrace and learn about one of these metamorphoses taking place. He stands exactly at this transition point from the old to the new, at the fulcrum moment of human consciousness. While in times before him people did not differentiate their experience of the natural world around from their own soul experiences, Pherecydes begins to differentiate himself from the surrounding world whereby his own soul life begins to comprehend and discern itself as a separate, independent being. While people previously experienced the forces in nature phenomena like thunder or wind to be the same kind as those within them when carrying out a particular activity such as moving about or raising an arm, Pherecydes does not experience himself as involved and as one with the world any more but begins to differentiate the forces around him from those active within him.

At the same time, his powerful imagery of the world demonstrates how he still holds on to the old consciousness cloaked in evocative Greek mythology. His cosmic imagery of the world[1]—a winged oak tree, freely floating in the centre of a universal mist of clouds and haze, unmoved and draped with a garment made of rich linen and embroidered with stars, rivers and land—palpably demonstrates how he still holds on to old mystical, pictorial portrayals. The world is still inhabited and worked upon by beings of Greek mythology while he is already trying to penetrate the riddles of the world and of human existence by thought. His differentiation into three primary and eternal principles—Zas (Zeus), Chthonie (or Chthonios, Earth) and Chronos (Time)—and his description of the origin of the world from this divine trinity clearly demonstrates his attempt to grasp his cosmology intellectually. When he speaks of Zeus as that whereby all is made and resembling the breath flowing though everything, Chthon as that wherefrom all is made and as the water putting pressure on all sides, and Chronos as that wherein all things are made, Pherecydes does introduce these three origins in abstract concepts. He describes the primordial principles and the generation of the cosmos out of them in images of living beings in a perceptible form. They are personified in such a way that we can only assume that he must have experienced the working together of these three forces directly and intuitively. He must have experienced himself in the unfolding events: Zeus transforming himself in producing Eros as the creator spirit of the world, Eros' union with Chthon and the beginning of measured finite time, and matter which then spilled over into the three elements of fire, water and air. The world is worked upon by the powerful gods of Greek mythology who are creating, fighting and celebrating in its history. Yet what presents itself to Pherecydes' soul life as images does not remain pure imagery. In differentiating the effects of the gods and events unfolding, he moves away from pure perception of the images and progresses towards experiencing himself as an independent, detached entity pondering over these images. This is what Rudolf Steiner calls the birth of thought life, which is expressed in Pherecydes less in a truly conceptual version as with later thinkers, but still more as a general prevailing soul-mood. Pherecydes lives in two worlds, in imagination and experience of pictures on the one hand and reflection by means of thoughts on the other. He is at a unique point in time where he has living visions which are able to look into the world of causes, a world which is entirely closed off to us nowadays, but he is not able anymore to entirely share the imaginative realm of his forefathers. While still living partially in it, at the same time, he pierces through man's existence in the world by thought:

> Pherecydes arrives at his [world outlook] in a different way from that of his predecessors. The significant fact is that he feels man to be a *living soul* in a way different from earlier times. For the earlier worldview, the word 'soul' did not yet have the meaning that it acquired in later conceptions of life, nor did Pherecydes have the idea of the soul in the sense of later thinkers. He simply *feels* the soul element of man, where the later thinkers want to speak clearly about it (in the form of thought) and they attempt to characterize it in intellectual terms.[2]

Thus at the threshold of human consciousness he still sees into the world with clairvoyance, while his (near) contemporaries have already more abstract concepts belonging to the ego. Aristotle characterizes Pherecydes as someone who combines the mystical with the non-mystical by mixing myth and philosophy, as someone who stands midway between poets and philosophers.[3] One can do justice to Pherecydes' cosmology only when considering that knowledge meant something different and was derived at very differently before and after his time. Otherwise, his work, often criticised as 'unphilosophical', would be understood as endorsing a peculiar form of childlike mysticism or to represent not much more than projections of human experience.

Pherecydes is not a rational thinker who relies on his own intellect and judgement alone. Thinkers after his time are much more philosophers in the modern sense. They clearly have a different grasp of the world and a very different understanding of what it means to know something about the world. So while Pherecydes is reported to have been one of the teachers of Pythagoras and many of the teachings of subsequent philosophers such as Heraclitus and Plato can be traced back to him in their roots,[4] they clearly have moved away from visions of the elemental world and on to much more independent sources of enquiry.

With Pherecydes as the bridge between what is nowadays labelled 'mythic' and 'Presocratic' thought, thinkers before him still lived entirely within the mystic realm in which no differentiation was experienced between the world and the thinker's thoughts as such. All was experienced in impressive, all encompassing images. Thus we know indirectly about the teacher of Pherecydes, whose name remains unknown to us, and we can approximate to an understanding of her being and her way of seeing and experiencing the world.

Within the context of the incarnations of Marie Steiner von Sivers, the person of Pherecydes' teacher is of great interest. Rudolf Steiner, who refers to her as '*die Namenlose*' (literally translated 'the nameless one', the feminine German article referring to a female incarnation), indicates that she is yet another incarnation within the incarnation sequence of this book:

> Among the pupils of the Orphic Mysteries was the lovable personality of whom I am speaking, whose earthly name has not come down to posterity, but who stands out clearly as a pupil of these Mysteries. Already in youth and then for many years, this person was closely connected with all the Greek Orphics during the period preceding that of Greek philosophy—a period of which no account is given in books and the history of philosophy. For what is recorded of Thales and Heraclitus is an echo of what the Mystery pupils had accomplished in their way at an earlier period. And one of the pupils of the Orphic Mysteries was the individual of whom I have just spoken, whose pupil in turn was Pherecydes of Syros...[5]

Without any more details on the individuality of Pherecydes' teacher, we may but only indirectly attempt to approximate to her being. With her student so clearly standing at a fulcrum moment of consciousness, giving birth to a new consciousness while still being connected to the old mystical mode of consciousness, one might wonder what precisely might have been her involvement and contribution in this process. With Rudolf Steiner specifically mentioning her as Pherecydes' teacher he lets us wonder about her own state of consciousness. She might have, in fact, been at a very similar stage, sharing with her student the new onset and teaching him what needed to happen. However, since Rudolf Steiner so clearly refers to Pherecydes as being the individuality concluding the decisive step for humanity, this renders the mention of her very surprising. Why would Rudolf Steiner have specifically mentioned her if Pherecydes has indeed concluded the step? Or else, we may conjecture whether she, having preceded him, despite still being in the old imaginative mode of consciousness instinctively knew of the decisive change in consciousness about to take place. In this case, she must have realized his potential and guided Pherecydes so that his own particular mission could be fulfilled and that the impending progress for evolution could take place. We wonder to what extent she might have been aware of the change she helped to bring about and how necessary it was for humanity. Whichever her own state of consciousness was, whether mindful or oblivious to both her impact on her student and the wider consequences for humanity, both Aristotle and Rudolf Steiner clearly acknowledge Pherecydes at this fulcrum moment of consciousness. Thus we can but assume that the individuality of '*die Namenlose*' evidently was instrumental in helping her student gain the later state of consciousness.

We have already previously encountered this motive of helping with the downward journey, away from the cosmic consciousness, more and more into the physical world in Euridice's snake bite and the poison of entering the physical world. As a great leader of humanity, she is the guide into the world of the senses. She is actively involved in leading humanity out of a clairvoyant state into the sense-perceptible world, a process whereby humanity's clairvoyant capacities become increasingly dormant.

In the chapters that follow, we will see how this relates to Rudolf Steiner's path of opening up a new way of knowledge. It is a path of reawakening those dormant capacities, but now in an entirely new way through cultivating certain soul attitudes and developing one's inner life, in particular increasing the activities of thinking, feeling and willing in a fully conscious way towards higher knowledge and insights into higher worlds.

8
Hypatia of Alexandria

New Perspectives on her Personality

Rahel Kern

Hypatia's savage death—murdered, dismembered and burnt by mobsters in an act of hatred and fanaticism—is often better remembered than are her outstanding achievements as the last carrier of pure Greek Hellenism in the realms of philosophy, astronomy, astrology, mathematics. Fearing for their own lives, scientists, scholars, poets and philosophers who had built and contributed to the culture and civilization of the metropolis fled the city following Hypatia's death. Her tragic death marks the end of free enquiry and ancient science and indicates the demise and decline of Alexandria,[1] the major city of ancient learning. The great era of Greek civilization, starting with Alexander the Great's[2] vision of linking Greece and the rich Nile valley by founding Alexandria, ends with the death of this pre-eminent individuality.

Speaking about Hypatia's death, Rudolf Steiner directly links her tragic destiny with the founding of Alexandria several centuries earlier. Concluding his account of her life, he closes his lecture on 27 December 1910 by pointing towards a connection to the metropolis of Alexandria:

> Symbolically, so to say, there is indicated here [in Hypatia's tragic destiny] something that is deeply connected with the founding of Alexandria by Alexander the Great—although it happened a long time after the actual founding of the city.[3]

In order to shed light on to these two parallel events in different epochs of time—Alexandria's glorious founding and the cataclysmic death of one of its most extraordinary thinkers—this chapter will begin with a short discourse on the founding of Alexandria, which was the prosperous capital and centre of learning that Hypatia was born in about six centuries later. As her home city and main place of activity, Alexandria then provides the backdrop for the second part of the chapter which will look at her life and work.

★ ★ ★

The time of Alexander the Great and his establishing the metropolis of Alexandria clearly bears characteristics attributed to the Archangel

Michaël. When defeating the dragon he is often depicted with sword and shield with the Latin inscription *Quis ut Deus*, the Latin phrase asking the emblematic question 'Who is like God?'. Michaël is the true protector and servant of mankind during dark times when humanity is at risk of undue attachment to the material world resulting in man's becoming hard and rigid in his being. Fighting the dragon, Michaël makes hearts beat faster, grants strength, courage and spiritual purpose. The *Book of Revelation* describes how he defeats the forces of evil throwing Satan to earth along with the fallen angels: '... there was war in heaven. Michaël and his angels fought against the dragon, and the dragon and his angels fought back. But he was not strong enough, and they lost their place in heaven.'[4] He is the archangel of the sun powers, endowing us with spirit and helping us to preserve our divine sun spark.

At the time of Alexander the Great, his influence as a cosmic intelligence was of great importance for humanity and for the following epochs of time. Independently of the course of events and occurrences on the outer plane of documented history and possible time differences between them, it is the inner pattern going through the centuries which makes some of them kindred spirits. So even though Hypatia's dates of life do not coincide directly with Michaël's leadership, her life and destiny are closely connected to the impulse of Alexandria and need to be seen within the light of the archangel's regency and activity.

★ ★ ★

Alexander III of Macedon was born in Paella, Macedon in July 356 BC on the night the temple of Ephesus stood in flames. His birth thus coincided with the fateful fire destroying the outer building enclosing the human wisdom of ancient times in this sacred site. In an act of arson the flames destroyed the site with its sacred images of the great goddess, the carvings in relief and columns; but while they destroyed all outward structures, they released everything spiritual that had gone into the temple and site since ancient times. Rudolf Steiner describes how this wisdom emanated from the venerated temple walls and was written into the cosmic ether. What formerly had been contained and nurtured within spiritual centres was now spread far and wide across the world. The burning of the temple was a sign that the concentrated wisdom would now live within the souls of those who had received it and who, from this point in time, would need to spread it wherever their destinies led them. It is a cosmic event in which the ancient mysteries disappeared and from which time onwards human beings had to live separated from the divine hierarchies. Michaël enters here as the carrier of the sun powers, inspiring us to grasp our own consciousness and to take our spiritual development into our own hands. Michaël is the inspirer of philosophy, of independent human enquiry and the search for truth. With the coming of the Michaëlic period, which started *circa* the sixth century BC, there was a change in human consciousness, most noticeable in the teachings of the philosopher Aristotle.

Aristotle realized this change in human consciousness was taking place when he formed his ten categories of quantity, quality, relation, space, time, position, activity (or action) and passivity (or suffering). Inspired by a strong vision of what had taken place at the time of the burning of the mystery centre of Ephesus years before, he was able to read out of the ether the fading away of clairvoyant revelations and man's future state separated from the divine hierarchies. This experience provided him with the impetus to formulate his 'cosmic script':

> Expressions which are in no way composite signify substance, quantity, quality, relation, place, time, position, state action, or affection ... Not one of these terms, in and by itself, involves an affirmation; it is by the combination of such terms that positive or negative statements arise.[5]

These ten categories encapsulate the secrets of the cosmos and of man. If treated in a living way, they can reveal themselves as the cosmic script and can lead to spiritual knowledge. Fundamentally speaking, Rudolf Steiner points out that all that anthroposophy has brought forth (and could ever bring forth) is experienced out of these concepts as they comprise all secrets the physical and the spiritual worlds contain.[6]

Aristotle found in Alexander a student who carried his wisdom out into the world. With both Aristotle's and Alexander's lives clearly standing under the sign of the archangel Michaël, the impulses living in Aristotle's philosophy and the inspiration behind Alexander's deeds and actions are closely linked in their mission of spreading Michaëlic impulses, which will be elaborated in the following.

★ ★ ★

Alexander grew up in a household that admired the Greeks and he enjoyed an upbringing that grew wholly out of the Greek stream of wisdom. When he turned 13, Alexander's father Philip II engaged the Greek philosopher Aristotle to tutor his young son, leading to an intimate student-teacher relationship that lasted for the next seven years and considerably influenced Alexander's outlook. Under Aristotle's tutorship and instruction, Alexander gained an interest in philosophy, medicine and science.

Alexander's journeys into the Asian continent and his campaign of conquest shortly after the assassination of his father in 336 BC (when the 20-year-old Alexander took the throne of Macedonia) have to be understood in the light of the teachings of Aristotle. He embarked on his conquests not just with a small and efficient army consisting of 30,000 foot soldiers and 5000 cavalrymen, but also took engineers, surveyors, architects, scientists and even historians on his expeditions. These were not just of a military nature, as he thereby introduced Aristotle's natural sciences and Grecian culture to the East. The small fraction of Aristotle's natural sciences remaining to us today is what Alexander carried with him to Asia. After eight years of military victories coupled with political and diplomatic skills, Alexander was the ruler of a massive empire incorporating Asia Minor, Syria, Egypt, Babylonia and the Persian Empire. During this time, shortly after being crowned Pharaoh in Memphis in 331 BC, prompted by a dream he also founded Alexandria, the new capital of Egypt, at the mouth of the Nile which he named after himself. Although its design was heavily influenced and determined by him, he did not stay long enough to see it developing into an illustrious and cosmopolitan city, graced with elegant architecture, statuary and broad avenues and known for its clever financial policies and sciences. Though Alexander never lived to see its full glory, its cultural significance and impact far outweigh that of any other city founded by him.

The significance of Alexandria is by no means limited to the particular time when the metropolis stood in its fullest glory. The founding of Alexandria fundamentally affects the development of the fourth cultural epoch by bringing together the three most important streams of culture in one centre: the pagan-Grecian, the Christian and the Mosaic-Hebrew stream. In its variety of cultures, traditions and faiths, Alexandria came to serve as a true meeting place for East and West. It is probably here that the word *cosmopolitan* realizes its full Michaëlic meaning—not just in the sense of an international, multiracial nation but in the sense of citizens of the cosmos. Welcoming respect for other cultures and an open-minded pursuit of knowledge, Alexandria attracted the greatest scholars of all three different streams who lived and worked side by side in the metropolis. Alexander devoted considerable sums of money to finance the enquiries of Aristotle and established centres of learning which allowed the tradition of ancient knowledge to be preserved. When, aged 32, he died from a fever in June 323 BC—the much older Aristotle died shortly after in March 322 BC—civil unrest tore his empire apart and the throne of Egypt fell to Ptolemy I[7] who took over the regency and continued to support the Greek sciences and arts, thereby mingling

Hellenic traditions with the legacy of the Pharaohs. He made a permanent endowment to science by setting up a foundation dedicated to the sciences, the Museion in Alexandria. Conceived as bringing together the whole of the earlier Greek science, art and literature, it represented a magnificent, most influential academic institution in antiquity, a place that allowed scholars from all disciplines to engage in lively and free exchange of thoughts and to carry out their respective studies of research. Like a veritable temple it attracted many prominent academics and preserved all branches of Greek culture. Scholars studied and explored as a community areas such as physics, literature, medicine, astronomy, geography, philosophy, mathematics, biology and engineering. With the sciences being under the overall care and protection of the state, which also employed hundreds of professors, it was not just established knowledge which was being collected but new research was also encouraged and financed. The grounds of the Museion was the place where new knowledge could be generated and cultivated. It was meticulously designed, and included libraries, zoological and botanical gardens, observatories and dissection rooms. The community of scholars of the Museion studied the entire cosmos, in the sense of the Greek word *cosmos* meaning the order of the universe as a harmonious system that is deeply interconnected. Many of the fundamental principles of European science and culture, which are still important until today, were established here.

Under the Ptolemaic dynasty Alexandria became the cultural and economic centre of the ancient world. When it ended with the death of Cleopatra VII in 30 BC and Egypt became a protectorate of Rome, the seat of political power shifted, yet Alexandria retained its status as the most impressive metropolis of the time. Throughout the Hellenistic period as well as in the times of the Roman Empire it remained the intellectual centre of the Roman Empire. Under the early Ptolemies, the city became an important foreign trade port for the whole of Europe, and also developed a flourishing trade with India and the East. The ensuing and increasing wealth of its population soon brought creativity and the arts to Egypt. While Alexander asserted his power, bringing the world under his influence, Ptolemy I saw a need to adopt Egyptian culture and become one with the people he ruled. Respecting Egyptian religion and beliefs, he brought about a synthesis between the existing Egyptian culture and the newly introduced Greek culture. It can be argued as to how far he entered into a real cultural exchange with the Egyptians or whether the splendour of the once vibrant city of Athens was merely transferred to Alexandria, thereby looking to preserve Athenian culture and traditions.

It is clear though that the Greek influx of culture—the philosophy with all of its nuances of intellectual life, the sciences and the variety of magnificent visual and performing arts—transformed Alexandria into a Greek city, but one situated on the African continent.

★ ★ ★

The rise of the metropolis Alexandria as a city on a lavish scale, as the world centre of culture, learning and commerce took place under the rulership of the archangel Michaël. And when Michaël gave up his dominion over the cosmic intelligence in 246 BC, the golden age in the Greek-Roman empire finally faltered.

During the early Christian centuries the intellectual and cultural life with its Greek spirit and strength of mind, previously so alive in Alexandria, was lost by a decline of the once treasured values and a continuous sliding into decadence. Attempts by the Church to establish religious uniformity across the entire Roman Empire through not just spreading but also enforcing Church doctrines had a truly devastating effect on all Hellenistic sciences. Church dignitaries associated these directly with paganism and condemned them as evil. Astronomical predictions and prophecies were suddenly feared as putting a limit on God's scope of action, scientific research as encroaching upon His habitat and philosophical views as dangerously undermining His omnipotence.

Up until AD 312 when Emperor Constantine the Great converted to Christianity and declared it the official religion of the Roman Empire, only a small group of Christians lived in Alexandria's racial melting pot and represented merely one of the many religions vying for popularity. With much disquiet and civil unrest throughout the centuries, Alexandria was by no means a peaceful place and, being in the minority, Christians often suffered terrible persecution. When the official status of the Christian churches changed in that year, it represented a dramatic change. Devout Christians, who until that point had often fought to defend their faith in the face of strong opposition and under threat of their lives, now suddenly belonged to a newly privileged and rapidly spreading faith. However, such official state endorsement had an impact on the values and outlook associated with the Church. Away from an inner, spiritual understanding of Christ as experienced by the early Christians, the focus of the state Church concentrated on its legitimized claim to political power. Introducing one single state religion presented Constantine with a chance to unify and consolidate the Roman Empire by virtue of a commonly shared system of beliefs and doctrines. One might wonder whether his motivation behind imposing Christian doctrines was linked to his own personal striving for power, in the sense that in a distorted interpretation an omnipotent God placed at the top of a clear celestial hierarchy could be used by him as a justification for an earthly and personal quest for power. As a monotheistic religion with a strong hierarchical presence in heaven, it carried the temptation to apply its divine order directly on societal structures on earth. As such, it may have offered Emperor Constantine the ideal justification to insist on his own person as being the supreme leader on earth, thereby demanding absolute and unconditional obedience from his followers. His politics and jurisdictional system certainly reduced Christian values and beliefs to an external obedience and to an adoption of laws as the only acceptable and correct way to think and act with regard to religion and the state. Many Christians in Alexandria, once persecuted for their faith, now succumbed to the lure of power and turned into persecutors raging against Gentiles and Jews. Ethical and religious differences between pagans, Jews and Christians came to the fore with conflicts, civil disturbances and bloody uprisings shaking Alexandria to its very core. The bigoted outlook and ever-increasing dominance of the institution of the state Church led to an extensive destruction of everything pagan. Countless synagogues and temples were burnt and increasingly non-Christian public figures were threatened and banned from holding public office. Needless to say such disintegration of the old Alexandrian social order and collapse of moral values also had a devastating effect on its once proud intellectual life.

★ ★ ★

It is at this low point in ancient history that Hypatia, a woman of outstanding personality lived and initiated a quiet revival of the old ideals and studies in Alexandria. Born in Alexandria in AD 370, she was the daughter of a Greek, Theon of Alexandria,[8] one of the most educated men in the city and a well-known astronomer and respected mathematician of antiquity. Together with her brother Epiphanius, who later also became a mathematician, Hypatia received a thorough education from her father. It is said that he planned every aspect of his children's upbringing with greatest care, aiming to bring them up to be 'perfect people'. Born at a time when the ancient ideal of education strongly discriminated against women, the entire educational system held to the Aristotelian conviction that women have not the same intellectual capacities as men and all academic institutions available to men were barred to women. Women were therefore wholly dependent on lessons from fathers or husbands, who provided the only prospect for them to obtain even just a basic education. Despite the prevailing misogyny of the time however, Theon set out to teach and educate both children alike. As an advocate of free thought and proponent of autonomous intellectual enquiry, he instilled in them a passion for cultivating the mind and fostered their mathematical, scientific and philosophical training. No religious dogma or system of thought should ever prevent rational enquiry and discovery of scientific truths. Hypatia herself is reported to have passed on her father's saying 'reserve your right to think, for even to think wrongly is better than not to think at all'.

Already very early on it became apparent that Hypatia had exceptional gifts and a great aptitude for her father's sciences. Having initially received home tuition, she continued her education at the Mouseion of Alexandria, possible for her since her father was a member of this library.[9] Here Hypatia began to study philosophy intensively; presumably this would have taken on the mathematical-scientific expression of Neoplatonism. It seems that she became acquainted with the teaching of Plotinus[10] still in its original form and must have felt a strong connection with his approaches to thought. Nowadays, Plotinus is considered to be the archetypal philosopher whose pure thinking is executed with and distinguished by moderation, discipline and absolute consistency.

Hypatia also seems to have spent a short period of time in Italy where she received further training, as well as in Athens where she was presented with the laurel wreath and philosopher's cloak, an honour awarded only to exceptionally outstanding students. It is reported that on her return to Alexandria she proudly wore the cloak when taking part in public events or when walking through the city publicly, interpreting works of the great philosophers and teaching those who gathered around her. During her educational travels, her reputation for her intellectual brilliance and wisdom had spread throughout the entire Roman Empire. Leaving a lasting impression on many men for her beauty and grace, as well as through her astuteness, wit and ingenuity, her reputation preceded her when she returned to Alexandria in AD 400 at the age of 30. She was famous not only for her comprehensive and deep knowledge of philosophy, surpassing that of the most learned thinkers of her time, but also for her eloquence of speech and ability to explain straightforwardly even the most complicated of ideas. In particular, she gained a reputation for her knowledge of astronomy, which at that time represented a specialized field of mathematics rather than the study of planets as physical objects. Seen as a field of enquiry lifting the mind out of the physical and towards the divine, it was regarded as being a way of leading the mind closer to God and to discerning His will, which would then also allow one to accurately predict future events. She was also proficient in other systems of mathematics, most notably geometry and arithmetic, and, judging by comments from contemporary mathematicians, she surpassed her father in those fields. According to them, her father Theon would have been an outstanding mathematician had it not been for his own daughter overshadowing him. Hypatia was also well versed in practical sciences such as mechanics and studied mechanical laws not only theoretically but put them to practical use in the development of technical devices. Worth mentioning here are the astrolabe, a measuring device to ascertain the position of the stars and used to cast horoscopes, and a hydrometer, indicating the specific gravity of liquids.

Upon her return to Alexandria, she was appointed the head of the Mouseion where she then held a chair and was officially commissioned to teach philosophy, mathematics and astronomy. It suffices to say that, in an era historically determined by misogyny, it is more than unusual for such a post traditionally reserved for men to be held by a woman.

While it proves impossible to apprehend exactly how far her teaching influence reached and who was amongst her studentship, there are some mentions of specific names. Many letters composed by Synesius Cyrene,[11] later the bishop of Ptolemais, do not just speak of Hypatia's excellent reputation as a teacher but also mention several of her students, many of whom were very influential and wealthy individuals. Besides himself, amongst her studentship there were his younger brother Euptius, who later became his brother's successor as bishop, their uncle Alexander, as well as Synesius' closest friend Herculian and his younger brother Olympus, a wealthy landowner in Syria and pious Christian. Other students included Euoptius, assumed to be another brother of Synesius, and also a later bishop, Ammonius, who was to be on the Alexandrian city council, Heysichius, later duke of Libya and also bishop, Athanasius the sophist, Theodosius the grammarian, and many others only known to us by name.

As common practice in her time, Hypatia accompanied her lectures with written texts and guides for her students and also wrote commentaries on well-known works.

Within the field of mathematics, her written work is thought to have included a 13-volume study on the *Arithmetica* of Diophantos, who had taught mathematics in Alexandria a century and a half before Hypatia's time. Nowadays, Diophantos is considered by number theorists not only as the 'father of algebra' but is also said to have introduced many mathematical operations which, in regard to their ingenuity, can only be compared to modern theories. It is widely accepted that Hypatia's formulation of alternative answers and raising of new problems within the theory of numbers were incorporated into Diophantos' later works. It is further known that she wrote an eight-volume treatise on the *Conic Sections* of Apollonius of Perga,[12] a commentary which includes a collection of astronomical display diagrams and which attempts to explain, amongst other things, the irregular orbits of the planets. The conics represent one of the principles fundamentaly important for the breakthrough from the geocentric to the heliocentric view of the world. It is further believed that she collaborated with her father Theon on various revisions, such as the *Almagest* by Ptolemy,[13] a collection of his works which encompassed all astronomical and mathematical knowledge of that time, and the *Elements* of Euclid (often also referred to as *Stoicea*)[14] in which the author deduced properties of geometric objects and established his elementary number theory. His methods became the model for all later mathematical theory. Even in the light of modern mathematical developments, Hypatia's extensive studies and commentaries still represent most intellectually challenging works.

Although none of her written work survived—probably not surprising given her destiny—it can be deduced from various mentions and attributions in works by her father or other contemporaries that she also undertook her own original research. Considering Hypatia's intellectual destination and prowess, it is indeed highly improbable that she would have limited herself to interpretations and would not have developed her own independent thoughts or views on philosophical matters.

★ ★ ★

Within the arena of philosophy, Hypatia is most likely to have been a proponent of Neoplatonism, the dominant philosophical movement at her time. In contrast to the earlier thinkers Plato and Aristotle, Neoplatonism does not regard matter as uncreated but as a principle that emerged from God. This in itself is an indication that Neoplatonism and Christianity are intimately linked and nowadays philosophical literature in the main strongly emphasizes the parallels between their respective understanding of the world. Both the Greek and Neoplatonic understanding of the world reflect on the existence and living presence of God. Both encompass awareness of the sanctity of being and ultimately focus on God as the eternal force upon which everything is resting. Such belief and conviction in God was neither simple faith nor based on any specific creed demanded by a Church, but was instead derived purely by logical and consistent thinking.

In the centuries in question, however, logical thinking and conscious questioning could not be seen to have any place in religion. For the large part, Christianity was introduced into wider society as a religion promoting a literal interpretation of the Bible and demanding unquestioned obedience to God-given laws and commandments, usually involving penance and world-renouncement. Such went, ironically, hand in hand with earthbound values becoming increasingly important, particularly amongst wealthy Church officials. Progressively gaining prominence, the Church stigmatized any other approach to religion engaging the intellect to be 'pagan', 'heretical' and 'blasphemous'. From the Church's point of view, the entirety of the Hellenistic sciences—especially the sciences of philosophy, mathematics, astronomy and astrology—were manifestly incompatible with the Christian faith. Under the rule of emperor Theodosius, the so-called 'Tolerance Edict'[15] was repealed in AD 391, resulting in widespread destruction of pagan temples and cults. Unqualified antipathy against all Greek-Hellenistic culture was on the rise. Ever-increasing power and dramatic influence of the Church on all aspects of life led to persecution of Hellenistic sciences. This included for example a ban on consulting soothsayers and mathematicians. In a movement against scientific teachings and in order to speak about God once again in what the Church must have experienced as, a demystified universe of science, some Church representatives even reverted to old theories, insisting that the earth is shaped as a flat disc with the heavens arching over it like a bell-jar.

As a non-Christian and firm promoter of a Greek mindset and spiritual content, Hypatia clearly epitomized everything that Alexandria's Church dignitaries vehemently fought against. Nonetheless, Hypatia never swayed in her devotion to the sciences. With characteristic determination and admirable composure she continued pursuing her research, passing on knowledge and refusing to be distracted from her research by any of the turmoils and conflicts between Church representatives on the one hand and supporters of Hellenistic beliefs or education on the other. Dedicated to her scientific and philosophical pursuits, there is no evidence whatsoever that Hypatia held any particular political interest. She also never made religious faith the subject of philosophical debate or contention and on no account differentiated between different religious communities when welcoming students of pagan, Jewish and Christian backgrounds alike. Her focus remained firmly on the content of Neoplatonic thinking, which, with its often spiritual and cosmological aspects, can only be an indication that she must have been aware of the spiritual wisdom encompassed within Neoplatonism. For teaching of philosophy did not limit itself to passing on different philosophical opinions or solely instructing specific schools of thought in late-Hellenistic society; students looked up to their tutors as spiritual guides, often forming close and lifelong connections.

Hypatia's open-mindedness in this regard to her students' backgrounds and religious convictions is most apparent when considering her deep friendship with one of her most prominent students, Synesius of Cyrene. He met her when he was still a pagan and was first introduced to Neoplatonic philosophy by her. When he later converted to Christianity and eventually was appointed Bishop of Ptolemais in AD 411, by no means did it alter his heartfelt connection with Hypatia. In his many letters, which cast much light on the social and intellectual life of the fifth century, he addresses her as his 'divine teacher' and 'august mistress',[16] expressing the utmost respect for her and referring to the spiritual strength he owed her. In his book *Concerning Dreams*, he indirectly sums up just how much he is indebted to Hypatia and how big a part her teachings played even in his career within the Church: 'For this reason also is the wise man akin to God because he strives to approach Him in knowledge, and occupies himself in thought, in which the divine essence has its meaning.'[17]

In a letter, probably written in AD 395 when parting company from a close friend, he directly refers to Hypatia:

> If Homer had told us that it was an advantage to Odysseus in his wanderings that he saw the towns and became acquainted with the mind of many nations, and although the people whom he visited were not cultured, but merely Laestrygonians and Cyclopses, how wondrously then would poetry have sung of our voyage, a voyage in which it was granted to you and me to experience marvellous things, the bare recital of which had seemed to us incredible! We have seen with our eyes, we have heard with our ears the lady who legitimately presides over the mysteries of philosophy.[18]

Hypatia's close friendship with Synesius discloses the paradox of her murder through the hands of zealous Church representatives—a paradox because many principles underpinning Church doctrines and subsequently endorsed by the Church are in fact based on Neoplatonism. The formulation of the doctrine of the Trinity, for example, to which Synesius of Cyrene significantly contributed, are based precisely on those principles which he first encountered and was taught by his teacher Hypatia.

★ ★ ★

Although Hypatia did not have any personal political interest, her influential teaching position let her also gain extraordinary social and political authority. Her large loyal circle of students included many men of political importance, flocking to her and asking for advice in all sorts of political and governmental matters. Alexandrian officials as well as visitors from across the entire Roman Empire gathered around her to listen to her views and opinions:

> There was a woman at Alexandria named Hypatia, daughter of the philosopher Theon, who made such attainments in literature and science, as to far surpass all the philosophers of her own time. Having succeeded to the school of Plato and Plotinus, she explained the principles of philosophy to her auditors, many of whom came from a distance to receive her instructions. Such was her self-possession and ease of manner, arising from the refinement and cultivation of her mind, that she not infrequently appeared in public in presence of the magistrates. For all men on account of her extraordinary dignity and virtue admired her the more without ever losing in an assembly of men that dignified modesty for which she was conspicuous, and which gained for her universal respect and admiration.[19]

Her position as a female consultant in political and governmental meetings meant that she was the only woman present in such gatherings, as participation in public and political life was ordinarily reserved for men. The statement of Thucydides[20] that the best women were the ones least spoken about was still widely regarded as valid. While Hypatia consulted with political and social leaders in Alexandria, her female contemporaries lived their lives confined within their families, far away from any glare of publicity.

With the increasing misogyny of the Church and its missionaries, Hypatia's situation became ever more sensitive and vulnerable in connection with her independent lifestyle. The *Suda Lexicon* reports that she moved freely about the city, speaking openly in public and explaining the teachings of Plato, Aristotle and other philosophers to anyone wishing to listen. Representing views that were considered to be of a heretical attitude, freely expressing scientific opinions clashing with the Church's system of belief outrightly, she also lived in an extremely unusual manner from a societal point of view. Remaining unmarried throughout her life, she evaded the common social understanding by not living in dependency on a man. Her life represents the true ideal of a scientist living in chastity, which however inevitably presented a direct challenge to the ideals and beliefs of her time. Time and again, she is described as a beautiful, unmarried woman, surrounded by many admirers, as an extremely intelligent and articulate thinker, with a depth of knowledge and understanding outshining her contemporaries, a promoter of revolutionary ideas. And with great social and political influence, she must have looked a dangerous rival in the eyes of the most powerful political and clerical representatives.

★ ★ ★

Throughout its history, bitter tensions, unrest and bloody conflicts arose in Alexandria, largely due to the Roman hegemony which Alexandrians never accepted without resistance:

> The Alexandrians are more delighted with tumult than any other people: and if they can find a pretext, breaks forth into the most intolerable excesses; for it nor is it scarcely possible to check their impetuosity until there has been much bloodshed.[21]

From AD 412 however, animosity and unrest between Jews, pagans and Christians soared. This aggravation is closely linked to the appointment of the new bishop Cyril with the situation increasingly worsening once he took up his position. Cyril considered it to be his own personal mission to 'cleanse' Alexandria of both Neoplatonism and Judaism, and his behaviour in carrying out this task was ruthless. Portrayed by historians as a fanatic and overly ambitious man, he fostered terrible hatred towards paganism and its ancient origins. His strong lust for power led him to use a group of Coptic monks to pursue his very own selfish and merciless schemes. Officially these monks were appointed as nurses, with the mission of containing the spread of infections diseases. Similar to martyrs, these monks originally decided to risk their lives in fighting deadly diseases, for which there existed no known cures. Exposure to disease-stricken areas when treating victims who had fallen ill or when arranging burials for those already passed away often cost them their lives. Besides this official function as nurses they also acted as unofficial spokespeople for the inhabitants of Alexandria, whereby they were frequently responsible for causing great unrest and endangering the security of entire cities. It is reported that Bishop Cyril used these monks as personal mercenaries and built them into his own private army which he unscrupulously relied upon to pursue his political goals by militant means and by initiating riots or acts against non-Christians.

Within this volatile mixture of power, political intrigue and religion Bishop Cyril embarked upon a dangerous dispute with the governor Orestes. As representatives of Church and state respectively they became bitter political rivals, both ultimately fighting for control over the city of Alexandria. In an escalating conflict, Cyril's Coptic monks plotted to assassinate Orestes. Even though Orestes was spared such a hateful fate, the situation in Alexandria became ever more volatile. Hypatia now also involuntarily became involved in this vicious power struggle. The source of Socrates Scholasticus reports that Orestes was well acquainted with Hypatia and, in his role as Roman governor, greatly valued her advice. Such political influence and unequalled position as an educated, independent woman must have stirred Cyril's deep hatred for Hypatia. His conviction grew that Hypatia's friendship with Orestes at heart prevented his Church from gaining absolute power over the entire city of Alexandria. Political intrigues and rumours accusing Hypatia of practising black magic began to spread, her occupation with astronomy and astrology clearly adding further fuel to such accusations. Even several hundred years after her death, in AD 700 Bishop John of Nikiu still described how Hypatia allegedly attempted to seduce people into exercising Satanic practices and blames her for the prefect's recalcitrance:

> And in those days there appeared in Alexandria a female philosopher, a pagan named Hypatia, and she was devoted at all times to magic, astrolabes and instruments of music, and she beguiled many people through her Satanic wiles. And the governor of the city [Orestes] honoured her exceedingly; for she had beguiled him through her magic. And he ceased attending church as had been his custom... And he not only did this, but he drew many believers to her, and he himself received the unbelievers at his house.[22]

With violence escalating and the struggle for power between Church and state growing ever more severe, Socrates Scholasticus describes in his account the brutal murder of Hypatia in AD 425 as a direct result of the civil unrest experienced by the city. During the Christian festival of Lent, more than 100 monks, under the leadership of the Church dignitary Petrus, raided Hypatia's carriage. It is reported that she was overpowered and dragged into a nearby church whereupon the monks tore her clothes off and ripped the flesh from her bones, using oyster shells[23] and their bare hands. Her remains were dragged through the town by the seething mob, before eventually being set alight inside the church. The description is reminiscent of a ritualistic killing and can be likened to the witch-hunts that occurred only much later in history.

The extent of Cyril's direct involvement in Hypatia's murder is unclear, even the *Suda Lexicon* refers to two different sources:

> [Hypatia] suffered such treatment on account of envy and because of her superior wisdom, especially in the area of astronomy; some say the envy was on the part of Cyril, while others claim that these

events took place on account of the innate rashness and proclivity towards sedition among the Alexandrians.[24]

And elsewhere in the *Suda*, Cyril's direct involvement is clearly stated:

> He [Cyril], was so struck with envy that he immediately began plotting her murder and the most heinous form of murder at that. For when Hypatia emerged from her house, in her accustomed manner, a throng of merciless and ferocious men who feared neither divine punishment nor human revenge attacked and cut her down, thus committing an outrageous and disgraceful deed against their fatherland.[25]

Until today, it is only possible to speculate over the involvement of Cyril and whether he was directly responsible for Hypatia's death by personally ordering her murder. It is, however, certain that her murder was committed with his knowledge and acceptance; various historians intimate that his role was much more active, particularly as it was Cyril's private army of monks who carried out the deadly attack.

The subsequent charges filed against Cyril were dropped in Constantinople—this certainly has to be partly attributed to corruption and partly to special arrangements being introduced for dealing with growing numbers of cases involving murders of Jews or pagans. Those in positions of power contented themselves with restricting the political rights of the Church's 'nurses' and introduced a decree which called for their numbers to be restricted. It undoubtedly did not affect Bishop Cyril's standing within the Catholic Church. Pope Leo XIII, recognizing his contribution in theology as a leading writer on Christian controversies in the late fourth and early fifth century, canonized him and appointed him as the 'Doctor of the Church', an extremely rare and honourable title.

★ ★ ★

The impact of Hypatia's death on the intellectual life in Alexandria and the profound effect on the intellectual history of both the East and the West is immense. Her entire being and teaching embody the corpus of her time's mathematical, scientific and philosophical wisdom. She not only played a fundamental role in the development of scientific and philosophical understanding of her time but her areas of enquiry and pursuit are part of the foundations of modern European culture and philosophy. With her death, the intellectual life of antiquity drew to a close and it was to take several centuries before any of her scientific and philosophical impulses were to reappear again in human consciousness. It was the end of the Greek-Hellenistic culture and the classical Greek world as a whole. Although recent research suggests that there were some Neoplatonic successors of Hyaptia,[26] by far the majority of 'pagan' philosophers and scientists abandoned Alexandria and fled to Persia where they were much welcomed. Bertrand Russell concisely sums up the impact of Hypatia's death with the words: 'After this Alexandria was no longer troubled by philosophers.'[27] It was indeed not only the end of the intellectual life in Alexandria but for the entire Roman Empire. When in AD 640 the troops of Caliph Omar conquered Alexandria, ushering in a period of Islamic domination, the Hellenistic culture had already disappeared for good.

★ ★ ★

The brutality and cruelty of her murder stands in perverse contrast to Hypatia's noble being. The fury of the thunderous mob, the uneducated and raw extremism of the Coptic monks, the deep-seated hatred of the ecclesiastical dignitaries and their fanatical faith clashes with her noble, pure and light-filled nature. Amidst wildly fanatical, brutal beliefs and ferocious, relentless brutality, Hypatia's light seems to shine through the centuries. Representing the highest form of purity and virtue, wisdom and ingenuity, she stands virgin-like at the turn of the fourth century. Her brutal murder does not represent brave martyrdom for her convictions or beliefs; her whole light-filled being symbolically represents a decisive turning point for humanity. The secret wisdom of initiation, previously strictly guarded in mystery centres, now experiences a proud revival with her individuality emanating a wisdom and purity that still stemmed from ancient times. Yet her life was not just a proud revival of the wisdom of a passing world. In her pure being, her inherent wisdom was now projected onto the physical plane and as such she was far ahead of her time. She surrendered herself to the destructive forces, sacrificing her wisdom and giving herself up to a most cruel death—a death that puts before humanity a most pregnant symbol of the dissolution and sweeping away of the old. In the Orphic image of her limbs being torn out of her body, the old faculty of clairvoyance is torn away from the sense world in a fundamental transformation of human consciousness.

Living and working in Alexandria, she had been in direct connection with the Aristotelian stream and was under the influence of the archangel Michaël as had Aristotle and Alexander prior to her. As referred to above, Aristotle had been at a turning point in human consciousness—being able to read from the ether he saw the end of the decaying ancient mysteries, he experienced the fading away of direct clairvoyant vision and knew that man now had to live in separation from the withdrawing divine hierarchies. His cosmic script is his gift to humanity in which he attempts to formulate the fundamental secrets of the universe and man, now in a conceptual language suited to a more intellectual consciousness. In thoughts, he expressed what initiates had received in earlier times in clairvoyance. Grappling with the new conceptual language, he expressed in those concepts all that Rudolf Steiner brought forth in the beginning of the twentieth century:

> Then even as Aristotle and Alexander used the fire of Ephesus when it flamed forth anew in their hearts, when it flamed forth in the cosmic ether and bore down to them anew the secrets that were afterwards gathered up into the very simple concepts—then even as they could use the fire of Ephesus, so will it be our part to use what has also been carried out into the ether—for we may say so in all humility—in the flames of the Goetheanum; namely all that has been intended and that shall be intended with Anthroposophy.[28]

Aristotle knew of the separation from the divine spiritual world and saw that humans from then on had to live fully in the physical world, focusing all their activities onto the realm of nature.

Hypatia's destiny now has to be understood in the very same stream—foreseeing later developments of humanity (however consciously or unconsciously may be left aside here), she becomes a symbol of how the horrors of destruction and dismemberment must be suffered in entering and recognizing the meaning of the sense world.

Epigram

Palladas

Όταν βλέπω σε, προσκυνῶ, καί τοὺς λόγους,
τῆς παρθένου τὸν οἶκον ἀστρῷον βλέπων·
εἰς οὐρανὸν γὰρ ἐστί σου τὰ πράγματα,
Ὑπατία σεμνή, τῶν λόγων εὐμορφία,
ἄχραντον ἄστρον τῆς σοφῆς παιδεύσεως.

When I see you, I worship you and your words,
 Seeing the starry house of the Virgo,
 All your deeds are dedicated to the heavens,
 Hypatia, demure ornament of learning,
 Immaculate star of the wise culture.[1]

9
Albertus Magnus I

The Cultural Hinterland of Scholasticism

Rahel Kern

Whereas our human grasp allows us to begin apprehending an event in its entirety—to see its beginning and end, from the first hesitant patterns slowly appearing, to the changes effected and the rippling on long after the event itself has passed, to comprehend the patterns emerging, its counter-images mirrored in events still to come—and with some due distance after the passing of a decent period of time, this is what the Roman God Janus, standing at the sentry of each new year, has under his tutelage. With one bearded face directed eastwards, eyes cast on all those happenings in the past, the other face gazes westwards, already looking at all things ahead in time. His stern yet gentle eyes speak of the passages, movements and changes he has presided over, the growing up of young people, the stepping in and out of doors of homes, the progression from the past to the future, all the endings he has witnessed. Looking simultaneously into the past and the future, the two-headed deity is looking back to a previous condition and at the same time forward to a future vision. He stands as a powerful reminder of the presence of the beginning and ending in all things.

One of the transitions that Janus has stood guard over is the slow decline of the Roman Empire which occurred over several centuries, and he probably paid particular attention to AD 529 which stands like a pivot point within the events of the gradual disintegration of Rome's political, economic, military and other social institutions. Some notable dates leading up to this date include the Battle of Adrianople in 378, the death of Theodosius I in 395 disintegrating the Empire, the crossing of the Rhine in 406 and subsequent invasion of German tribes, the death of Stilicho in 408 leading to the breaking up of the Western army, and the forced abdication of the last Emperor, Romulus Augustus, in 476. His abdication and deposition is the culmination point at which Rome ultimately fell and which made the complete collapse of the entire Western Imperium Romanum inevitable. It is the moment in history that is traditionally seen to be marking the end of classical antiquity and the beginning of a period of a dark night of history, the beginning of the European Middle Ages.

Accompanying these events within the military, political and economic arena, was a societal and cultural decline and, as a result, previously highly influential, most sophisticated and culturally advanced schools across the entire Roman Empire were shut down:

- In the middle of the third century AD the old 'peripatetic school', founded by Aristotle c. 335 BC in Athens and named *Lyceum* named after Apollo Lyceus, fell into decline and died out.
- In the fourth century, following the murder of Hypatia and closure of the Mouseion, scientists and philosophers fled the ancient city of Alexandria.
- In the fifth century (AD 529), the Academy in Athens was closed by the Roman Emperor Justinian, a place which had been founded by Plato in c. 387 BC and which had persisted throughout the Hellenistic age as a sceptical school and in the Roman period as a centre for Neoplatonism. Justinian, known to have been an enemy of all wisdom passed down from ancient Greece, made it his mission to banish all Aristotelian-Platonic thinking. This closure did not just lead ancient philosophy to come to an end; it made it completely disappear from the Occident.

The year 529 and the closure of the Academy of Athens marks the end of the Hellenistic cultural world. It denotes a moment that deeply affects Western history, in all its culture and civilization. The period now following is characterized by people's need and search for security and protection, by fighting for basic survival and attempts to reconstruct their lives in increasingly dark times. And while Janus would have watched ancient philosophy coming to an end and gradually disappearing completely from the Occident, he would have also—presiding over the beginning and ending in all things—watched a new era quietly announcing itself.

In the same year of 529, as Justinian banished the Plotinistic philosophers from the Roman Empire, and consequently drove out all awareness and conception of spirit-reality, a space opened up—away from all the demands and requirements of the daily struggles for existence—in which activities such as contemplation and learning could be pursued, a space that was to allow for cultivating and deeply influencing the development of European civilization and culture over the next few centuries.

The person behind this new dawn for humanity is the son of a Roman noble of Nursia, Benedict of Nursia. Drawn to Christianity from a very early age, he established the very first monastery in Europe. The abbey was founded in Monte Cassino in 529 and sits atop a large rocky mount, among the mountainous hills to the south of Rome, with the blue waters of the Mediterranean in the distance. Centuries later, Monte Cassino was to become the childhood home of Thomas Aquinas. And some further centuries later, Rudolf Steiner, accompanied by Marie Steiner-von Sivers, visited the place just before Whitsun 1910, shortly before giving his lectures on the 'Fifth Gospel' when he spoke of the impending appearance of Christ 'in the etheric'.[1]

Although Benedict preferred a quiet, contemplative life and there is no evidence that he had any plans for spreading his teachings to monasteries outside the dozen which he established over his lifetime, he is generally regarded as the founder of the Benedictine order and father of Western monasticism. It was his order of St Benedict that set out in the sixth century to promote the idea of monastic life outside Italy and evangelize other European countries. After Benedict's death, it was the order's mission to evangelize England. The foundation of the first English Benedictine monastery in Canterbury in 597 fundamentally influenced the history of the Church in Britain. Other countries quickly followed over the subsequent centuries and Benedictine communities were soon to be found in almost every country of Western Europe. Remaining the only monastic order until the end of the eleventh century, it played a fundamental role in spreading education, the arts, civilization and evangelization. Benedict's influence was of such magnitude that the centuries following his life and death are often referred to as the 'Benedictine centuries' and he was honoured by the Roman Catholic Church as the patron saint of Europe.

The rule laid down by St Benedict, which receives candidates into the order with the solemn commitment of a vow of obedience, of stability and of a monastic manner of life, has been greatly influential and remains until today the most common rule for monasteries. A further legacy is Benedict's emphasis on balancing prayer, work and study. Each day is divided into roughly the same hours of prayer and liturgical activities, manual and craft work, as well as study of the scriptures and commentaries thereof.

With studies being an essential part of the daily routine of all monks, monasteries became the guardians of knowledge and enquiry. What had been taught in open schools in previous centuries now withdrew behind quiet monastic walls. Despite being usually regarded as having played an inhibiting role with regard to free scientific investigations throughout centuries, the Church also played a role in allowing much of the ancient wisdom and learning to be preserved. While Western Europe was very much at a cultural low point and the Dark Ages prevailed outside monastery walls, the clergy and monastic orders presented the only literate group of people. In reclusion from the world, monks not only cultivated works within the religious and cultural arena but were also highly engaged in scientific studies, such as the study of metals and botany, and actively pursued technological innovations, farming and even geometry and mathematics.

Benedict's twin sister Scholastica (c. 480–547) founded a convent just five miles south from her brother's Abbey of Monte Cassino in Plombariola. Described as the first Benedictine nun, she presided over the female order, probably under the direction of her brother and following very similar rules to his community. And whereas this is not recognized as a historical fact, we can wonder whether her name is already an indication of what role the Benedictine order was to play later in the development of medieval thought. With its strong emphasis on learning from its first inception, it endeavoured to reconcile medieval Christian theology with the philosophy of the ancient classical philosophers. Eventually, Western monasticism developed into Scholasticism in the twelfth century.

The Benedictine order was founded in a period of military ventures and Crusades, invasions, unjust warfare, treachery and cruelty, bringing much suffering and a general decline of cultural and intellectual values. The derogatory term *Media tempestas* (Middle Ages) was first introduced in the fifteenth century and is derived from the view that this period is a deviation from the classical learning. With no real content of its own, it stood in between the classical ancient times and the modern times of the Renaissance. Throughout the centuries the Benedictine order presented in medieval Western Europe the only place in which intellectual and cultural values were preserved and cherished.

This holds true despite some shorter periods of time throughout the centuries that stand out as periods of significant cultural renewal and revivals of learning. For example, during the late eighth to ninth centuries, the reigns of the Carolingian rulers Charlemagne and Louis the Pious is a period of intellectual and cultural revival. Due to the efforts of Charlemagne, who gathered the elite scholars and great minds of his time at his court, there was much intellectual activity. Despite the very warlike side of his nature, he also became known for promoting and encouraging learning independently of social status. As a devout Christian, he had learned Latin and Greek, studied grammar, rhetoric, dialectic, astrology and mathematics (however, it is also claimed that he never mastered reading and writing himself). In 787, he decreed that every monastery had to establish a school where monks were to teach children without remuneration. These schools greatly contributed to raising the level of education of the general population during the eighth and ninth centuries and throughout his empire became the forerunners of universities, which shaped what would later become the academic landscape in Western Europe.

Now the gaze of Janus once more. While monastic life was able to carry through the thread of learning from the fateful year 529 onwards, the real intellectual revitalization, going hand in hand also with social, political and economic changes, did not occur before the twelfth century, at the outset of the High Middle Ages, but in the thirteenth century at the apogee of the Middle Ages. Inventions and technological innovations allowed architects across the Continent to demonstrate what could be achieved with features such as the pointed arch, the ribbed vault and the flying buttress. Many churches, abbeys and cathedrals across the Continent most powerfully put on show the development of Gothic architecture, setting it clearly apart from classical buildings. A vernacular literature grew up, particularly in Italy, where it culminated in writings such as Dante's *Divine Comedy*. Towards the end of the century, Dante's friend Giotto also started painting in a new way, linking the old Byzantine icons with a novel Italian development. And while the earliest universities, which had developed in Salerno in the course of the ninth century and Bologna in the eleventh century, were still closely linked to religious schools, such schools became much more organized. Towards the end of the twelfth century, they began to centre on certain courses of study and were not as closely linked to monasteries in their set-up. The first bona fide university was established in Paris in 1221. Because of their teaching fraternity, it is from within the monasteries that the revival of science and ancient philosophy spread in Europe. Foremost amongst the scholars influencing the development of scholastic thought and foreshadowing modern science in the thirteenth century was Albertus Magnus.

10
Albertus Magnus II

His Life's Path and Meeting with Thomas Aquinas

Rahel Kern

I can do no more than intimate that the individuality who incarnated as Hypatia, who brought with her the wisdom of the Orphic Mysteries and gave personal expression to it, was called upon in a subsequent incarnation to take the opposite path: to bear all personal wisdom upwards again to the divine-spiritual. Hypatia appeared at the turn of the twelfth and thirteenth century as a significant, universal spirit of later history, one who had a great influence upon the knowledge that brings together the science and philosophy.[1]

These are the words with which Rudolf Steiner introduces Hypatia's subsequent incarnation for the first, and only, time in a public lecture. It is through inference that this statement is believed to hold true of Albertus Magnus. An entry in one of Steiner's notebooks, which was discovered at a much later date, seems to confirm this. This phenomenon of mentioning Albertus Magnus not directly is, indeed, characteristic of Steiner's references to Albertus in both earlier and subsequent lectures. Considering that Rudolf Steiner widely lectured and wrote on Scholasticism and the development of medieval thought, and given Albertus' stature and prominence within medieval philosophy and theology, such reserve is astonishing. Indeed, one might come to believe that he would have hardly mentioned Albertus at all if it were not for his student Thomas Aquinas with whom he couples Albertus together. And while there are numerous lectures dedicated specifically to either the personality or the philosophical contribution of Thomas Aquinas, Steiner seldom singles out Albertus. One wonders why Rudolf Steiner represents Albertus only in conjunction with Thomas Aquinas, who, taking the centre stage, seems to leave Albertus Magnus in his shadow.

The following will try to throw light upon this question by looking at Albertus' life and his spiritual friendship with Thomas Aquinas.

Albertus was born into a knightly family in Lauingen, Germany in 1200. Not much is known about his childhood and youth, but he later remarked on his close connection to nature. There are, for example, comments on his childhood about observing the habits of fish in the family's estate on the Danube. Such a joy of observing phenomena in nature and an active interest were to accompany him throughout his life. His formal education started most probably at the University of Padua in northern Italy, where he is said to have studied grammar, logic and rhetoric. It is reported that he is also likely to have attended courses in medicine and jurisdiction. During this time he met Jordan of Saxony,[2] the second general Master leading the recently founded Dominican order. The order has its roots in the religious movement of the late twelfth century, which reacted to and challenged the wealth, struggle for personal power and ensuing corruption within the Church. Members of the Dominican order lived a simple life in apostolic poverty. As such, their lives present positive examples and inspiration of how new values and virtues can be introduced and adopted. One of these values was knowledge and the pursuit of intellectual striving and teaching. From the very moment of its inception, Dominic sought to closely connect his newly founded order with schools, which at that point in time were just in the process of developing into universities. And it is here at the university in Padua in 1223 that Albertus meets Jordan of Saxony, who had himself joined the order only three years before. Already then, Jordan had developed a reputation for emptying university lecture halls of their most talented students by drawing them to the order as novices. Not only did he demonstrate a fervent eloquence in speech when giving his most inspiring sermons, his kind and charming character also reflected the ideals he had chosen to dedicate his own life to and his living example served as inspiration for many. During his lifetime, Jordan's preaching is said to have prompted over a thousand young men to enter the order. Albertus was one of them and Jordan received him into the order in the same year that he met him.

Albertus subsequently moved to Cologne, Germany to continue his studies in theology and complete his training for the order by 1228. Soon after, he began teaching and lecturing throughout Germany and started publishing his first works. Throughout his life, Albertus produced an immense literary work, which demonstrates profound knowledge of and immersion into the ancient thinkers as well as contemporary philosophers and theologians. Besides a number of works in which Albertus developed his own thoughts and visions, he wrote commentaries on the Bible and prepared extensive commentaries which could be described as philosophical encyclopedias of Christian and intellectual thought, constantly collecting, paraphrasing and systematizing thought constructs throughout his life. Here are just a few of the thinkers who deeply influenced Albertus' philosophical theological outlook:

- Dionysius the Areopagite,[3] a mysterious thinker whose name goes back to the Acts of the Apostles. He started believing and was converted to Christianity after hearing St Paul speak to the crowd about the 'unknown God'. His writings were regarded as being among the most important Christian works for centuries. Albertus, who believed the Areopagite's work to be inspired by the Holy Spirit, wrote commentaries about all of his letters and books, which nowadays count amongst his greatest contributions. Drawn from Dionysius, Albertus later presented and advanced the idea that positive knowledge of God is possible, but that such knowledge will always be obscure and imperfect. Through contemplation one can know that God *is*, but not who God is. Certain aspects of God will always be unknowable by the intellect alone and it is thus easier to state what God is not than to positively affirm what he is. But, according to Albertus, this does not imply a contradiction between one's ability to only ever make relative affirmations of God while being able to deny certain aspects of God absolutely.
- Origen (AD 186–253), who was banned as a heretic by Justinian in the fifth century, nearly 300 years after his death, in the same move in which Justinian had closed the Academy of Athens trying to bring uniformity to the religious life by eliminating any unorthodox elements. Origen taught and wrote within the earliest Christian times; it was a period when the Pauline threefold understanding of the human being as consisting of body, soul and spirit was still well and alive and humanity was understood to have entered from higher worlds through the planetary sphere into the earth sphere. Being a highly learned scholar on the one hand and giving prominence in his teachings to Christian revelation on the other hand, he searched for higher knowledge in the hope to gain deeper comprehension of the mysteries of Christianity. This combination of study and divine revelation surely must have made a deep impression on Albertus; it is a theme that emerges again, in a more formed and conceptualized form, in the Scholastic undertaking.
- Boethius (c. AD 480–525) is regarded as the first Scholastic and is known for his explicit articulation of one of the central tenets in Scholasticism, preserved in the following words: 'fidem, si poteris, rationemque coniunge' ('link up, as much as you can, reason with belief'). Boethius was also the first to envisage a translation of Plato and Aristotle's entire works. His translation of Aristotle's logical work became very influential, but he did not manage to complete a translation of his entire works, a project which Albertus was to undertake and complete later.

Boethius was a great formative influence on Christian thought and pre-thirteenth-century philosophy. He is particularly known for his early medieval discussion of universals, and his distinction between God and *id quod est*, that which is. Both are debates which Albertus advanced in his philosophy.

- Augustine (AD 354–430), regarded as the father of the Western Church and whose thought not just influenced but dominated Christian thinking until the early thirteenth century. He regarded philosophy not as a branch of learning but as an inward journey, driven by a desire to know and be known by God. From the depths of human experience, he reflects upon himself and issues in life, always searching for God and inner transformation. His *leitmotiv* in his striving to understand the content of belief and Christianity can be summarized as: 'Understand, so that you may believe; believe, so that you may understand'. His writings, particularly his famous *Confessions*, must have made a deep impact on Albertus Magnus and moulded his outlook. The universal striving of the individual, the emphasis for a constant *exercitatio animi* (exercise of the mind) and the transformation and metamorphosis of the thinker in the sense of purifying the soul and cultivating moral attitudes are themes that emerge again in Albertus work.

Albertus also extensively studied Peter Lombard, Porphyry, the Irish theologian Johannes Scotus Eriugena and Islamic thinkers such as Avicenna and Averroes, who played a major role in introducing Aristotle's work to the Latin West. Already during his lifetime, Albertus was known for his learnedness and incredible wisdom, prompting comments by his contemporaries such as the following:

> There is one, who, should all philosophy disappear, would be able to create it all anew. This new inventor would resurrect it better than it had been before and would outperform the old philosophers through the grandeur of his mastery.[4]

In 1245, he was sent to Paris, the most important centre of theological education at that time, to complete his studies and receive his doctorate. Paris was then known as an energetic centre of excellence for academic studies and Albertus encountered an entirely new intellectual world. People had a growing desire for knowledge and the city attracted the intellectual elite from all over Europe, who gathered to study and discuss new ideas. Even though it was a time when the Church authorities put prohibitions in place at universities against privately or publicly lecturing on some of Aristotle's writings, seeking thereby to protect the Christian doctrine, many scholars were keenly interested in the study of logic and Aristotelian philosophy. Faulty translations and misleading commentaries alarmed authorities to such a degree that they issued a decree forbidding the reading of Aristotle. In Albertus' time, there are indications that many scholars were already entering into a dialogue with Aristotelian philosophy, and Aristotle as the greatest master of logic already had a particularly influential place within Parisian intellectual life. Albertus Magnus was convinced that the objections to Aristotle were groundless and would cease only if his works were purified from the errors in translation and false commentators were refuted. This led to his ambitious decision to produce commentaries upon all of Aristotle's works. In his writings, he later attacked living adversaries and refuted false commentators. In particular, he authored two treatises against Averroes who had propagated the false Aristotelian view that philosophy and religion, being two different areas of enquiry, could hold opposing views, and who tried to cancel out individual responsibility by claiming that all men have but one soul.

Albertus held numerous teaching posts and, during his lifetime, taught many prominent students. Among them was Ulrich von Strassburg[5] who was influenced greatly by his teacher and developed the thoughts which had their origin in the teachings of Albertus into his well-known Doctrine of Divine Ideas (in his *Summa de Bono*). His most famous student, however, was Thomas Aquinas, whom he met in Paris in 1245. Thomas, after early studies in Monte Cassino from the age of five, had moved to the university of Naples where he met members of the Dominican order which, after much family resistance, he eventually joined in 1244 aged 19. He remained under Albertus' direction for the next three years. It followed an extraordinarily close spiritual friendship and most remarkable working collaboration for the next 30 years (1245–74).

An anecdote tells of how Albertus very early on recognized Thomas' genius and foretold his greatness to come. As a thoughtful and taciturn student, he initially made a poor impression on his fellow students and teachers, who thought him dull. But when Albertus got to know his work, he is said to have exclaimed: 'We call this man a dumb ox, but his bellowing in doctrine will one day resound throughout the world.'[6]

Albertus became to be known as 'Doctor Universalis', referring to his superior understanding and knowledge in all major subjects ranging from natural sciences to philosophy and theology, and was later even given the appellation 'Magnus', Albertus the Great. Thomas Aquinas, however, became known for his purity and virtue. Thomas was often referred to as

'Doctor Angelicus', the Angelic Doctor, who devoted his life entirely to penetrating the divine truths and who throughout his lifetime gained a unique understanding of theology and philosophy. The Catholic Encyclopedia reports that the Parisian doctors who were Albertus' contemporaries referred to him as the 'morning star, the luminous sun, the light of the whole Church'.[7] And indeed, in paintings the sun is a common attribute placed on the chest of Thomas. The National Gallery in London exhibits the 'Demidoff Altarpiece'[8] which, on one of its panels, depicts St Thomas with a sun radiating on his chest, a large open book in one hand and holding a church in the other arm.

Albertus and Thomas moved to Cologne together, where Albertus was appointed regent of studies at the Studium Generale that was newly created by the Dominican order in Cologne in 1248. The Studium Generale consisted of a study of the seven liberal arts; the term 'liberal' hereby refers to the 'free man' pursuing such studies and the term 'arts' is to be understood in the sense of 'skills'. They were divided into the Trivium ('the three roads') and the Quadrivium ('the four roads'). The Trivium consisted of grammar, rhetoric and logic. The Quadrivium consisted of arithmetic (the number in itself), geometry (the number in space), music and harmonics (the number in time), and astronomy or cosmology (the number in space and time). Each of these seven arts was essentially understood to be useful in comprehending the nature of God, each in its own and distinct way. As a collective, they offer a canonical way of depicting the realms of higher learning and organized learning for the ultimate purpose of understanding philosophy, the meta-study uniting all branches of knowledge. The origin of the seven liberal arts lies in antiquity and is believed to go back to the Old Testament in which wisdom is described as a house with seven pillars:

> Wisdom has built her house, she has set up her seven pillars. She has slaughtered her beasts, she has mixed her wine, she has also set her table. She has sent out her maids to call from the highest places in the town, 'Whoever is simple, let him turn in here!' To him who is without sense she says, 'Come, eat of my bread and drink of the wine I have mixed. Leave simpleness, and live, and walk in the way of insight.'[9]

Each of the seven pillars are here taken to represent one of the seven arts. The history of the seven liberal arts is a history of the development of education from Plato's time in classical Athens to Cassiodorus[10] as the first Christian to use the term 'seven liberal arts', Alcuin[11] who specified them as part of the Carolingian Renaissance in the eighth and ninth centuries, to their adoption amongst the fraternity in the Middle Ages, and up to their full flowering at the cathedral school at Chartres in the twelfth century.

The year 1248 was also that in which the foundation stone was laid for the Cathedral in Cologne. Both Albertus and Aquinas are believed to have been closely connected to the cathedral. It is likely that Albertus was involved in the architecture and planning of this tall and up-reaching Gothic building. Aquinas, who wrote some gravely beautiful liturgical church hymns, most probably composed his well-known 'Pange lingua...' specifically for the opening ceremony of the cathedral. Towards the end of his life, Albertus made his will leaving his belongings to the cathedral—his books for the library, his vestments for the vestry, and his financial means for the completion of the cathedral's choirs.

Albertus and Thomas remained together in Cologne until 1252, in which year Thomas was then sent to Paris for teaching duties. Albertus, who by that time was already a revered philosophical authority in Cologne, stayed there and began his extensive work on Aristotle. Even though Albertus only had a very limited understanding of the Greek language he managed to get access to original Greek translations from a fellow monk. It was his intention to make Aristotle's entire work accessible to the West, a goal which he pursued relentlessly. He paraphrased and annotated the entire works of Aristotle and wrote long commentaries, some works he even made comments on for a second time. It was his aim not only to present the reader with the content, but also to make Aristotle's thought intelligible and accessible. He therefore inserted his own insights and, at times, suggested updated accounts that show both a deep understanding of Aristotle's thought and an exceptionally high level of learning and familiarity with philosophical and theological matters of his time. His commentaries, comprising 40 volumes altogether, followed in succession over the next 20 years.

In 1254, Albertus had to interrupt his teaching when he was elected the prior provincial for the German-speaking province of the order. Such a task required him to spend long stretches of time travelling through the province visiting Dominican convents and priories. Practising ministry and common life while living in individual poverty meant that he travelled only on foot. During his three-year office, he visited nearly all of the by now 40 Dominican convents and 20 women's cloisters. Given such frequent journeys and extensive travels across Germany and, later, across Europe in order to study, teach and lecture in various cities, he spent a large proportion of his life walking in nature.

One may take a moment to reflect what effect such frequent and enduring exercise might have had on Albertus—not just the immediate benefits to his physical condition and overall health, but also possibly more far-reaching effects. Rudolf Steiner repeatedly refers to the metamorphosis of the limb system into the head region from one incarnation to the next. While physically speaking limbs and head are very distinct from another, on a spiritual level they are of the same substance but in very different developmental stages in time. What arms, hands, legs and feet are in one incarnation metamorphose into the different parts of the head in the following incarnation.[12] Considering Albertus' extremely well-exercised legs and Marie Steiner-von Sivers' lifelong work with speech (located mainly in the jaw region), one wonders whether this might serve as a demonstration of the metamorphic connections.

His extensive travels by no means meant that his research and writing came to a halt. He always found time to pursue his studies and continue writing, and such long walks gave Albertus ample opportunity to observe and experience phenomena in nature. Many of his writings give precise and accurate descriptions of what his watchful senses and keen mind explored, and such observations are reflected throughout his botanical writings. These are most detailed empirical observations and careful descriptions, in which his words portray most accurate plant anatomies, indicate a clear grasp of a taxonomic scheme for plant evolution, as well as advocating practical advice on planting trees, cultivating vineyards, and so on.

His remarkable gift of observation, the utmost attention paid to the minutest details and meticulously precise descriptions often remind one of a Goetheanistic approach, in the sense of impartial and unpretentious devotion to a particular phenomenon. This is also reflected in his extensive commentaries on chemistry, including distillation, liquefaction, coagulation, and on geology, including a compilation of minerals and their properties, observations about fossils, stability of mineral forms, and so on. His works in the natural sciences further embrace descriptions of the animal kingdom which he, following the lead of Aristotle, also wrote on voluminously. His monumental work *De Animalibus* is a vast tomb of descriptions that Albertus acquired in his lifetime of observing, testing and recording the lives of all sorts of weird and wonderful creatures. Albertus here portrayed various animal forms, and his observations range from the different laying habits of flies to equine and canine veterinary medicine. There are also observations on castrated, philandering priests who nonetheless manage to produce children, reproduction and embryology (from an external anatomical point of view), adaptations of animals to their respective environments, questions such as whether bats have legs and birds have bladders, and much much more. It represents the epitome of an Aristotelian scheme classifying the animal world.

> Further, eggs differ according to their shape, for some are pointed and some are broad and rounded. Some have either shape, one at each end. In these, the rounded, wide part leaves the bird first, because this one is turned to the outside, and the sharp part leaves last, for this one is turned towards the diaphragm. For this reason too, this end is harder, and somewhat wrinkled in hens' eggs from the heat.
> Aristotle says that long eggs with a sharp head produce male birds, but rounded eggs that have a roundness in place of the sharp angle produce females. But this is entirely false, and the flaw was due to improper copying and not to the saying of the philosopher. For this reason, Avicenna says that males and roosters are produced from rounded, short eggs, and hens are produced from sharp eggs, and this agrees with the experience which we have had with eggs, as well as with reason.[13]

Not only does this example show his keen eye for and interest in details, but also his meticulous attention to detail when it comes to misleading commentaries or faulty translations of Aristotle. As will be elaborated in the following chapter, Albertus had a particular mission of making the true Aristotle known and in particular refutes Averroes.

In addition to his commentary work on Aristotle, he also wrote about 30 theological works and scriptural expositions preserved as handwritten manuscripts. These include a commentary on Peter Lombard's *Sentences* and on the writings of 'Dionysius Areopagita', his *Super Matthaeum* (Commentary on Matthew), and two treatises against Averroes; one one of them his famous refutation of Averroes' psychology in his *De unitate intellectus contra Averroistas* (On the uniqueness of intellect against Averroists).

Albertus was not only an indisputable scholar, who could practically apply his knowledge in the sense world; he was also known for his inner meditative work and devotion. He was a master in putting inner experiences into vivid and familiar images gathered from his own experiences and simple, clear words that would reach and captivate the hearts of many. Throughout his life he regularly preached to large congregations and crowds that used to gather for his sermons. It is said that the churches were often not big enough to hold all people flocking to hear him, attracted by the simplicity and wisdom in his words and his sympathy for the needs and problems of those listening.

In the years 1254 to 1257, Albertus was the provincial minister of the entire Teutonia province of the Dominicans, an area covering most of modern Germany and stretching north as far as Antwerp, and in the south down to Vienna. Again, in staying true to Dominican poverty, all travels were on foot. When he resigned the office in 1257, he returned to Cologne as the regent of studies—he had been longingly awaited there in order to help out with a dispute between the citizens of Cologne and Archbishop Konrad von Hochstaden. As an increasingly public figure, with a reputation for his impartiality and sound judgement, he was frequently trusted to advise on a variety of local affairs, intervene as peace broker and adjudicate on conflicts. This particular diplomatic call resulted from a conflict he had already helped to resolve some six years before, but which now had escalated again. Once more, he managed to make a judgement that was found acceptable to both sides.

As appointed master of the Dominican order, Albertus travelled to Valenciennes in 1259 to attend a general chapter of his order, along with Thomas Aquinas and others. On behalf of his order he undertook an extensive discussion on the curriculum of the scholastic programme to draw up a plan for the organization of studies throughout the order. As a result of their work, the order officially adopted a policy of providing a full programme of studies, including theology and the arts, modelled on the curriculum of the University of Paris. With philosophy as one of the arts this represented a true innovation and also a personal accomplishment for Albertus. For years, he had insisted on the importance of philosophy and fought for changing the curriculum of the Dominican schools by introducing Aristotle and Neoplatonists such as Plotinus into the classroom.

In 1260, he received a papal letter from Alexander IV with the unusual and surprising request to accept his offer of appointment as bishop in Regensburg. The role of bishop is not just far apart from that of a scholar, but it also carries with it an obvious tension between the Dominican ideal of poverty and the economic wealth of the highly influential and powerful position of bishop. Despite grave concerns, Albertus obeyed the Pope's wishes and was consecrated. His predecessor had run up high debts, and Albertus' appointment involved putting in order the diocese's economic situation and restoring its spiritual condition, both of which had been neglected. Despite holding such a highly powerful position, he remained true to the simple and humble way of life. During his visits to the various parishes of the diocese, he acquired his nickname 'Bundschuh' (sometimes translated as 'Boots the bishop', 'Tied shoe'), referring to his unusual shoes and style of dress for a bishop as he held on to a life of poverty throughout his appointment. Once the reform of that diocese was sufficiently underway, Albertus handed in his petition for resignation. Being released from his duty in 1263, Albertus was then asked to serve as Pope Urban's legate and special envoy in the Germany-speaking countries. The Pope was devoted to his hope that, with the Dominican's help through propagating the idea, a Crusade could be mounted. Already in his 70s, Albertus preached this until the idea of such a Crusade was given up with the death of Pope Urban in 1264.

It is likely that Albertus then settled in Würzburg until 1267. Over the next few years this venerable and much respected old man travelled across Germany conducting various ecclesiastical tasks. Letters and documents give evidence of his many activities, including consecration of churches, chapels, altars, legal settlements and diplomatic peace-making, all over Germany—in Regensburg, Aachen, Esslingen, Strasbourg, and so on.

The final years of Albertus Magnus' life are closely intermingled with legend. While on one of his travels on 7 March 1274 he received the sad news of Thomas' death after he had fallen ill. It is reported that at the hour of his friend's death, prior to being told, Albertus sat at dinner with fellow monks and suddenly exclaimed that 'the light of the Church has been extinguished'[14] and could not restrain his tears. The prior who had noted down the exact day and hour of this incident could later confirm that Thomas Aquinas had indeed crossed the threshold at that very moment when Albertus had sensed his passing away. Thomas' death represented a very heavy blow for Albertus.

In 1277, he undertook a journey to Paris to defend the memory and philosophy of Thomas Aquinas, which is said to have been caught up in a bitter conflict between the departments of philosophy and theology and had come under attack from the university who wished to denounce it. Despite his fragile age—he was in his late 70s—he adamantly undertook a last journey to Paris, where he gave a captivating speech which was received with overwhelming agreement and enthusiasm.

Returning to Cologne, he continued working on his writings, watched the continuing building of the cathedral in Cologne and still received many visitors. Anticipating his own death, Albertus drew up his testament in 1279. Having lived up to an unusually old age and being already a legend in his own lifetime, Albertus Magnus died on 5 November 1280 in Cologne. Originally he was buried in the Dominican church but after the closure of the monastery he found his final resting place in the church of St Andreas in Cologne.

Theology as a Science

Albertus Magnus

[Theology] is of all sciences the most entitled to credence—certissimae credulitatis et fidei. *Other sciences, concerning creatures, possess* rationes immobiles, *yet those* rationes *are* mobiles *because they are in created things. But this science, founded in* rationibus aeternis, *is immutable both* secundum esse *and* secundum rationem. *And since it is not constituted of the sensible and imaginable, which are not quite cleared of the hangings of matter, plainly it, alone or supremely, is science: for the divine intellect is altogether intellectual, being the light and cause of everything intelligible; and from it to us is the divine science.*[1]

11
Albertus Magnus III

Scholasticism and its Resurgence in Anthroposophy

Rahel Kern

After the closure of the academy in Athens in AD 529, academics and scholars fled the Roman Empire. Most notably the seven teachers—Damskios, Simplikos and five others from different regions—escaped to Gondishapur, Persia, and took the last remains of Greek thought and wisdom with them. Throughout the previous centuries, Persia had greatly profited from the growth of and trade with the ever-expanding Roman Empire. While the Empire was increasingly unable to satisfy its own continually growing needs, it became more and more reliant on trade with the Persian Empire just situated at its periphery. As a result, its civilization was at its height, with scientific and cultural activities flourishing and prospering. The seven teachers found not just refuge there but a place where wealth and high standards of living provided a sound basis for spiritual and scientific enquiry. While the learning of the formerly great schools—such as the works of the Lyceum and the Academy in Athens—was lost to the West, it was now eagerly incorporated into early Islamic philosophy and was to play a major part in the philosophical and religious outlook of the Byzantine civilization. Especially Aristotle's philosophical outlook found high appeal and attracted much interest. From the moment of Aristotelian thinking entering the Eastern world, Islamic scholars noted his significance.

Aristotle does indeed hold an extremely significant position not just within philosophy but also within the development of human consciousness, a matter which is largely overlooked in mainstream academic philosophy. Nowadays it is common for philosophers and historians to regard the Presocratic Greek philosopher Thales[1] as the originator of philosophy and see all subsequent philosophical enquiries as an extension and expansion of his quest. 'Philosophy begins with Thales,'[2] wrote Bertrand Russell. Thales does indeed add a new aspect to human thinking by explaining natural phenomena like earthquakes or thunderstorms without reference to anthropomorphic gods. Rather than falling back on their divine will or mythology as did his predecessors, he relies purely on the natural phenomenon itself and uses rational principles to underpin his explanations. In this respect, Thales has been tremendously influential and has fundamentally changed how philosophers engage with their subjects.

The way in which his knowledge came about and how he came to be aware of it was however still reliant on clairvoyance. As we have seen, all early philosophers such as Thales, Heraclites, Pythagoras and up to Plato[3] essentially discuss wisdom from the ancient mysteries that—though reworked into more abstract concepts—have been prompted by clairvoyant experiences. Even Plato still discusses the content of occult teachings, previously strictly protected by the old mystery centres, and which he still directly experienced. Plato expresses this for example when discussing knowledge of certain self-evident truths, which he famously refers to in his *Meno* as the mind's 'innate sources of knowledge'. His student Aristotle, who is already in a different state of consciousness, challenged such innate starting points for knowledge. Aristotle did not have the capacity to see directly into spiritual worlds and does not report having any clairvoyant experiences. And precisely because he did not have such immediate insight through intuition or clairvoyance as thinkers prior to his time had, he had to fall back on his own individual thinking. His whole framework for knowledge is built purely from his own personal intellectual and reasoning capabilities. It is his working out of pure abstract concepts, thereby introducing logical deductions and syllogisms, that makes him the first philosopher in the strict sense. Aristotle marks the point in the history of consciousness at which humanity has undergone a profound shift away from the old clairvoyant world of the gods.

> But the essential characteristic of the philosopher, manifested for the first time in Aristotle, is the fact that he necessarily rejects all other sources (or has no access to them), and works exclusively with the technique of ideas. And since this may be said for the first time of Aristotle, it is not without good historical reason that it should be precisely this philosopher who founded logic and the science of thought. All other efforts in this direction had been of a precursory nature only. The way and the manner in which concepts and judgements were formed and conclusions drawn—this entire range of mental activity was discovered by Aristotle as a kind of natural history of subjective thought, and everything we meet within him is closely connected with this inauguration of the technique of thought.[4]

Aristotle accepted the Platonic view that for something to count as knowledge it must have a certain stability, and asserts that scientific knowledge concerns eternal truths, i.e. that of 'which cannot be otherwise'. However, he then challenged Plato in his *Posterior Analysis* on his innate starting points for knowledge and instead stressed the crucial role of sense perception in providing the raw material for knowledge. Insights into worldly affairs can only be gathered by close observations of the external sense world. In the first instance there needs to be sense perception, which then can be built upon and which needs to be accompanied by precise reasoning and judgement. As for something to count as knowledge, such input from the sensory world needs to be advanced by rigorous logical steps from premise to conclusion (requirement of deductive validity).

As already mentioned in the above, Islamic scholars noted Aristotle's importance from the moment when Aristotelian thinking entered the Eastern world and were extremely keen to integrate and assimilate his wisdom into their Eastern thinking. Many simply referred to him as 'the philosopher', thereby expressing their respect and admiration. Several circles of translators produced translations and reworkings of the original Greek sources. Given the culture of the Eastern Empire in Byzantium, many of these translations do in fact constitute an interpretation of Aristotle's thought, rather than a straightforward translation. In order to concur with the Semitic religious impulses of the Islamic philosopher-theologians, certain aspects of his philosophy were either omitted or altered. There are also to be found various pseudo-Aristotelian writings from this time, which heavily drew on Aristotle but distorted certain aspects to fit into the Arabic understanding of the world.

Between the sixth and ninth centuries, when Western European history experienced a period of cultural and scientific decay, Byzantine and Islamic civilizations flourished and Aristotle played a major part in shaping their philosophical and religious outlook. And it was from there, through the Arabic-Latin translations, that Aristotle first became known again to the Latin West. A large part of the corpus of Aristotle's work had been translated into Arabic, and it is from those Arabic translations that the first translations into European languages were grafted and brought into Latin Europe towards the end of the eleventh century (Italy) and in the first half of the twelfth century (Spain). It is such mistranslated materials due to Arabic exegesis and interpretations through which Aristotle entered European thinking. While Aristotle's logic was already known to medieval scholars at that point in time, Aristotle's natural philosophy, psychology, metaphysics and ethics had previously not yet been introduced. The Moorish conquests of the Iberian Peninsula in particular became a vehicle for transporting such distorted interpretations to the West with long-lasting effects on philosophy. In 711, the Arab governor of Tangiers, Tariq ibn-Ziyad, crossed what is now the border between Morocco and Spain with an army of Berbers, landing on the Rock of Tariq, Gibraltar. In different forms, the Moorish presence and occupation were to last for nearly 800 years until 1492, thereby profoundly marking the history and culture of Portugal and particularly Spain. The Arabs took possession of Spain; the sciences, trade, urban life and urban culture spread and Arabic influences fully permeated the European world outlook and ethos:

> One of the particular characteristics of the Arabic way of thinking is that it is first of all hair-splitting, abstract, and that it dislikes the concrete. It therefore prefers to look at all affairs in the world and nature in an abstract way. Not only that, it also has a kind of blossoming, even voluptuous development of fantasy. Just think about it for a moment, how this dry, abstract way of thinking, which even shows itself in the artistic realm of the Arabs, develops next to this fantasy about a kind of paradise, about a kind of afterworld with all the sensual joys from this world. These two things are happening side by side: dry, materialistic observation of nature and world affairs, and on the other hand a voluptuous life of fantasy... This way of conceptualizing has deeply entered into European life, especially into that of Southern, Western and Middle Europe.[5]

Throughout the Arabic occupation of the Iberian Peninsula, the municipality of Toledo had remained a Christian bishopric and developed into an important centre of Islamic learning. As cities with a more educated population began to develop in Europe, Christian scholars were eager to absorb the learning and knowledge amassed by the Muslims and many European scholars went to study with the Arabs. The widespread reintroduction of Aristotle from Byzantine and Arab scholars coincided with the development of the medieval university and a wider growth of an academic culture. In a similar way as to how Greek education and thought had once captivated scholars in ancient Rome, Arabic-speaking philosophers with their unique take on Aristotle now influenced the European Occident. Bearing a very particular world outlook such Arabic influence dominated the arena of philosophy and made its influence felt:

> The Arabic scholars came with their wonderfully chiselled Aristotelian knowledge and tried to attack Christianity from all different directions. Those wishing to defend Christianity only stood a chance if they were able to show that the instruments used by the Arabs were applied incorrectly. The Arabs gave the appearance that only

they alone had access to the right Aristotelian way of thinking, and could therefore direct their attacks against Christianity from this position of superiority. The Arabic interpretation makes it seem as if anyone sharing the Aristotelian point of view would of necessity have to be an opponent of Christiniy.[6]

It is not difficult to see that there is a patent incompatibility of certain Islamic interpretations with the Christian faith. Until 1260, the main interpreters of Aristotle amongst philosophers and theologians in Christian Europe were the two Islamic thinkers Avicenna[7] and Averroes,[8] who both described the world in Aristotelian terms but introduced their own modifications, supplied their own efficient interpretation or dealt with philosophical issues by twisting Aristotle's concepts to fit with a Muslim understanding of the world. An example of what this 'Arabic Aristotelianism', as it is nowadays called, propagated is the theory of the eternity of the world, and another is the pantheistic intra-mundane understanding of the world itself being God; both stances self-evidently challenge the Christian faith. It is no surprise then that the Church authority and the theological faculty of the University of Paris sought to protect the Christian doctrine by issuing prohibitions against Aristotelian lecturing.

In Albertus Magnus' time at the University of Paris, these prohibitions were still in place—and the Church's rejection of Aristotle due to mistranslations certainly contributed to his ambition a few years later to produce commentaries upon all his works—although there were gradual signs that at least certain people within the theological faculty had an earnest desire to open up more. The inauguration of a new curriculum that included the study of the Aristotelian corpus was only introduced at the University of Paris in 1255. After that, other European universities followed suit and, in fact, soon after positioned Aristotelian works alongside other natural science texts at the centre of their respective curriculums. With education becoming one of the highest ideals within European society, Aristotelian learning and teaching now became the starting point for any serious academic endeavour, be it philosophical, theological or scientific in nature. And European scholars and philosophers embracing and absorbing such newly gained knowledge of the ancients were now eager to reconcile Aristotelian thinking with both Christian theology and the teachings of the Roman Catholic Church. Given the societal impact and recognition of Aristotle as 'the master of those who have gained knowledge'[9] any thinker wishing to be taken seriously had no choice but to take Aristotle as his starting point. The early

Scholastics Albertus Magnus and Thomas Aquinas were foremost amongst the thinkers who made it their task to demonstrate that the wisdom of antiquity, and in particular Aristotle, could be linked with the Christian faith.

In order to understand the impact of Aristotelian thinking on subsequent schools of thought and in particular on Scholasticism, the following will provide a brief outline of some of Aristotle's thinking that directly influenced Albertus Magnus and Thomas Aquinas. As all philosophy aims to go beyond unreflective ordinary awareness of the world around us, this matter also stands at the very centre of Aristotle's enquiry. Aristotle was grappling with probably the most ancient debates and enquiries in philosophy that concern the ultimate nature of reality, with the question of how we gain knowledge of the spatio-temporal sense world around us, what constitutes true understanding and genuine knowledge, and how to achieve these.

Agreeing with his teacher Plato that any starting points for true knowledge need to be self-evidently true, Aristotle uses reason, logical analysis and conceptual clarification to build up his framework for genuine knowledge. As outlined in the above, Plato is still relying on the mind to have innate knowledge of certain self-evident truths which he then relies upon as the source of all further knowledge. In order to explain such, Plato introduces abstract forms over and above the ordinary world of particular objects encountered in sense perception—a realm of abstract (non-material) reality. In this account, particular objects occupying a single region of space at a given time are modelled after their universal archetypes. Plato understood these universal forms to be unchangeable, eternal and absolute and therefore never to be grasped through the senses but only through pure understanding. In order to attain genuine knowledge, Plato then argued that one needs to grasp the timeless and permanent universals of which the ordinary changing day-to-day particulars are imperfect instances. This underlying order behind the changing flux of experience had, with all due reverence to his much adored teacher, been heavily criticised and rejected by his student Aristotle.

In immediate contrast to Plato, Aristotle's explanation of how we come to acquire general universal concepts starts with the direct experience of particular things in the sense world. The ultimate units of reality are individual subjects, instances of universal essences. The latter have no independent reality in their own right; they simply exist in a particular subject. So whereas Aristotle completely concurs that knowledge needs to go beyond particular instances and means grasping universal truths, he surpasses his teacher by stressing the importance of sense perception as the starting point from which knowledge can be derived as opposed to innate information. According to Aristotle, knowledge develops naturally from sense perception as we notice and remember general similarities encountered in sense experience. Aristotle calls this faculty for grasping the universal in the particular *nous* (usually translated as 'intuition').

With Christianity firmly relying on the Scriptures or, better, the revelation of the Scriptures, it might be easy to think the Aristotelian claim that sense perception provides the raw material of knowledge would contradict a Christian understanding of the world. Albertus, however, clearly did not believe this to be the case. Building on Aristotle's framework, he stressed that any knowledge of the external world essentially needs to start with an exploration of the sense world. He goes on to argue that there is yet another qualitatively different kind of knowledge. This is knowledge of the spiritual world which we come to know about through revelation of the Scriptures. There are then two distinct domains—the domain of knowledge derived by sense perception and the domain of knowledge derived by belief—which are not contradicting each other, but simply represent two distinct types of knowledge. Each also has a distinct methodology of how to come to know about it. Albertus' approach was later fully developed into the Scholastic 'two ways of knowing' by his student Thomas Aquinas.

The ancient debate about universals and particulars as described in the above also influenced Aristotle's more general dispute about form and matter, whereby natural objects are seen to be compounds of matter and form. Matter might be taken to refer to individual substances, including spiritual and any non-physical substance making up reality. Form might be taken to refer to the way the substance is put together as a whole. In very simple terms, one could think of 'matter', the primary substance, as being a particular animal and 'form', the secondary substance, being the species.[10]

Albertus Magnus extensively commentated on Aristotle's metaphysics and took it as his point of departure. The term metaphysics is derived from the Greek *ta meta ta physika* and refers to 'the things after the natural things' or better 'the things beyond the natural things', i.e. it is an investigation into the nature of being as such. Albertus consistently built on Aristotelian metaphysics by starting from the study of nature.

Building on Aristotle's differentiation between form and matter, Albertus thereby differentiated between three distinct universals in regard to the sense world: *Universalia ante rem* ('universals before the thing') refer to universal exemplars in the divine mind before their creation. *Universalia in rebus* ('universals in the thing') refer to universal features inherent in the individual things themselves. *Universalia post rem* ('universals after the thing') refer to their universal names. As concepts in the human mind they are posterior to the particular things represented by these concepts. The differentiation into these three universals gives a vivid description of cosmic evolution and creation, from the state of being in God to the embodiment in the world or nature to being in the human soul. It is noteworthy that human cognition is expressed separately from the existence of being in the world—an indication of how human consciousness separates itself more and more out of an ancient experience as a unity with the world to the experience as a separate entity. Despite this separation, human consciousness is part of the cosmic happening. In receiving the ideas inherent in the world around us, human cognition is part of and has an active part to play within the wider cosmic happenings (from an ontological point of view only, i.e. there is no indication yet as to what kind of meaning this might have for the thinker himself). In other words, human thoughts are not just superimposed onto reality—it is implied that they are elements of reality.

Without going into the intricacies and intriguing details of some of the ontological/theological problems these three types of universals raise and to which Aquinas, amongst others, provided intuitive solutions for—such as the question of the nature of the relationship between God and his ideas, or the question of the compatibility of the diversity of divine ideas with the unity of divine thought itself, to name just a couple—what is of particular importance in this specific context is the fact that these universals presuppose God to be the ultimate origin of the universe. There are ontologically primary universals that exist before things, which precede all creation by existing as divine ideas. According to this view, everything we ever experience or perceive via our senses has its origin in the being of God. And furthermore, the particular things encountered in sense perception have certain features which we as human beings, firstly, are able to comprehend and, secondly, are able to signify by giving them universal terms. It is therefore in our thinking that the sense world and God come together. Thomas Aquinas further expands on this by speaking about the divine being behind the sense world in his *Summa Theologica*. For him, truth is the revelation of the real things and therefore something secondary that never is just by itself. Truth is subordinate to the divine reality which we are striving to uncover. And as a glance forward, yet a few centuries later Rudolf Steiner expands on this notion by guiding us step by step to the experience that reality, having been split into two by our senses, is created *within us* by uniting percept and concept; the act of knowing is a synthesis of percept and concept.[11]

Such epistemological differentiation into true reality on the one hand and our encounter of it on the other gave rise to what we now know of as the Scholastic undertaking. Scholasticism at its most basic began with a most conscientious and meticulous process of collecting and taking stock of what was already known in classical and ancient philosophy—such as Albertus' commentaries and paraphrases. It then went on to a most rigorous conceptual analysis of all concepts employed, drawing out distinctions, solving contradictions, and precisely defining all conceptual constructs. The exceedingly methodical approach employed by Scholastics had a tremendous effect on the mind in terms of sharpening their thinking abilities. Such Scholastic schooling was, however, not to be understood as a project of acquiring abstract information about thought constructs or of getting to grips with a particular set of problem-solving techniques. It was a genuine striving for discovery and revelation of true insight and took the form of exercising not just thought, but also the will and totality of one's being. Any such schooling was not undertaken for the sake of education but deeply involved and was intertwined with the self-transformation of the student. Philosophy was regarded as a way of life, both in its exercise and efforts exerted and in its goal of achieving wisdom itself. For real wisdom was understood not just to give rise to knowledge, but also to transform and positively change the thinker in the process. In this sense, one might say Scholasticism served the refinement of the medieval scholar: with philosophy ultimately hoping to allow insight into the highest divine truths, exercise of wisdom entailed a cosmic dimension (in the sense of the thinker belonging to a whole that goes beyond the limits of his/her individuality) and any such quest could not be based on intellectual principles and philosophical discourse alone. For early Scholastics, any such quests for insight necessarily had a moral component. Moral education became thus an absolute requirement and prerequisite. Striving towards knowledge and insight then became a way of life, practised at each instant. The noble Scholastic outlook and attitude towards life was a long path of self-discipline and self-transformation, involving practices of mediation, spiritual exercises, prayer and study.

Centuries later, Rudolf Steiner emphasizes this transformation in the pursuit of higher knowledge. He gives the principle that for each step taken in spiritual perception, three steps are to be taken in moral development.[12] Practising virtues are essential realities, not abstract concepts, and therefore critical to spiritual growth.

At the very heart of the Scholastic striving for divine truth and knowledge lay the experience of a deeply felt tension, which was brought about by the question of the relation between *fides et ratio* (between faith and reason), i.e. between the kind of principles held to be true on the basis of faith and the kind of principles taken to be truth-bearing on the basis of rational enquiry. Within that juncture of Western culture when this question flared up into a crisis amongst scholars—largely as a result of the reintroduction of the Aristotelian works in Latin translation—it called into question as to how far faith is independent of, if not outwardly adversarial towards, reason, and to what extent the latter is necessary or appropriate for the justification of religious belief. What is reason's appropriate jurisdiction vis-à-vis that of faith? There seemed an unbridgeable gap and conflict between the reliance on faith (Christian revelation) versus the reliance on rational enquiry (Aristotelian logic) in the pursuit of philosophical and religious truth. These questions were the starting point for Albertus and Aquinas whose philosophy brought about a new *modus vivendi* between faith and rational enquiry that does not only show that Aristotelian thinking, if Aristotle is correctly understood, tolerates but, even more, fully supports and justifies Christianity.

Building on his three universals as a threefold classification of things in terms of their function (in itself, in respect to understanding, as existing in one particular) Albertus Magnus goes on to differentiate between different types of objects of human knowing. According to him there are three different objects of knowledge which he designates as *naturalia*, *credenda* and *beatificantia*:

> The natural things that the intellect contemplates are received in a natural light, while the things that the intellect contemplates in the order of belief are received in a light that is gratuitous and the beatifying realities are received in the light of glory.[13]

This distinction between natural light and the light of glory thus gives rise to radically different types of knowledge. With the philosophy of Albertus and Aquinas being closely intertwined, Aquinas expands this in his *Summa Theologica*. With great clarity he differentiates between two different ways of knowing—philosophical and theological—neither of which he took to contradict or exclude the other. Their differences derive from their different sources and the basis of their respective sciences. Philosophical discourse is concerned with rational truths, such principles acquired through gathering empirical knowledge, analysis thereof and reflection on that which is based on experiential evidence. Brought about by the thinker's own, inwardly active reason, rational truths are in themselves not products of proof but are known by themselves (they are known *per se*, as opposed to *per alia*). They concern truths about the natural sciences, the external world, but also the existence of God. And they are truths which can be discovered and investigated without the precondition of faith. By contrast, theological discourse and sacred doctrine receives its principles from divine revelation—it is through grace that we come to know of it, and we can only experience and comprehend it with our faculty of faith. It concerns truths which God has revealed about himself in the creation and redemption of the world, such as the doctrine of the Trinity, the Creation, the incarnation of Christ, and the sacraments. Believers can, of course, reflect upon these truths as within any other science as they are, needless to say, governed by the same principles of rationality and thought, but they are characterized by being held true on the basis of faith. According to Aquinas, rational enquiry and revelation are two very distinct ways of knowing (*ratio cognoscibilis*), offering us different sciences and qualitatively very different kinds of truths:

> Sciences are differentiated according to the various means through which knowledge is obtained. For the astronomer and the physicist both may prove the same conclusion—that the earth, for instance, is round: the astronomer by means of mathematics (i.e. abstracting from matter), but the physicist by means of matter itself. Hence there is no reason why those things which may be learnt from philosophical science, so far as they can be known by natural reason, may not also be taught us by some other science in so far that they fall within revelation. Hence theology included in sacred doctrine differs in kind from that theology which is part of philosophy.[14]

Aquinas did not stop short at distinguishing between sacred doctrine and natural knowledge but also insisted that there can be no contradiction between doctrines of faith and true natural knowledge. He strongly rejected any kind of 'double truth', which some of his Parisian contemporaries developed and according to which Christian philosophers every so often have simultaneously to accept two conflicting points of view, namely when sacred doctrine contradicts that which is established in philosophy. Aquinas argued that since all truth ultimately comes from God and because of God's unity and inherent non-contradiction such a view of conflicting truths is impossible to uphold. He insisted on the harmony between the supernatural and natural order.

Our natural desire and quest for knowledge can ultimately only be fulfilled by God or a vision of God; it is only grace that perfects nature. This, however, does not imply that the quest for knowledge is in vain. Quite to the contrary, it means that we are called upon to enhance and train our capacity for natural reason by exercising and training our capabilities of analysis, reasoning, deduction and arrangement of content.

Despite the sources and subject matters of theology and philosophy being different, we need to employ the use of reason in both. Theological discourse is governed by principles of reason and needs to be tested by recourse to reasoning in the same way as any other discourse within the natural sciences or philosophy. In this respect, the subject matter studied in philosophy bears a likeness to the realities that are objects of faith.

Aquinas even went a step further by emphasizing how reason must serve faith (faith being that which we know by God's revelation) and by drawing out the dependency of grace on the natural order. Since grace is a quality added to nature, divine law presupposes natural law:

> But Sacred Doctrine makes use even of human reason, not, indeed, to prove faith ... but to make clear other things that are put forward in this doctrine. Since grace therefore does not destroy nature, but perfects it, natural reason should minister to faith (...).[15]

Reason has an immense role to play within the arena of faith. Faith builds on reason. According to Aquinas, reason prepares the minds of those receiving faith by providing the truths which faith presupposes. By acquiring knowledge through experience and gathering insights into the structure of external reality, such as nature, man, his actions and being *qua* being, in preparing ourselves we create the preconditions for God to reveal that which lies beyond the reach of natural reason and surpasses nature. In the same way as nature is to grace, reason is the precondition of faith—the *praeambula fidei* (preambles for faith). Aquinas maintained, for example, that the existence of God is not self-evident. Quite different from revelation, human reason can deduce the existence of God and thus prepare us to acknowledge the truths provided by divine revelation. One note here, that Aquinas' view is very unlike that of Anselm of Canterbury whose starting point is an acceptance of the Christian revelation as true. Originally, Anselm had intended to entitle his *Proslogion* as 'Faith seeking understanding', thereby clearly indicating that it is as a believer that he sought to understand. (This raises the question as to whether he ever meant his famous ontological argument setting out to prove the existence of God to convince unbelievers). For Aquinas and the Scholastics, thinking had therefore an essential task to fulfil, namely to prepare us up to the point where we are ready to receive divine revelation:

> We are trying to educate ourselves on the things that surround us ... When objects present themselves to us, we can perceive them through our senses. We are then forced to form definitions. Behind the things there lie the divine forces that we do not dare approach.

> We are striving to school ourselves from object to object, and thus, by confining ourselves to the sense-perceptible, finally arrive at the highest concepts.[16]

Once divine grace has revealed itself, reason should then endeavour to explain and develop these truths of faith, as well as propose them as an intelligible (scientific) way and defend them.

There has been much discussion about the extent to which Aquinas uses Aristotle's philosophy when elaborating his doctrine of faith as there are moments when he goes beyond Aristotle's thought, or even refutes and corrects him. What is certain, however, is that Aristotle became the guide that led Scholastics up to the threshold which they could reach by their own accord, with their own strength of reasoning, the threshold beyond which there lies the realm that is inaccessible to (Greek) thought. It is here—at the point within us where rational analysis and enquiry is expended, and where divine grace reveals insight into God's infinite and transcendent being and wisdom—that reason and belief come into contact with each other. It is within us that reason and belief border onto one other. Rudolf Steiner describes this with the following words:

> ... human thought with all its techniques falls short of penetrating, of itself, into those regions which embody the content of the highest revealed wisdom. The early Scholastic appealed to a certain fund of wisdom which transcends the technique of thinking; that is, it is only attainable in so far as thought is capable of elucidating the wisdom which has been revealed... He presses forward up to a certain boundary where revealed wisdom meets him. Thus the content of personal research and revelation becomes united in an objective, unified and monistic conception of the universe.[17]

With this, philosophy set limits to what can be known for the first time in the evolution of human consciousness. As defined in the above, universals *ante rem* as prototypes of things within the divine essence before their creation remain outside our human understanding; in thinking we are unable to directly share into or have any immediate experience of the content of divine thought. Only when these universal exemplars change into universals *in rebus*—now not any more categories of cognition but rather categories of being—can we hope to grasp them and thereby turn them into *universalia ante res*. Scholasticism hereby draws a clear limit with respect to truth that remains outside human cognition. On either side of this boundary to knowledge (*Erkenntnisgrenze*) there lies a particular kind of truth: the human version on one side and the divine one on the other.

And while it is in human thinking that world and divine thought meet—in other words, the being of created things represents the connection between human and divine cognition—the being of created things acts at the same time as a divider, clearly separating human and divine thoughts.

The Scholastic emphasis on thought and thought exercises carries a clear danger for philosophy to become a purely abstract and theoretical activity. Indeed, this is the turn that philosophy took since the Middle Ages. Philosophy moved more and more away from being directed towards people becoming fully developed human beings, towards a training to become specialists at applying well-studied theorems and constructing technical jargon. This can be seen in the famous debate about the nature and meaning of universals, originally stemming from Plato and Aristotle's debate as outlined above, and which was to carry on in more abstract forms well into the thirteenth century.

It is a debate about the nature or essence of universals, such as put forward by Albertus, and questions what such a 'concept' referring to a kind of 'being' denotes: Does it posit a reality or is it simply a name? Which one has more reality, the universal name or the individual feature of the thing referred to? Has the object in question been created out of the universal, or has the universal been given to the object after its creation? While early Scholastics such as Albertus and Aquinas were realists in the sense that they awarded universals being, i.e. they believed in their absolute reality, so-called nominalists took them to constitute no more than labels without any claim to being, i.e. they did not believe them to be real. With that, nominalism threatens to imprison human beings within their own mind without any chance of ever gaining access to independent and separate reality: If universals are mere names bestowed onto things encountered in sense perception, then these names do not make any claims about reality. They are then created within our own human minds, without any guarantee that the respective name denotes anything real or that a corresponding reality then does indeed exist.

Albertus Magnus and Thomas Aquinas stayed true to philosophy as an investigation into reality. Their interest in and reference to universals concerns, firstly, the question of what kinds of things exist (including physical/material and spiritual) and, secondly, the question of their nature and essence. But in this so-called 'problem of universals' philosophy shifts from ontological concerns about the reality of things towards epistemological concerns about how we achieve knowledge of them. According to this nominalist point of view, before being able to make any claims about reality and the nature of things one needs to establish how far humans have the ability to comprehend them in the first place. The fundamental concern has shifted to what we can know and how we can justify any claim to knowledge. In particular, the issue at stake is whether and how our convictions about the external world can be justified considering our own mental state. This represents a tremendous shift away from the traditional perception of philosophy as the meta-study providing the fundamental structures of reality from which sciences can take their starting points. Philosophy is no longer helping science to draw up the inventory of the world, but is reduced to a second order discipline that reflects on how science relates to reality and investigates the preconditions of experience. Eventually, this turned into the question of whether we can represent reality at all.

At the height of nominalsim in the eighteenth century, Immanuel Kant[18] argues in his monumental work *The Critique of Pure Reason*, published in German in 1781, for a clear and absolute limit to knowledge. Adopting an Aristotelian starting point in sense perception like the Scholastics, Kant limits human experience to the empirical world. According to him, sense experience presents the only way of finding out about reality in that our human capacities for knowledge are necessarily bound up with and limited to sense experience. It is therefore impossible to gain any knowledge whose justification does not depend on experience. Instead of being able to describe mind-independent essences of things, any statement about reality articulates never anything more than our necessary preconditions for the experience of objects, i.e. the essential features of the way we experience them. And any aspiration to ascend to the world beyond immediate experience—a world which he calls *noumena* or things in themselves—is doomed to failure. In the following metaphor, Kant condemns any attempt to describe the ultimate reality behind sense perception as mere speculation and deception:

> The light dove cleaving in free flight the thin air, whose resistance it feels, might imagine [absurdly] that her movements would be far more free and rapid in airless space. Just in the same way did Plato, abandoning the world of sense because of the narrow limits it sets to the understanding, venture upon the wings of ideas beyond it, into the void of pure intellect ... It is, indeed, common fate of human reason in speculation to finish the imposing edifice of thought as rapidly as possible, and then for the first time to begin to examine whether the foundation is a solid one or no[t].[19]

As there is, for Kant, no possible description of the world which can free itself entirely of some reference to experience, human reason is not capable of *a priori* knowledge, i.e. knowledge prior to and independent of sense experience. The thing in itself remains eternally unknown. One note here that if the nature or essence of things is inaccessible as a matter of principle, Kant did not just establish firm limits to human knowledge, but much more than that, established the impossibility of ever reaching any true insight. Philosophy can then never hope to provide any grasp of reality; it becomes a critical activity reflecting on the way we represent reality and concerned with setting limits to thoughts from within.

There is a fundamental difference between Kant's interpretation of limits to knowledge and the early Scholastics' understanding; for Kant, the limits to knowledge are absolute. This gave rise to the Kantian dogma that there is no other way of relating to the spiritual world than unqualified belief. For Albertus Magnus and Thomas Aquinas, there is a distinction between how knowledge is gained. However, their careful distinction between that which human beings are able to understand out of their own rationality on the one hand and that which needs to be revealed as a truth of faith on the other, while setting a clear boundary, does by no means constitute an absolute limit. Even though both Scholastics are adamant that mysteries of faith cannot be established by mere natural reason, such truths of faith can be grasped in principle. Although they cannot be discovered by oneself, nor is there hope to ever fully understand them with our intellectual faculties alone, personally gained truths serve as a pillar for understanding the truths of faith. Human reason and divine revelation are compatible and not contradictory.

Building on Aristotle's distinction between form and matter, Albertus gives a clear indication of the kind of interaction between the human soul and the objects of cognition. Universals *ante rem* are the essence of the form before it is instantiated in an individual object, universals *in re* describes the essence in the thing itself, and universals *post rem* are the essence of the form as an inner experience in recognizing such. There is an interaction between the human soul with the object. The mission of early Scholasticism could then be described as creating the kind of soul experience needed for such a differentiation.

This is essentially a path of initiation that the early Scholastics broke as new ground—a thorough development of the art of thinking, for it to become the foundation for a true understanding of reality.

Without assuming that the history of philosophy could have been changed or the development of human thought could have been altered, it seems that the natural continuation of Scholasticism would have been to push these boundaries and to extend the realm of that which can be known further and further.

> ... the most natural thing would have been to have increasingly expanded the technique of thinking, so that ever higher and higher portions of the supersensible world should have been grasped by thought.[20]

If the limits delineated by our expressions of thought are indeed not absolute as Albertus Magnus and Thomas Aquinas argued, the real question that then arises concerns how these limits can be overcome. The question then becomes: How to achieve knowledge of higher worlds?

A book by Rudolf Steiner under the very same title[21] is addressing precisely this question of how to push out the boundaries set by our embodied nature. For even if the essence of things is recognizable in principle, it does by no means imply that the world with all its mysteries and secrets is an open book waiting to be read. For we are, at every point in our lives, limited by our highly individual capacity to grasp and understand. More than anything else, it is a question of spiritual development and inner activity of where the precise boundaries lie at any point in time. In the above-mentioned work, Steiner extensively describes inner exercises that lead one's soul forces towards the experience of an extra-sensory spiritual world. His so-called 'auxiliary exercises' give ample instructions in the same vein as the early Scholastics. Rudolf Steiner's starting point for any such exercise is clear and rigorous thinking. Anthroposophy attempts to lead through the sphere of strict logical thinking, by continually strengthening the soul life, towards a transformation of consciousness.

> One cannot speak of a limit of knowledge. It may be that, at any particular moment, this or that remains unexplained because, through our place in life, we are prevented from perceiving the things involved. What is not found out today, however, may be found tomorrow. The limits due to the causes are only transitory, and can be overcome by the process of perception and thinking.[22]

Only a consciousness, able to change and transform itself can redeem thought from its own preconceived limitations. A transformed consciousness allows true research into what constitutes reality. In this sense, anthroposophy can be seen as a natural development out of Scholasticism. It is here that the two Scholastic areas of *fides* and *ratio* permeate each other when the limits of knowledge are extended into the realm of revelation, and cognition and belief are united. Extending consciousness out of its current limitations does then not replace faith but, on the contrary, opens up a space for revelations given in grace. With that, Rudolf Steiner lays the foundation for the *possibility* of true knowledge, a principle that seems to be infinitely demonstrated by his scientific spiritual research.

12
What was the Point of Gothic?

Architecture and the Development of Human Consciousness

Brien Masters

Though we could picture human consciousness in ancient Greek times as a flight of steps in the vast staircase that begins in the dim distant past with humanity's atavistic clairvoyance directly viewing the world of spirit, and 'descending' into the faculty of perceiving the world revealed by 'earthly' senses to the exclusion—some would hold, ultimately the occlusion—of that other world, we could nevertheless take it for granted that each step in that Greek flight embraced two elements of *vision*: the vision which nowadays we would broadly accord to the true experience (i.e. not illusory), utterly rare amongst our contemporaries, of some object in, or vista of, that metaphysical world (back to the top of the staircase); and the vision—the Greeks didn't need to change the verb, though my continuing with it here might seem odd—of the world of outer reality for which we moderns seek the optometrist's help if we find our personal possession of the faculty becoming myopic or otherwise going out of focus. Might we even go as far as saying: just as the poet began his epic with 'It sings in me', so also the non-blind Greeks could describe the way that the two worlds (that of outer objects and that of spirit *or of thought*) entered their consciousness: 'it appears in me' or 'in my field *of vision*'? Even if this is too much of an approximation for the keenly differentiating philosopher, it will serve our broad purpose, particularly if we can identify with the insight Rudolf Steiner brought to bear on the situation when he pointed out that:

> We do not [...] understand [...] Aristotle [...] unless we realize that, though he had almost arrived at an understanding of thought, free from all evidence of the senses, nevertheless, whenever he speaks of concepts, he still keeps within the meaning of traditional experience which regarded concepts as belonging to the outer world as much as sense perceptions.[1]

Augustine, on a *lower* flight of steps, 'felt compelled to rise to the thoughts free from sense perception, to thoughts which still kept their meaning, even if they were not dealing with earthly air and sea [...] thoughts which had a content beyond the vision of sense.'[2] Such descent and ascent in the same experience and in the thought life of humanity became the ardent study in the thirteenth century of Albertus Magnus (and by implication his pupil Thomas Aquinas), and it is both stimulating and illuminating to move from the metaphor of the staircase (above) into the realm of actual architecture, in order to follow how the process taking place in the evolution of human consciousness was manifest in the outer structures of iron, wood and stone, slate, glass and fresco.

The Greek temple, with its special proportions, provided a physical dwelling place for the god or goddess to which it was dedicated. What sacred entity Apollo and Athena provided for those in whose midst the temple stood, entered their consciousness—to whatever degree, depending on which step they stood on the Greek flight of stairs—as did the sculptures of entablature or frieze, the entasis on the pillars, the steps below, the tympanum above and all the other details of the building. The two sides of the coin of vision worked together in the currency of consciousness. Though infinitely exalted, the process of consciousness was akin to the everyday, to that which enabled the Greek to perceive his next-door neighbour's finer nature and physical body.

With the early Christian basilica, to experience 'the god' the worshippers had to enter the building—leave, as it were, the outer world of perception and enter the sacred space in which their personal consciousness could be imbued with the super-earthly. The catacomb provided the same consciousness-opportunity though through different means, due to Christian persecution in the first two centuries AD. Yet we find there, cut off from the everyday sense world, images of Orpheus and Jonah, and symbols of Christ, which presumably helped those who were followers of Christianity to raise or enhance their consciousness to something of a Pauline/Damascus state, to one degree or another. However, whilst we may consider the Christianizing of thought-life to be an entirely new direction in the spiritual life on earth, the 'tread' of consciousness which embraces it continued in its foreordained direction.

If we allow ourselves the short cut of juxtaposing the early basilica and the most lofty of Romanesque cathedrals, we have the architectural equivalent of the next major flight of stairs which takes us to the end of the twelfth century. This stage of development is arguably epitomized in Chartres with, on the one hand, its millennia-old spiritual tradition[3] and, on the other hand, its leap forward from Romanesque to Gothic, backed by the Continent-wide famed School of Chartres,[4] a jewel of outstanding culture in the Middle Ages. As the flames leapt into the sky, tragically destroying its Romanesque cathedral—the last of several built on the same site to be destroyed—it seems the flame of the development of human conciousness leapt forward, the destruction of the old liberating the possibility of the new and thus creating the new style of Gothic architecture.

We, with our earthly senses and our aesthetic feeling, see *the pointed arch* as that which symbolizes Gothic architecture's most outstanding feature; it is the essence of its crowning beauty. When Rudolf Steiner investigated what the pointed arch—superseding the rounded Romanesque arch—represented spiritually, he discovered in it more than aesthetic beauty. The barrel vault of the Romanesque cathedral, studded with gold stars painted against an ethereal blue (with the rounded arches of its windows on all sides) represented, one could say, the vault of heaven. In divine service, the yearning souls of cleric and of congregation gathered beneath the vault were 'lifted' up by it as into spiritual realms, borne upward by the ritual, the sculptured and stained-glass images, the otherworldly flow of the plainsong echoing on high, in the transepts and in the side aisles. At the end of the service the worshippers, be they ecclesiastical or otherwise, re-entered their daily life with renewed religious conviction and fervour. However, as the end of the (twelfth) century gradually approached, the realization that the experience of and access to the spirit on these occasions was dwindling became more and more acute and of great concern in a society in which the church provided the bedrock of culture. The Romanesque figures sculpted at the west façade of Chartres cathedral—permeated on the one hand with a transcendent mood in their whole demeanour, but on the other hand a look of unrelieved sorrow that distancing from the divine was the direction in which human consciousness was inexorably leading—are frequently cited as indicative of this development.

With the pressing question 'What next?' came the positive answer 'Strive to regain what is being lost'. Gothic architecture became the means of doing this. The point of the arch represented the breakthrough. With the barrel vault having changed, so to speak, from symbolizing that which reassuringly overarched earthly life—the spiritual world—to that which cut it off from its divine source, it became necessary to *pierce through*, i.e. point the arch upwards. And it worked! The arch, together with the upwardly soaring fluting of the great pillars which bore the load of the roof, the vast sea of colour pouring in through the glass windows from sunrise to sunset which transformed the stonework, the floor, the interior sculptures and every object that stood there into a flood of dappled beauty, the sheer extent of the glass itself—the huge flying buttresses outside enabled the stone wall structure to be trimmed down to relatively narrow roof supports allowing the windows to assume hitherto unknown significance in the sense- and soul-impressions of those who were worshipping within—the super-earthly content of the stained glass, depicting saints in heaven high above and biblical scenes from the Old and New Testaments in the lancets below, all creating otherworldly dimensions of space and time ... all this had the effect of jerking the soul and spirit of those who entered 'the house' out of their increasingly dungeon-like body.[5] The experience—a direct spiritual descendant, one might say, of that which the images of Orpheus and Jonah had conjured in the souls of the early Christians, in meditative defiance of the whole religious infrastructure of ancient Rome, sought in the seclusion of the catacombs[6]—was referred to by contemporaries as 'taking heaven by storm'. And as Gothic spread across Europe in the decades that followed (Chartres was essentially rebuilt between 1194 and 1220) the architecture emphasized and enhanced those features here characterized, in which was vested the potential for recompensing the atrophying of natural spiritual awareness that was enshrouding the consciousness of the West.

In what might be described as his greatest sequence of lectures in 1924—as distinct from the specific *cycles* of lectures which also took place during the same year and which characterized the bulk of his work on spiritual-scientific topics that had bearing on the daily life and occupations of his listeners—Rudolf Steiner concentrated on themes which all had a bearing on karmic relationships. This sequence has been published in eight volumes. In the second volume are lectures in which Steiner shares his research precisely into the period here under consideration. We find there descriptions of the thought life of the Neoplatonists, the so-called Chartres masters who taught in the last decades of the Romanesque period and who were the clients, so to speak, for the stonemasons and other artists/artisans who undertook with astonishing success the inconceivably vast 'programme' of construction of the Gothic cathedral of Chartres, which has miraculously survived the ravages of war and iconoclasm that have come and gone through the ages, and which stands there on its hill jutting above the surrounding plain of La Beauce for all now to see—as well, of course, of the dozens of other Gothic buildings of like impact that sprung up and whose influence washed like waves of cultural new birth across Europe into the thirteenth and fourteenth centuries.

In the same lecture sequence, Steiner recounts how, once Gothic had been born, transferred one could say from the minds of the Neoplatonists into its soaring buildings of unprecedented spiritual grandeur, as these 'masters' excarnated, the Scholastics began to incarnate. One envisages a mighty crossing over of souls in the spiritual world, a crossing over of ascent and descent, with Albertus Magnus descending chronologically in the lead. He is also attributed with having achieved that point in the edifice of human thinking which sought to answer the question 'What is our relationship to a world of which all that we know is derived from concepts which can only arise in ourselves out of our own experience as individuals?' This is the question which Rudolf Steiner encapsulated in lectures on Scholasticism in 1920.[7] In these lectures he discusses at length the contribution of Albertus and Aquinas to the development of human consciousness. In the present architectural context—the change from the rounded Romanesque arch to the pointed Gothic arch—perhaps it would be appropriate to give Albertus the accolade for spiritually giving the impetus which broke through the semicircle with the first tip of the Gothic 'point', while according Aquinas the accolade of having developed the full edifice that followed. On a similarly lighter note, G.K. Chesterton, in his slim biography of Aquinas, makes an astute observation: 'A very learned Anglican once said to me, not perhaps without a touch of tartness, "I can't understand why everybody talks as if Thomas Aquinas were the beginning of the Scholastic philosophy. I could understand their saying he was the end of it." Whether or no the comment was meant to be tart we may be sure that the reply of St Thomas would have been perfectly urbane. And indeed it would be easy to answer, with a certain placidity, that in his Thomist language the end of a thing does not mean its destruction but its fulfilment.' Be all that as it may, here we shall pursue further the contribution of Albertus Magnus, as the one who strenuously begins to reconstruct the staircase of consciousness, starting not at the topmost step but *at the bottom*.

13
The Mission of Drama

And its Alignment with Music Drama and Mystery Drama

Brien Masters

In his lecture cycle *The Christ Impulse and the Development of Ego Consciousness*,[1] as well as elsewhere, Rudolf Steiner points out that in ancient Greek times the language contained no word for conscience. For example, in Aeschylus' play *Eumenides*, at the point where Orestes has murdered Clytemnestra his mother, his consciousness is raised briefly to a clairvoyant state—something that was already fading in the population as a whole—so that he sees himself surrounded by those beings who severely chastise him for his murderous action, the *Erinyes*. These were sometimes staged as female goddesses of vengeance with snakes writhing on their heads, like Medusa, and with blood streaming from their eyes. Later on, when Euripides wants to portray a similar situation with similar consequences in his plays, he uses the Greek word for conscience to convey to the audience what the culprit is going through. This not only informs the audience of the state of soul the actor is portraying, but the experience, albeit engendered theatrically, brings about *the birth of conscience* in the soul of the onlookers. Steiner connects this with the mission of drama, pointing out, by way of substantiation, that no word for conscience can be found in the Old Testament. Conscience becomes a faculty of soul through the theatre.

When lecturing in Stratford on Avon, Shakespeare's birthplace, in April 1922, Steiner turns once more to drama, and comments that the mission of drama is to bring about some form of metamorphosis in the human soul. He goes into no further detail regarding Shakespeare; perhaps research will tell what Shakespeare's mission was at that crucial point in the age of the consciousness soul[2] in which his consummate genius was at work.

In so far as Shakespeare's plays took time before they became part of household parlance, they could be said to differ from their equivalent in Greek times where, in the theatre situated in the sanctuary of Asklepio at Epidaurus, in Athens in the theatre of Dionysus on the slope of the Acropolis and in the theatres in many other cities, vast swathes of the population watched the plays. The popularity of the theatre meant that the metamorphosis of soul implicit in the action and language permeated the entire population in such a way that it had 'come to stay'. The famous Greek plays which have come down to us—not all are extant—were translated into Latin, the Romans referring to the Erinyes as *The Furies*. So the process, beginning in classical Greek times, quite apart from anything else that was contained in the experience of the theatre, continued for about a millennium when, in the sixth century AD the Roman theatres were closed down.[3]

After what appears to be a lull of some three to four centuries, drama re-enters the cultural life of Europe in a way that is externally as far removed from the vast crowds of ancient times as could be imagined. At Easter time in the ninth century, when Christianity was taking firm root in religious / cultural life, there occurred at the appropriate place before the Introit of the Mass a minute enactment: designated priests would make their way to the altar where they were in full view of the congregation, clad in vestments that indicated their identity—three dressed as the three Marys coming to the place on Golgotha where the sepulchre in which Christ's body had been laid to rest, and one dressed in white as an angel. There they spoke the three sentences recounted in the Gospel in which, as answer to the women's enquiring looks, the angel says: 'I know that ye seek Jesus who was crucified; he is not here, he is risen.'[4]

This seedlike glimpse of things to come was eventually moved from the Easter Mass to Matins, and grew over a lengthy period of time into the medieval pageants which were performed at the crossing point of nave and transept in the cathedrals, then brought out to the west end and performed in front of the west façade, and finally taken on stages erected on wagons (hence *pageants*) round the city to certain stations where the population had gathered to watch. As this process took place, moving from a very brief liturgical drama 'performed' at the Easter Mass by priests to additional enactments of biblically derived texts—or incidents alluded to in the scriptures—the rubrics that described how the scenes were to be dramatized (gestures, props, costumes, movements and often even the tone of voice) were specifically indicated.

In England this culminated in the fifteenth century with the widely famed mystery plays, each scene of which was performed by one of the guilds—in 1210 the pope had forbidden the clergy to be further involved in the acting. The York cycle was the first to be fully developed in 1430–40, followed by the Wakefield cycle in 1450, the Coventry cycle in 1468, and finally the Chester cycle in 1475–1500.[5] Through this medium the people, crowded outside the west end of the cathedral, in the market place and at other strategic points in the city, witnessed the whole sequence of scenes that stretched from the Creation of the world to the

Last Judgement (alpha to omega). Following some time after Easter is Corpus Christi—a day connected with processions with which both Albertus Magnus and Thomas Aquinas have been long associated—on the Thursday following Trinity Sunday (a further separation between town and ecclesiastical gown?).

Shortly after the institution of Corpus Christi was the year in which Simon de Montfort faced the reigning monarch of England, Henry III—at the Battle of Lewes in East Sussex—with those barons who regarded the king as having overstepped his power and authority, and the honour accorded him by their sworn allegiance. It was a battle which, on being won by de Montfort and the lords of the land who rallied around him, led to the first parliament coming about—which in turn led to the constitutional monarchy which survives in England as a remarkable variant of democracy.

The inexorable change in humanity's state from the alpha of the non-personal permeated-by-divinity to one in which the independent ego inserts itself into life can be seen throughout history in an enormous range of variations. In a further step away from medieval feudalism in England, the revolt of Wat Tyler, who led the peasants into London in 1381 to voice their claims to Richard II, could be cited. On the Continent, one of the most impressive instances of this is Martin Luther, defiantly sticking to his argument—against the tsunami of papal power that the Roman Church had gradually accrued unto itself—with his memorable ego-utterance 'Here I stand; I can no other.'

The next 'scene' in this narrative that takes the process a step further is on Italian soil. The Academy that was set up by Count Bardi and his associates in Florence promulgated a new genre of music in which drama (rather than poetic texts for madrigals or solo lute songs, or religious texts such as the Mass and those to which motets were composed, or verses which were sung to melodies by the main body of the worshipping congregation in the Protestant north, etc.) formed the main part. We know this genre as *opera*. At its inception, based on the principles of the New Music,[6] the genre consisted of the story being declaimed by solo singers accompanied by a harmony instrument—keyboards of various kinds, lutes and other instruments that produced harmony through strumming—with a bowed bass part supporting the bottom line. Within little more than a decade it had developed into full-blown opera, with an impressive following in which aristocrats vied with each other to put on performances which excelled in elaborate décor, orchestration and costume. Monteverdi's *L'Orfeo*, produced at the court of Mantua in 1607, one could say was the ambassador of the movement in full and formal regalia, which resulted in public opera houses with considerable repertoires spreading across the land and sustained by significant public support.

The Greek myth of Orpheus and Euridice was amongst the most used stories to be fashioned as a libretto and was, in fact, set to music by Peri himself and other contemporaries; it was still enjoying popularity as a basis for the libretto in Gluck's time.[7] Other mythological themes from the classical tradition were also favoured, which is not surprising in one way since the genre came at the crest of the wave of the Renaissance. But the same principle can be seen in the application of opera in seventeenth-century France[8] and in the masques that were popular across the Channel in England after the Restoration. Such themes in England, too, were taken up by the Baroque composer and entrepreneur who made London his home, Georg Friederic Händel. In the output of this composer we note two important components: the slow discontinuation of employing at considerable expense the feted Italian opera singers, and the introduction of oratorio, works based on Old Testament themes during Lent, scored for soloists and orchestra, similar to opera but with an increasingly prominent role for the chorus. Oratorio became a genre in its own right, reaching a climax in Baroque Britain with Handel's *Messiah*.

At this point it will be advantageous to our argument if we extract some important threads that weave in one way or another through the foregoing. Firstly we are concerned with the stage, with whatever degree of spectacle there may have been. (This manifestly does not apply to oratorio but, as we shall see, the genre retains important threads in the emerging pattern.) Secondly we are concerned with the fact that what took place on the stage had a developmental effect in the souls of the audience/congregation/onlookers. Thirdly we are concerned with art forms based on narrative, i.e. stories that speak to the 'middle system' of the human being. Fourthly we are concerned with popular forms of entertainment (which, it could be said, applies to the levering of the medieval mystery drama out of the immediate precincts of the church).[9] Fifthly we are concerned with narratives that have bearing on the moral/ethical life of the people. And sixthly we are concerned with metamorphic changes which are the result of such theatrical experiences that contribute something permanent and salient to the overall evolution of human consciousness.[10]

We shall return to these threads in common, but with them in mind let us trace a few more stages in the development of opera per se. The immense popularity of Italian opera, though mingled with other elements in England, continued south of the Alps throughout the eighteenth century, with operas being written with Italian titles by Mozart such as *Cosi fan Tutte*, *Il Serraglio*, *Le Nozze de Figaro* and *Don Giovanni*, to name those with 'lighter' libretti. Some would say that the content of these works was fatuous and unworthy of Mozart's incomparable art. Here we may leave that argument essentially on one side, but not without pointing out that in his Italian operas, within the seeming candy-floss, it is that which is noble and worthily human that triumphs over the peccadilloes and over the even more outlandish flaws in human nature that brings each work to its climax.

Then at the crown of his career, in 1791, Mozart produced *Die Zauberflöte*. Musically, of course, its hallmark is one hundred per cent Mozart, but its libretto was the result of Schikaneder's wish to put on a show which was lucrative and which connected to the national *Singspiel*, rather than following Italian fashion. (We will come to the Egyptian element in it, presently.) His own brilliant pantomime-like handling of the part of Papageno was also a significant factor in its initial theatrical success, if we are to take the long-term view. He and Mozart were both Freemasons, a fact which, in our endeavouring to find threads which run through this narrative, gives us a further clue as to what is going on.

Within Greek culture, the Greek soul, highly sensitive to art in all its forms, experienced, as we have seen, within the drama that which influenced the ego as such, that member within our human being wherein we experience conscience—the *still small voice*. And it is the ego, after all, which carries the impulses from one epoch to the next of that which contributes to the progress of human evolution, albeit *first imbibed by the soul via the senses*. Then comes, within orthodox Christianity, the enactment of that moment which signified for each ego the renewal of life in a way that had not occurred before, nor will occur again: the resurrection from death on the cross by a divine being. Through the fact of the resurrection—irrespective of 'belief' in it or not—each ego on earth is endowed with forces to support its outer and inner progress, as well as faculties which, if developed, can attain access to ever more that flows from the Sun Being, Christ. Even the Ascension and Pentecost were subsidiary from this point of view and, interestingly enough, only started to feature quite late in the medieval liturgical drama.

Through the strength thus gained, the human being is deemed to be equipped to go through its next evolutionary step: the onset of reductionist intellectualism at the further cost of that form of consciousness which had led away from atavistic clairvoyance. This is what came about in the seventeenth century with its vast U-turn away from medieval spirituality towards natural science, leading to the view of the world that denied reality to anything that the senses (let us call them the phenomenologically stimulated senses, touch, hearing, taste, sight, smell) could not perceive and measure in rational terms. As a *counterbalance* to this, not just on the stage, but within the medium of music, came opera, opera with its preference for mythological themes to begin with, and its inauguration with the myth of Orpheus, whose higher being (Euridice), it will be recalled, suffered the 'poisoning' of consciousness brought about by an overwhelming focus on the outer phenomena of earth.

It goes without saying that the theatre, be it drama or opera, engages the sense of hearing too. However, hearing is the lower of the four higher senses. The theatre thus appeals to the whole human being: amongst the lower senses, movement and balance; amongst the middle senses, sight and warmth; amongst the higher senses, hearing, the word and thought. Such involvement of the human being, whose interested absorption in what is going on onstage (as well as in all that is evoked via the imagination offstage), is a major factor in the process whereby the mission of theatre/drama, to bring about transformational experiences that will project into the inner life of the onlooker in a metamorphic way, is achieved.

What follows next? The human being needs a reminder that that world of spirit from which its consciousness has been torn away was indeed formerly accessible—*through initiation*. But this cannot be done to begin with in a widely effective way through philosophy or preaching—or only for a limited few. To get the message, however subconsciously across, it needed the popularity of a vaudeville style of music and genre. Freemasonry knew of the 'what', but only the genius of Mozart, piggybacking on the inspiration of Schikaneder's libretto, could come up with the 'how': the butcher-boy-whistleable Papageno ditties and the almost trite simplicity of the magic bells music, alongside the *Sturm und Drang* mood of Tamino's conflict with the dragon in the opening scene, the star-worshipping coloratura of the Queen of Night, the religious (though not sectarian) majesty of the Sarastro arias and the priests' choruses ... and once all that has tickled every taste bud that the soul's tongue could possibly wish for, comes the initiation scene, played before a by now captive audience on unaccompanied flute. And its message? Higher consciousness was once attained through initiation. It *is* a human faculty—or *was*. And the unspoken corollary is: how do we go about its reinstatement, not by putting the clock back to Ancient Egypt but in a way that is suitable for modern consciousness?

The next part of the wave of development resembles a trough rather than a crest at first sight, though it is moving towards the same distant shore. The desperation of the human state bereft of its former spiritual insight is ignored—be it through apathy, neglect, atrophied ability, or whatever. The answer therefore: awaken the ego to its dire state as acutely as possible. In *Fidelio*, Beethoven follows a popular trend—though his personal popularity flows mainly from elsewhere in his oeuvre, of course. At the time when Europe's germinating evolutionary seed was sending down ever deeper roots came the thirst for power; an overblown ego, might one say, had its sights on what was essentially world-dominance: Napoleon. In the wake of his campaigns, victories, the slaughter of thousands of young lives, the homelessness of bereft families, the toppling of leaders of nations and his nepotistic replacement of them, etc. came the phenomenon of the *political prisoner*. The weak sought to gain influence with those who had bloated their strength through evil means.

Dozens of plays and operas took up this theme—an awakener it seemed so that the population would realize what was going on. Often the archetypal political-prisoner rescue plot was overdressed in absurdly exaggerated situations. But Beethoven, whose initial admiration changed into disdain for Napoleon, contented himself with the simplest of all versions. Florestan is chained in the deepest and darkest of dungeons by Pizarro who was ready as soon as convenient to destroy and obliterate all trace of the good that obstructed his evil way to power. The situation is saved by a faithful woman, Florestan's wife Leonore, disguised at the beginning of the opera as Fidelio. Through faith, courage, love and willingness to sacrifice she prevails. A more powerful metaphor of the human state would be difficult to imagine and, judging from the effort that Beethoven put into the opera's composition as well as writing the several overtures he wrote for it, he must have seen it as a symbolic awakener for the Ego of at least his contemporaries.

The final step, as far as our present study is concerned, can be seen in the work of Richard Wagner. From Romantic beginnings (*The Flying Dutchman, Tannhäuser, Lohengrin*) which follow on to some extent from the direction in which Weber had gone earlier with *Der Freischütz* and *Euryanthe* and which one observes are parallel with the romantic novel and its explosive popularity—as if the vast swathe of Western humanity is relieved to find at least something in life that is not the product of the Gradgrind of industrialization and its counterpart, the mechanization of thinking—Wagner moves towards his unparalleled *music dramas* (incidentally, no longer termed opera), particularly *The Ring* tetralogy with its return to the world of myth and its inescapable message to take the spirit seriously. The final step in his mission is *Parsifal*, first performed in 1882. The Grail theme plaits all the strands with which we have been concerned: the importance of the Ego; Parsifal's search for the Grail castle is lifelong and central to his whole being; that which exists on the spiritual plane but does not follow in the footsteps of the sectarian Church's insistence on blind, unquestioning belief in the authority of an institution; and that whereby the sense world and its retardation of human advance (Amfortas' wound) can only be overcome by persistent inner work, flawless integrity and unswerving virtue. There is a strong flavour of that in Skryabin's *Prometheus* and in his unfulfilled dream of 'a fusion of all the arts, but not a theatrical one like Wagner's [for Art] must unite with philosophy and religion in an indivisible whole to form a new gospel. [For that], it would be necessary to build a special temple—perhaps here, perhaps far away in India. But mankind is not yet ready for it.'[11]

It surely cannot be without significance that Richard Wagner's building on the *Festspielhügel* in Bayreuth finds its apotheosis in Rudolf Steiner's Goetheanum—he having the opposite view to Skryabin as to whether mankind was 'ready for it'—built on the hill in Dornach, via the link of Eduard Schuré and Marie von Sivers (as she then was). The former is dedicated to what we might conceive of as the mystery drama—with music, whilst the latter is built, as the House of the Word, with the performances of Steiner's Mystery Dramas in mind in its main auditorium. With Steiner's presentation of the reality of repeated earth lives, the next long step in evolution is placed before the human ego. With it, it could be said, three missions merge: that of drama, that of Rudolf Steiner (at least one of the foremost aspects of his mission), and that of Marie Steiner-von Sivers.

Dialogue at the Sepulchre on Easter Morning

The above is a transcription of a manuscript dating from c. 950 and originating from St Gall. The Introit proper to the Mass follows on.

14
Heads and Tales

Being Aware of Both Sides of the Steiners' Spiritual Coin

Brien Masters

In 1920 when the original Waldorf School in Stuttgart was about to add the first Upper School class to the Lower School provision it had established during the previous academic year, Rudolf Steiner gave a lecture course to the teachers to prepare for this event. Often referred to as *Education for Adolescence*, it contains much insight into the nature of the thresholds of child development at ages 12 and 14 and indications for addressing the young person's needs at this time.

In the ninth lecture, when focusing on the step from the second to the third septennial phase, Steiner urges the necessity of accompanying the maturation of the physical body—the sexual maturity which enables the human being to reproduce its own kind—with studies of an aesthetic nature. In very broad outline these studies were the history of the visual arts (Class 9, age 15), the history of literature (Class 10, age 16), the history of music (Class 11, age 17), and the history of architecture (Class 12, age 18).

The actual educational and general cultural value of these studies is self-evident, but the thinking behind the suggestion in relation to child development and education goes deep. At 14, with the emancipation of the forces in the astral nature of the human being, and the child's interest in all new fields of existence that awakens as a result (the astral being, the vehicle for sensation that we have in common with the animal kingdom), closest of all to that astral awakening is what is happening to the child him/herself, day-by-day, hour-by-hour: the development of the physical body.

Although this is not the physical body's final development (there are still some years of *growth* to come during adolescence), the stage reached is at the highest level of maturity. At the same time, with the fourth member of the human being, the ego, still having some way to go in life before it can enter into its full potential of discernment, responsibility, self-control, 'control' of the lower members, judgement of right and wrong and so on, the danger exists that the astral awakening will become focused with undue concentration on the physical—its appearance, the ramifications of pubescent maturation etc.—*at the expense* of other aspects of life. And the study of the great works of art, especially in these four fields of the visual arts, literature, music and architecture, points the adolescent's consciousness powerfully towards that core of human nature which is directed to the polar opposite of the physical.

The all-absorbing questions of why the Egyptian built pyramids, or why Rembrandt painted such intense chiaroscuro, or why the *Odyssey* appeared when it did and in the form that it did, or why Beethoven's style had the impact on society that still continues today—and a thousand similar questions—lead far beyond the purely physical.

We may deduce from this that something occurs in the beholding (be it visual, aural or otherwise) of art that is more than merely what the senses register in whatever way it is conveyed to human consciousness, and that that something works upon an organ (let us call it, without attempting to define it) that has direct access to the supersensible world. In relation to our present theme, there is the remarkably corroborative fact that it was *the involvement in beholding the art treasures of the world, aided by Marie von Sivers' expressed insights, which enabled Rudolf Steiner to evolve a form for spiritual science in which the results of his spiritual research were couched in a way that he found most appropriate for his (Western) contemporaries.*

Leaving aside the intriguing question of how that may have happened and what organ—of the initiate—was affected, and how the nature of that resultant form can be characterized etc., we may formulate the principle: art and its (penetrating) beholding has a significant contribution to make to the human being's advancing relationship to the spiritual world. (The term 'advancing' is still relevant even if the region of the spiritual world in question is opposed to the furtherance of evolution—as with demons who would divert cosmic evolution from its divinely ordained purpose.) It was surely this general principle which prompted Rudolf Steiner to adorn the meeting place for the Theosophical Congress in Munich in 1910 with red drapery and introduce sculpture onto the rostrum, and—leaping some years—the same principle which was behind the performances of eurythmy in connection with later anthroposophical conferences. There were, of course, other artistic components too. These were performing arts which were practical, however demanding, when spiritual science was 'taken' beyond the Goetheanum, Dornach, where, in addition to the performing arts, participants also drank in the architecture, its sculptural forms, and the wealth of colour in the paintings on the underside of the two cupolas, and through the coloured daylight which streamed through the stained glass windows on either side of the auditorium and elsewhere. Rudolf Steiner described in his lecture of 28 December 1914 the experience of being inside the Goetheanum building, '... the thing of importance is what the soul experiences in its deepest foundations when, lingering in the building, it flows out to the boundaries of its forms.' This may be seen as a step further than that which obtained in the Gothic cathedral, when the building created a sacred space in which the soul's devotion was quickened. The 'new principle' in the Goethanum is the creation of a building which provides what Steiner describes as 'rather like a cake-mould which is there ... for the sake of the [cake inside] ... the experiences induced in the soul by the forms of the building as the soul flows around them'.

The question then arises: Why 'The House of the Word'—how Rudolf Steiner referred to the Goetheanum—rather than the House of Art, or the House of Wisdom, or some such?

To consider this let us look at two aspects of the word. The Old Testament's (mythological) testimony to the creation of the world makes it clear that the speech of divine beings is a creative process of limitless magnitude. Consider for example: 'And God said, "Let there be light!"' What that must have sounded like in the coming-into-being of light is beyond human comprehension in our present state of development. Nevertheless, we are concerned in some dimension with *sound*—whether we call it the Music of the Spheres, the Logos, the voice of God or use some other designation.

In sound we have an entry into the *inner* nature of the sounding object. For instance, when gardeners tap a plant pot they are able to ascertain how dry the soil inside is. Similarly, our inner soul experience comes to expression through the vocalic content of language. Thus, when the vowels sound—sound which *we* bring into the outer air—we potentially have a spiritual route which can connect us to the sun forces (AU), to the Mars forces (É), to the Saturn forces (U) and so on, to each of the planetary Intelligences. This route is a soul route. To imbibe the inner quality of sound emanating from the zodiac we need to travel via the consonants: V (Aries), R (Taurus), H (Gemini), F (Cancer), T (Leo), B (Virgo), TZ (Libra), S (Scorpio), G (Sagittarius), L (Capricorn), M (Aquarius), N (Pisces).

These two spiritual 'sound tracks', however, do not lead us to words without further ado. Words depend on our own inner activity. Returning to the mythological account of creation in the book of Genesis, in Ch. 2:19–20 Adam is accorded the task by the Elohim of naming the animals. The combination of vowel and consonant sound forth: as in *lion* and *tiger*, *eagle* and *dolphin*, *rabbit* and *hippo*... And we may take it that, as this was the first deed of Adam—Eve was not yet created from Adam's rib or named by him (as we learn from verses 21–3)—the deed is in full accord with Adam's pure spirituality, before it has been sullied by the Fall. Thus in language, at least at its root, we have the collaboration of the divine and the human. The gods speak creation. And the jewel of their created crown—ADAM (the Hebrew for human being)—performs the first act of human freedom vouchsafed by the gods: naming the created world.

A Greek temple was so proportioned through mystery wisdom that it provided a 'house' (quasi-physical body) for the god to whom it was dedicated: Athena, Apollo, and so on. The wrath of Christ Jesus was directed against the 'money lenders and those who sold doves' who had desecrated Solomon's Temple in which the Covenant was housed. The Gothic cathedral was experienced as the House of God, when the people were inside worshipping in the service of the divine. A house of ill-fame (now an archaic term) was a former name for a brothel in which the (divinely endowed) act of creation was viewed as abominably denigrated. In a CD, the sound is technologically entrapped in a prison-house. Wordsworth used the expression 'prison-house' to encapsulate the process of the child's descent from divine worlds—'Heaven lies about us in our infancy'—to the world of sense-perception, the world in which the sense perceptions of the boy-become-youth 'fade' from being able to apprehend 'the light and whence it flows' from its heavenly source to 'the light of common day'. The Goetheanum, with its rostrum placed beneath the intersection of the two cupolas, themselves in 'divine proportion', had at the far east end the Representative of Humanity *facing* speaker at the rostrum, actor speaking in the Mystery Drama, reciter speaking poetry—all of whom in turn face the audience (*audio* = to hear or to listen) whose inner activity of beholding the spirit through *higher senses* is quickened thereby.

Though Rudolf Steiner, in drawing spiritual-scientific correspondences between the arts and the members of the human constitution, places eurythmy and 'the seventh art' above painting, sculpture, architecture and poetry from which one might conclude that the 'word' is not at the pinnacle of the hierarchy of the arts, seen from the viewpoint outlined above it becomes clear that this first free deed of Adam—to take the sounds of the cosmos, and in combining them, forming them into syllables (which comprise the names of the 'creatures' of the created world)—places the word, so to speak, as the spiritual regent of the arts. With the consonants being symbolizing sound-images of the outer, *material* world, there is of course the danger that speech will become too anchored in outer matter. With the vowels embodying both the essence of the planets and their reflection in the human soul, there is the danger that their over-dominance will kite-fly speech too close to the *spirit*.

Hence the need for humans, who are 'all-too-human' in speech—as in other respects (despite its pre-Fall origin)—to have a 'guide, philosopher and friend' when entering into the word; and hence the positioning of the 'Group' in which the Divine Logos (the representative of Humanity) creates a space of grace between the consonantly subdued and fettered-in-matter Ahriman and the vocally omnipotently, detached-from-earth Lucifer; and hence *The House of the Word*. With this, let us take a seat in the auditorium.

One might hazard a guess that most of the members of an audience listening to a violin concerto—probably enjoying the performance if it is a concerto they love and perhaps being stunned by the display of virtuosity of the soloist—will probably not be marvelling at the fact that such a tiny instrument can be heard even on its own let alone over and above the 'voice' of a symphony orchestra—in such a huge space as a modern concert hall seating thousands. This remarkable acoustical phenomenon is due to the shape of the wooden part of the violin, which makes no sound of its own but is designed to enhance the sound of the strings of the instrument. Leaving aside what amounts to the mathematical mystery of how the great violin-making pioneers such as Antonio Stradivari and Andrea Guarneri evolved the prototype for this by now familiar shape, we are left with the elementary, two-component principle of a musical instrument: there is the *source* of the sound, and the means of enhancing its *resonance*.

The human voice, in so far as it is an instrument of sound, is no exception. In the vocal chords is the source of the sound and in the cavities of the chest and head the sound resonates, the combination of which enables us to recognize (because of the uniqueness of every human being) whether it is our bank manager on the other end of the phone, a granddaughter or a friend who is inviting us to a birthday celebration. But despite the *personal* nature of these phenomena, thus far they only address the physical aspect of human speech. When children play Chinese Whispers, getting what they say often hopelessly and amusingly muddled through giggling, by cutting out most of both source and resonator, they produce sound which may be regarded as related to, yet *sub*sidiary to, speech. Let us turn to the opposite: what may be regarded as that which uses speech but adds to the word a *superior* element.

At one end of the scale there are elements in daily life such as public announcements in a train station. They may well be recorded. Even if the quality of the sound grates in some cases, we rely on the accuracy of *information* they convey: a delay in the arrival of our train service, a platform alteration, the carriages in which we need to travel if our destination has only a short platform and so on. At the opposite end of the scale (at least for our present purposes) is the language spoken by an initiate, which strives to convey, to the extent that present-day vocabulary accommodates it, the result of his spiritual research—a field of 'knowledge' just as factual as the platform number from which a train is due to depart but relating to a sphere of experience which, though having spirit reality, may be well beyond the listener's ken. Mystery wisdom can only be accessed directly through spiritual means. The source of the sound which conveys that *spirit reality* is clear: the research-informed words spoken by the initiate. What about the resonator which stirs in the soul of the listener—not outer sound (as in the concert hall)—but direct awareness of that spirit reality in a way similar to an awareness of the physical reality stirred in me if I hear someone speak the words 'your front door'?

This depends on several factors. The one most pertinent here is the degree of openness of soul. Openness itself has two components. The first is a prerequisite, it could be said: the *will* to listen and to hear. The second concerns the soul-equivalent to hearing *ability*—the opposite to deafness. One may hope that each human being will have retained sufficient traces of his or her divine origin to be aware that at least the words of the initiate convey more than knowledge informed by rationality and derived from the sense-perceptible world. Those traces, however, vary: in one they are stronger; in another they are weaker. Their variation can also be experienced in each person: the times when we have 'ears to hear' and the times when those 'ears' appear deaf.

It was to address this ability that connected with the soul's openness to the spirit that the life-long work of Marie Steiner-von Sivers was directed in the performing arts. It was the *way* she developed—and taught others to develop—a quality of speech that *kindled the spark of spirit-hearing ability* in the soul of the listener which, when listening to recitation, or a dramatic production, or the speaking of a text for a eurythmy performance, built a bridge of artistic-aesthetic appreciation from the soul of the listener to what the artist was conveying. And this faculty, when once awoken and *applied to listening to the initiate lecturing*, built yet another arch of the bridge: an arch that spanned from earthly consciousness to that of the spirit. These are the two sides of the Steiners' coin.

15
Redemption of the Senses

Fading 'Into the Light of Common Day' and Beyond

Rahel Kern

One of the deepest and most profound subjects of enquiry within all branches of knowledge from philosophy to the sciences is the being of man himself. It is certainly one of the oldest aspirations of humanity to explore and investigate the nature of itself, of human beings as such. Any such enquiry also always concerns the inherent relation of human beings to the cosmos—and with man being part of two worlds, this implies a twofold enquiry into the natural world on the one hand and the spiritual world on the other.

The relation between man and cosmos is not static and constant; on the contrary, it is dynamic and changes throughout the centuries. There are developments within the flow of time that reveal themselves in manifold ways within the development of the peoples within different cultures, their changing myths, their different mystery centres and initiation practices; it also reveals itself within the life and succession of people as the bearers of new knowledge and insight, as inaugurators of new cultures and religions, as teachers and initiates.

> She creates forms ever new. What is, never was before, and what was, never returns. All things are new, yet it is always the old ... All in her is eternal life, becoming, movement, and yet she moves not onward. She is eternally transformed, and there is no moment's stopping in her. For 'stay' she has no concept, and she has set her curse on standstill. Yet she is firm.[1]

This constant, ongoing development that Goethe describes here within the context of the organically metamorphosing nature realm also holds true of our human relation to the cosmos. Our appreciation of and engagement with both the natural sense world and the supersensory spirit world constantly changes and evolves as our consciousness changes. As a matter of fact, it is a relation that is deeply and intrinsically dependent on the development of human consciousness, denoting here not merely an intellectual consciousness, but referring to a complete, soul-permeating, moral and spiritual consciousness.

As an ongoing, ever-changing process, this transformation and evolution of human consciousness that we have traced throughout the centuries is naturally also manifest within the different incarnations of an individuality. Each particular incarnation reveals a specific step within human thinking and consciousness, from Atlantean clairvoyance through to our modern-day intellectualism. The present karmic study into the being behind its latest incarnation, Marie Steiner-von Sivers, traces a descent of consciousness from spiritual heights into the physical world and an ascent from outer sense perception up again into the world of the spirit.

The Orphic incarnation represents a macrocosmic Ego, which still dwells out in the deep wisdom of the cosmos and has not been born on the earth as an individual human ego. Up until 3000 BC, the beginning of Kali Yuga, the spiritual world still spoke directly through people, who, in the sense of acting as immediate 'translators' and conveyers for the spiritual world, had no personality as we conceive it now but directly passed on received messages or intentions in their actions and thoughts. Expressed in an engaging pictorial language, the myth of Orpheus and Euridice conveys the laws active within the change from the old supersensible, purely spiritual consciousness of the old prophets towards a more earthwards, sense-directed experience of the world. The more Orpheus gains awareness of the physical sense world around him and begins to live in the material world, the more he forfeits connection to a clairvoyant experience of the spiritual heights. The bite of the viper, resulting in his beloved Euridice being snatched away and abducted into the underworld, speaks of this loss and his terrible experience of bereavement when entering into the physical realm. Incarnating into a physical body entails developing a relationship with the physical world via the senses. This opening up of the sense world always implies sacrificing and leaving behind the previously experienced macrocosmic unity. Presented in a similar image as the Egyptian god Osiris, whose body was torn into 14 pieces and scattered throughout Egypt, Orpheus is also ripped apart, limb by limb, as he is entering the sense-perceptible world. The impact of deeply incarnating and meeting the forces of the physical world has the effect of literally tearing away and destroying his supersensible consciousness.

The next incarnation indicated by Rudolf Steiner relates to the teacher of Pherecydes of Syros in the sixth century BC, whom he portrayed as 'a last straggler endowed with the clairvoyance of earlier times'.[2] We thus know indirectly that, as the teacher of Pherecydes, this person was still seeing behind the physical sense world to the real causes that lie beyond what we nowadays perceive with our senses. It is a stage in the evolution of consciousness before (abstract) thought grasps and takes hold of the outer world. It is still a pre-personal stage; the thought-bearing ego has not made its appearance yet. However, in Pherecydes we can see a first merging of the old imaginative clairvoyance with sense perception in as far as he moves beyond pure perception and description of these perceived images towards a contemplation and reflection about them.

A major step in the evolution of consciousness is achieved in ancient Greece where Orpheus' song and his ability for music awakens the full personality. It is a time in which individual human beings give rise to and voice thoughts truly brought about by themselves as never before. The full individuality appears, gaining more and more importance:

> The significance of personality constantly increases the nearer we come to the Greek epoch, when the ego works and weaves in the ego. In the strong and forceful figures of the Greek epoch the stamp of personality is complete. It is with the Greeks ... that what can at first be bestowed on the individuality only from higher worlds withdraws to the greatest extent, while what a man expresses in his personality as his proper humanity comes to the forefront.[3]

Towards the end of the Greek period, Hypatia and her contemporaries represent full personalities. In Hypatia, the old Orphic wisdom is revived and brought back to life, transformed and delivered through her personality. However, even though she has now taken up a full personality in this incarnation, her destiny itself is much wider and symptomatic of what is occurring for humanity. The Orphic experience of being torn apart reverberates in the very same pregnant image when, repeated now in this incarnation, she endures yet another tragic death. The faculty of clairvoyance is, again and now representative for all humanity, torn to pieces, when she completely enters into the sense world as an independent thinker.

> ... the revival of the old Pagan wisdom of Orpheus transformed into personality could be experienced in Alexandria in the figure of Hypatia. World-karma was working in the truest sense symbolically. What had constituted the secret of her Initiation was now projected, mirrored, on the physical plane. And here we come to an event that is symbolically significant in the case of many things that have taken place in historical times. We come to one of those events that is seemingly only a martyrdom, but is in reality a symbol in which spiritual forces, spiritual intimations are coming to expression. (...) In this event, important secrets of the 4th Post-Atlantean epoch are reflected. This epoch, destined as it was to represent the dissolution,

the sweeping-away, of the old, contained so much that was great and significant, and with paradoxical grandeur placed before the world a most pregnant symbol in the slaughter—one can call it nothing else—of Hypatia, the outstanding woman at the turn of the 4th–5th centuries of our era.[4]

Her martyrdom and dramatic death are significant as symbolizing the descent of human consciousness into the sense world, at a point in time close to the Mystery of Golgotha. Within a wider context of the development of human consciousness over centuries, this is a turning point in time and a pivot point in the history of humanity, between the descending forces into the physical material world and the beginning of the ascending forces.

Such descent into and ascent from nature can also be found in the outlook and philosophy of Albertus Magnus. His great connection with nature from a very early age onwards, his many journeys on foot across medieval Europe and plentiful nature descriptions and observations tell of an interest in the sense world and what later became the Goetheanistic approach of immersing oneself in the sense phenomena. Albertus, however, does not remain on the phenomenological level of observation and description but lifts it up and connects sense perception with the highest spiritual insights and Christian truths, as can be seen in his philosophy and his contribution to the development of early Scholasticism which has the intention to connect and interlink the realms of rational sense on the one hand and the realm of supernatural divine truth on the other. The mediator between these two realms is a fully developed, morally responsible and free-thinking person.

Within the immediate church environment, Albertus is said to have been involved in the inauguration of a Christian festival that might be taken as a representation of bringing about this connection between the realm of nature and Christian revelation. There are several, differing accounts of how the ritual of Corpus Christi came about, where it drew inspiration from, how its decree was issued and how it became an institution. It is said to have been celebrated for the first time in Cologne in 1246 before becoming an annual feast. The symbolism and public statement of the festival captures the attempt of bringing together the two realms: the body of Christ is displayed on a monstrance in the form of a consecrated host and is carried in a procession led by the priest out of the inner church building, through the local streets of the respective town and right into the nature of the surrounding fields and countryside. Divine revelation and the nature realm are symbolically joined. Thomas Aquinas composed the Mass and office for the festival, which is a beautiful canticle that has since become a classic piece in church liturgy. It begins with the words *Pange lingua Gloriosi Corporis Mysterium*, which in literal translation reads as 'Sing, my tongue, the mystery of the glorious body' and which carries on 'and of the precious Blood, shed to save the world, the fruit of a noble womb, by the King of the nations'. The words speak of the doctrine of transubstantiation or, in the words used in the above, of the physical incarnation of a divine-spiritual being. Again, it is the spiritual supersensible world merging with the physical sense world. The famous sequence of the Mass, the *Lauda Sion*, further reveals the Scholastic undertaking of the confluence of rational human reason and divine revelation: 'Taught by Christ, the Church maintains that the bread's substance changed into flesh, the wine to blood. Does it pass your comprehending? Faith, the law of sight transcending leaps to things not understood.'[5]

Such attempts at joining nature and spirit realms, at interlinking reason and faith, occurred at a time when people experienced themselves to be far removed and cut off from spiritual reality. It was a crisis point in time, when people experienced themselves shut out from higher knowledge and limited to the world of sense. In the religious and church realm, this finds expression in the use of relics and reliquaries in devotional practice. It can be seen as an attempt to provide a bridge between the unattainable heaven and earth, to re-enliven the lost connection to the spiritual world through veneration of the physical remains and traditions handed down. Even though relic veneration can be traced back to the Roman period in the fourth century, it peaks in the late medieval period and became a central part of Christian worship. Throughout Europe, skilled goldsmiths and the finest craftsmen placed objects associated with Christ and the saints into beautifully ornate containers, which were opulently decorated and displayed costly materials such as gold and silver in which were set precious gemstones. These priceless reliquaries with their sacred contents were used both for public ceremonies as well as assisting in personal prayer. Particularly around the year 1250, people experienced more and more a boundary between the physical world of sense which they were able to apprehend and the spiritual world to which access had been lost.

> The most eminent minds of that time [about the year 1250] who were striving after some kind of higher knowledge could only say to themselves: 'What our reason, our intellect, our spiritual knowledge are able to find out is limited to the physical world around us. With all our human endeavour and power of perception, we cannot reach

a spiritual world. We only know of it by accepting the information concerning it which our forefathers bequeathed us.' This was the time when direct view of the higher worlds was obscured. That this can be said of the era in which Scholasticism flourished, is not without significance.[6]

It is Scholasticism in its early form as developed by Albertus Magnus and Thomas Aquinas which attempts to break through this experienced boundary, at a time when the old clairvoyance is completely lost.

A new form of seeing the spiritual world was needed, a new form of clairvoyance that now goes hand in hand with initiation as the guide of spiritual sight. Within the spiritual evolution of mankind, the year 1250 holds a pivot point. Rudolf Steiner repeatedly draws attention to this year as the point in time when people's view of the spiritual world was completely clouded over and a new element entered the spiritual guidance of humanity.

This year 1250 is of momentous importance in history... [It] was a point of time especially adapted for conveying to mankind the mysteries which come to direct expression in the connection of the Spiritual with the working of Nature. Hence we see that this year 1250 was the starting-point of great and detailed elaborations of what was formerly only believed, only divined: it was the starting-point of Scholasticism, which is greatly undervalued today.[7]

Though Steiner does not elaborate on the starting point in this lecture, it is clear that the year 1250 holds a truly significant position in the revival of a new clairvoyance. This clairvoyance does not rely on the lower soul forces any more as in previous centuries and millennia—the conditions of acquiring knowledge of higher worlds have evolved. The new, true modern esotericism requires the higher faculties of soul to work their way to such knowledge. Scholasticism played a major role in this.

Looking at our development since then, it is noticeable that people's attention was drawn towards and is increasingly bound up with the senses. The focus of consciousness has shifted more and more down into the sense-perceptible physical world. Hence all branches of the sciences that study the external structure, the history and the origin of the earth came now to full bloom, with many disciplines gradually emerging as independent sciences. Botany saw a thorough classification and precise identification of native plants, sea voyages of exploration returned botanical treasures, leading to a rigorous process of naming, description and classification. Geology saw a systematic study of the mineral content of the earth and into the processes by which it is shaped and changed, including detailed examination of the structure and function of rock layers and examinations of fossils contained in them. Botany and geology are two prime examples of how sciences have this outward directed search for truth. The thoughts and concepts arising out of such studies are immediately linked with and correspond to facts in the external sense world—they reflect how people conceptualize the earth. One might describe this development by saying that thoughts increasingly rigidified until they became mere conveyors of facts and carriers of ever more detailed specific information relating to particular occurrences or circumstances. Spiritual content, beyond dogmatic presentation, was therefore less and less prevalent.

And in the same vein, not just thoughts but also our habitual use of language became more and more inflexible and rigid. Words have moved away from being nuanced, plastic expressions carrying all sorts of shades of possibilities towards increasingly specific denotations of lifeless, abstract facts. The rigidifying effect of the intellect on language can be seen in phenomena such as reduction of words, word attrition and contraction of meaning.

While initials were already used in Rome before the Christian era, acronymy as a linguistic process has spread widely only in the twentieth century. Our progressive tendency towards word minimalism has gone so far that certain abbreviations or contractions of phrases are often pronounced as words in their own rights, and the etymology of the words they originally derived from are more and more forgotten. Examples of such acronymy replacing full phrases are the term 'laser' which originated from the words 'Light Amplification by Stimulated Emission of Radiation' and the term 'radar' which was coined by the US Navy in the 1940s as an acronym for 'Radio Detection And Ranging'. Common knowledge often does not recognize that these have entered our vocabulary under the false identity of regular words.

This goes hand in hand with a loss of diversification in the sense of a reduced active vocabulary. Virginia Sease points out how there is an attrition in vocabulary at least since the 1990s whereby younger generations lose the shades of distinction and subtle differentiation the English language would naturally provide.[8]

Then there are phenomena such as contraction of meaning whereby words become more specific and exclusive in what they denote. The further back we go in history, the more complex language becomes in the sense that words still have their concomitant meanings; the closer we get to our current time, the more differentiated language becomes due to a process of words losing their meaning. Owen Barfield describes the process of words contracting in meaning as follows:

> ...so that, for example, a single word combining the meanings 'spirit', 'wind', and 'breath' in a unified manner subsequently splits into three separate words, each with a more restricted meaning. Narrower meanings conduce to accuracy of communication, and result from rational analysis. Broader meanings support fullness of expression, and result from imaginative synthesis.[9]

This evolution of language is a demonstration of how human consciousness has evolved; the earlier unity was accompanied by a perception of the world as greater unity, while the development of our later differentiation of language goes along with a more fragmented, disintegrated experience of reality. In our current state of consciousness, contractions of meaning occur passively, as opposed to expansions in meaning which require a strong inner activity from us, such as in poetry.

Throughout her life, Marie Steiner-von Sivers actively worked with speech and endeavoured to find the lost spirit quality again that once lived in each spoken word. In her recitation and drama work, she consciously works with the breath, the rhythm of speech, its intervals and melody, its subtle overtones and undertones. Through working with such fine substances, she overcomes the general use of words as mere expressions of intellectual thought and carriers of intelligibility. Speech becomes a true art form. Marie Steiner-von Sivers describes the nature of speech as a mystery, which can, through sensual and artistic perception of the word, enable human beings to find the way back to the spirit:

> If we consider speech merely as simply a means of communication, as the garment of an intellectualistic content, we kill it off as an art. We tear it limb from limb by just adapting it to our reasoning, instead of allowing our reasoning to be illuminated by its light. Then the life of its sounds disappears grey-on-grey drabness, instead of glowing in the manifold hues of a refracted diamond, with its rhythms, its melodies, the sculpture of its outlines, the architecture of its impulse, the strength or the calm of its metrical beat, the dignity of its cadences, the power that holds all these together and parts it asunder, and throws them again into a whirling vortex, till the movement sweeps on to a Dionysian revel, or flows bright and crystal-clear in Apollonian dance...[10]

One notes here how she describes the process of losing the spiritual connection within language and speech in Orphic terms of limbs being torn out and Dionysian flow of melody. In entering and turning towards the sense world, mankind frees itself more and more from the connection with the spiritual world, evolves into separate and independent individuals. After having passed through the low point of losing the living awareness of the spiritual world, the task today is about re-establishing this connection. Marie Steiner-von Sivers brings her quest in connection with speech succinctly to the point in the very opening sentence of the same article:

> In speech man grasps his divine nature. The sounds of speech are creative forces that unite him with his origin and enable him to find once more the paths to the spirit.[11]

Her written word shows a similar adeptness of capturing spiritual aspects within the sense world and a talent for bringing it, within the constraints of indifferent lifeless ink and paper, into exceptionally delicate and skilful nature descriptions. Like Albertus Magnus, she has a deep connection with nature and, particularly at the time of her visit with Rudolf Steiner to Penmaenmawr in 1923, she composes remarkable descriptions of the Welsh countryside, nature's beauty, the elements alive in the sea, of Druids and the Celtic culture.

> And yet behind the hills the past stands there alive, preserved in those tremendous images that even today attract the searching human being. He wends his way up those steep slopes towards it, not shunning battle with the whistling wind that goes shooting out of the ravines. Soon he is splendidly rewarded. The strand of the bay vanishes from sight. Radiant yellow and deeply shining violet are spread far around, hanging in meadows of gorse and heather. An overpowering blaze of colour waves up in flames and dies into repose. And yet Nature here is too stark for any pleasant lingering. The struggle with the wind becomes more of an effort; each step must be fought for. Soon only stone is around us, arid grass and moss. You have to brace and defend yourself in order not to be blown down; you plunge onwards and breathe in new strength by drinking the lines and colours of the distant horizon. The Druids did not make it easy for their pilgrims.[12]

Gifted with such delicate awareness and perception, it is no surprise that Marie Steiner-von Sivers shys away from the coarse naturalism with which she comes into contact in her Parisian student time. Within the theatrical world, she encounters a vigorous pursuit of continual and intense sense stimulation and an (over-)indulgence in details. Marie

Steiner-von Sivers could not habituate herself to it—it is not at ease with her exquisite sense of perception for subtle changes in the human voice and landscapes, her appreciation of natural beauty in colouring and lighting, her immediate awareness of spirit reality such as in later rehearsals of Eurythmy. Such continual overemphasis of the senses continually desensitizes perception as it is taken up into perceptual habits and creates new dispositions and inclinations, and over time leads to an imprisonment in the world of sense. All her creative endeavours strive to reduce the force of modern over-sensual stimulation. It is a striving to gradually lift—both the audience's and the artist's—perception and consciousness (the forces of the fully incarnated personality) out of the mundaneness of everyday into higher spiritual spheres by intensifying and refining these. Such striving to lead the ego towards a conscious grasp of the spirit can be seen in all her engagement with the different arts—from creative speech in recitations and recitals, theatrical stage performances, and her involvement in the Mystery Dramas, to the establishment of eurythmy, to her role as 'inspiratrice' for Rudolf Steiner when he designed the architecture of the first Goetheanum.

Artistic striving towards the spirit and the process of engagement in artistic work is hereby twofold. There is a process proceeding from the external sense world to the inner soul world in impressions. The Latin word impression literally means 'pressed in', referring to the external sense world affecting and stirring the inner life of the person, e.g. when experiencing the beauty of nature for example. However, there is also a second process which is often overlooked and which has a gesture from the inner to the outer. Rudolf Steiner expresses this in the following:

> Beauty is not the divine in a cloak of physical reality; no, it is the physical reality in a cloak that is divine. The artist does not bring the divine on the earth by letting it flow into the world; he raises the world into the sphere of the divine.[13]

In her artistic efforts, Marie Steiner-von Sivers does not mirror the external but her knowledge of the spirit has its source in a deeper stratum of soul. It is an inner experience that finds its way into an external manifestation of that spirit in art.

Whereas the external world impresses itself onto our present-day consciousness and without that any active or conscious efforts are needed from us, this second process requires an active involvement and is an ability that consciously needs to be acquired. It is an ability which needs to be acquired along the path of heightening one's soul activities.[14] It is important to note that any such increase is not a result of speculation or engaging in hypothesis, but a gradual progress along the path of self-knowledge towards an experience (albeit a spiritual one). It is the knowledge of the spirit as an inner experience.

It is where these two opposing processes (outer-inner and inner-outer) meet and grapple with each other that the full reality can be grasped. It is then that the sense world can be the point of departure towards supernatural, extrasensory experiences. The spiritual world is therefore not behind the appearances of the sense world but in them as the other half which together creates full reality.

Viewed from the perspective of spiritual science (*Geisteswissenschaft*), what we see exemplified in the sequence of concrete incarnations in connection with the Orphic mysteries—*Die Namenlose*—Hypatia—Albertus Magnus—Marie Steiner-von Sivers—is a gradual entering into the physical sense world and with it a changing connection to the spiritual world which brings with it different challenges and changing conditions for recognizing humanity's relation to the cosmos. The journey takes us from an initial Orphic unity with the cosmos, in which the soul's experiences were naturally part of the spiritual world, to the fully developed personality in Hypatia, thinking out of her very own individual resources and solely relying on her own judgement, to Albertus Magnus now entirely cut off from a direct experience with the spiritual world and continually striving by an all-encompassing training of his thought life, moral conduct, meditation and prayer to prepare himself for a moment of divine revelation, and finally in Marie Steiner-von Sivers, an individuality consciously developing a rich inner life to reinstate the living soul connection with the spiritual world and giving her own personal life almost entirely to in her relentless endeavour to encourage people onto their own individual path towards self-knowledge. Her life was dedicated to and intimately linked with anthroposophy, towards awakening people to the relation with the cosmos in a deeper sense.

> Anthroposophy is a path of knowledge, to guide the spiritual in the human being to the spiritual in the universe.[15]

16
The Karmic Background of Marie Steiner-von Sivers

Tracing how Awareness Filtered Through

Brien Masters

As we have seen, Rudolf Steiner drew attention to the esoteric significance of Hypatia in the first of a cycle of six lectures given in Stuttgart entitled *Occult History*. This was on 27 December 1910. The first appearance of this in English translation—and it is the English-speaking world we are primarily seeking to address here—did not appear until 47 years later, i.e. in 1957. It is currently (2011) out of print. That is to say, a generation and a half had passed by before the content of the lectures was available to the public. Moreover it is unlikely that any English person was present at the lecture in 1910 and, even if they were, it is hardly likely that, at the age say 70 or 80, any comment they may have made or recollection they may have shared would have caused vast ripples to flow through the anthroposophical membership of the English-speaking world. Even the world of letters beyond anthroposophy has very little to say about Hypatia. The 1947 edition of the *Encyclopaedia Britannica* includes a short article; its references are mainly nineteenth century and, of course, include the 'romantic' novel by Charles Kingsley of 1853 (eight years before Rudolf Steiner was born!).

As for the pupil of Hypatia, when she was incarnated earlier as an initiate in the Orphic mysteries, namely the presocratic philosopher Pherecydes of Syros, Andrew Welburn notes in his *The Mysteries* that Steiner was 'highly unusual' in drawing attention to the important place his philosophy holds in the development of human consciousness in ancient Greece at the point where that *pictorial* form of consciousness, that related to the plethora of Greek myths, was beginning to merge with a more prosaic form of consciousness characteristic of Classical Greek and Hellenistic times.[1] Here again, one could say, Steiner is well in the vanguard of those who placed Pherecydes amongst the most significant of Greek thinkers. However, the veil of non-identity of his teacher is not drawn aside by Steiner; thus, Hypatia in that earlier incarnation remains the 'nameless one'. We can discover little of Hypatia's train of karma, therefore, through these slender tricklings.

Moving forward from Hypatia is, at first, still more enigmatic. Two days after the said lecture, on 29 December Rudolf Steiner refers to a subsequent (it might not have the been *the* subsequent) incarnation of Hypatia. He concludes with 'then we see how the powers operating in the course of history penetrate into the successive incarnations of particular individualities'.[2] 'Particular' maybe, but *who?* There could, of course, be several candidates for that 'significant, universal spirit....' but this is not the place for speculation. Steiner apparently did not intimate—certainly not clarify—*why* he could 'do no more than intimate' who Hypatia was in that subsequent incarnation. Whilst it may feasibly have been possible for the akashic record not to have been accessed for the name of the initiate who was Pherecydes' teacher—so long ago, and at a time in evolution when the initiate's personality stepped completely into the background, so that nothing could obscure their performing the pure will of the gods—surely *so* prominent a spiritual leader as recent as the twelfth/thirteenth centuries cannot also have been 'nameless'? Surely Steiner must have been aware of his or her—probably the former, given the historic context—identity. Why only 'intimate' rather than press his point home (either in that lecture or a later one in the cycle, or even at some future date when he returned to the subject) by using the 'great influence' that the person—as a *known* person—wielded, in order to substantiate his point?

It can hardly have been because the opportunity did not present itself. Referring to the influence in the twelfth/thirteenth centuries in such terms could hardly have been pointing to anything other than that of the Scholastics. And if the significant person we have before us here (albeit unnamed) *was* a prominent leader amongst the Scholastics, it must have given Steiner plenty of opportunity to refer back—or, what is more likely, he would have been proactive in the matter and made a point of it on some occasion, either directly or as some relevant aside.

Perhaps the most striking elaboration of Scholasticism of subsequent years occurred in the lectures of 1920 entitled *Die Philosophie des Thomas von Aquino*. These were brought out in English translation in 1956 in an edition which consisted not merely of the original text of the three lectures and brief editorial notes, but a highly illuminating commentary which took various forms (a lengthy précis of each lecture, an Epilogue and Appendices, and other well-researched footnotes which included substantial references to theologians and other writers whose lines of argument supported Steiner's) written by the prominent prelate Canon A.P. Shepherd of Worcester cathedral.[3] Even so, and considering how widely well read Shepherd was in Steiner's oeuvre, there is not the slightest hint that one of the Scholastics (and Steiner draws attention preeminently, from the opening sentence onwards, to Albertus Magnus and

Thomas Aquinas) might be the reincarnated individuality to whom Steiner attached such importance, in her earlier incarnation as Hypatia, in the evolution of consciousness.

Although these lectures on Scholastic thought came off the press a year before those on *Occult History*—and the publisher was Hodder and Stoughton, rather than one of those closely linked with the anthroposophical movement across the world—the respective dates were 1956 and 1957. As the editors/translators were well known to one another through conferences and in other ways, it would be unconvincing to argue that Shepherd was unaware of the reference of 29 December 1910. One may therefore assume that he was being spiritually tactful in making no reference to the karmic connections. Even taking into account the fact that the prestigious position held by Hodder and Stoughton was more than likely to result in the publication reaching a wider audience than the comparatively in-house edition of *Occult History*, this still leaves us with an open question—something to the effect: Was it considered of relative unimportance to draw attention, even tangentially, to Steiner's 1910 remark? Or it simply may not have 'clicked', even to a mind as astute, erudite and all-embracing as Shepherd's, even though karmic connections were being leaked at the time (not in a negative sense) into the public domain. These were revealed through the publication of Steiner's lectures on karmic relationships, delivered during most of 1924. The first volume to be published in English translation was in 1953 and the other seven volumes, no less, followed in subsequent years, three of them in the 1950s when all the above was astir.

A gap of 45 years occurs before the next significant tessera of the mosaic appears. This was in a book by Wilfried Hammacher entitled *Marie Steiner*,[4] in which he quotes from a notebook of Rudolf Steiner in which it becomes clear that 'the Scholastic' whose identity he could 'do no more than intimate' in 1910 was, in fact, Albertus Magnus. It is also noteworthy that only four years before this research of Hammacher's was published Peter van Manen had published a short monograph on Marie Steiner[5] in which he clearly had not come across the authenticity of incarnation sequences which links Hypatia with Albertus. The full mosaic picture, therefore, took 88 years (1910–98) to emerge. The tesserae for the subsequent incarnation of Albertus were by this time already extant though tucked away in the memory of a few individuals. They resonate a) with Rudolf Steiner's main mission in life, to awaken a vision of karma; and b) with the *way*—or rather, ways—in which he put this awakening task into practice. 'Ways' plural needs qualifying. It is as if the overriding principle is that the awakening of an individual to his or her own former earth life (lives), should occur as much as possible from within—as if there is an occult law to the effect that only in this way would it be a positive experience with a positive outcome. (The minimal outcome seems to have been summed up by Steiner: Those who awaken to such a vision attain an experience of the enduring ego which, consequently, will arise in ego-consciousness in the next life.) The ways in which Rudolf Steiner prompted such awakening individual by individual would make fascinating (as well as spiritually vital) research. Suffice it here to give a few examples before focusing again on our main concern: Hypatia-Albertus.

It is well recorded[6] that Dr Walter Johannes Stein's inward awakening to his previous death was confirmed by Steiner as a genuine reality. In this case there is nothing to suggest that Stein was prompted either through something that he had read on the period in which the death took place (that of the Portuguese discoveries in the East) or likewise heard, or through a remark that Steiner had made which brought him to the brink at which his consciousness broke through the veil which otherwise denies entry to the past. In the case of Graf Ludwig Polzer-Hoditz, it was definitely Rudolf Steiner who took the initiative, more than once suggesting to the Count that he concern himself with the personality whom he had been in a former incarnation.[7] With Dr Willem Zeylmans van Emmichoven, it was on their first meeting, Zeylmans being introduced to Rudolf Steiner by his wife who was studying eurythmy in Dornach, that Steiner's welcoming remark—'I have been waiting a long time for you to come'—flung open the door, so to say, which made possible a view to the vista of past lives, but left it to the course of Zeylman's life journey so that the ego itself could a) decide whether to look through the door; and b) having decided to do so, discern what he saw there relating to his ego's past.[8]

How different it was in the case of linking a (then) present incarnation with that of Albertus Magnus. The process has come down to posterity through incidents that have been told by various parties—the other two being Rudolf Steiner and Marie von Sivers (who became Steiner's wife in 1914). It transpired that when Steiner was lecturing in Cologne, he went with Marie von Sivers to visit the church of St Andreas quite close to the railway station, in which the tomb of Albertus Magnus was situated, Cologne being the focal point of Albertus' work during the last phase of his long and productive life. It seems that this mini-pilgrimage (if that is the right concept) was a regular occurrence—given that visits to Cologne were not all that frequent, and that Marie von Sivers was not all that keen, though Steiner was insistent. First it was recounted how, in 1911–12, after visiting the tomb, Steiner and von Sivers, in the presence of Helene

Röchling, took a few steps away from where they had been standing, at which Steiner asked: 'Do you remember the work we were engaged in together at that time?' Her reply was short, 'Not very distinctly,' at which he commented, '*But* [the seemingly emphatic: *doch*] you were my teacher back then.' It is also reported that Günther Schubert had received confirmation directly from Rudolf Steiner of the connection. Even more intriguing, perhaps, is the story of Anna Samweber who, also beside the tomb of Albertus in Cologne had a clairvoyant experience that pointed back to Marie Steiner's previous incarnation. On recounting this to Marie Steiner, the latter gave a little laugh and told her about the visit(s) she had made to the tomb and the comments of Steiner's about her (as Albertus) being his former teacher. This, of course, reflects what has come down as a firm historic fact that Albertus' prominent pupil was Thomas Aquinas. It also reflects what is contained in the esoteric material that came into the public domain after Ita Wegman's death, from which it is clear that Steiner himself was previously incarnated as Aquinas (and Wegman as Reginald of Piperno).[9] W.J. Stein's letter to Marie Steiner on 12 April 1927 brings further evidence of these connections via other 'witnesses': 'Frau Linda informed me once that Dr Steiner had confirmed [to Fräulein Johanna Mücke...] that in Albertus Magnus dwelt the same individuality as Hypatia.'

All the above—and there is more, not included here—is placed by Hammacher in a copious footnote.[10] Without casting any doubt on the verbal/anecdotal evidence, for some reason he does not include it all in the main body of his text. Perhaps he had literary reasons for not doing so—it would have seemed too discursive or even a diversion impeding the flow of his argument and spiritually well-founded. Yet his whole book basically depends on the link between Hypatia and Albertus being accurate. It therefore seemed not just appropriate but vitally relevant here to place such evidence alongside that which we have from the stenographed lectures in which Rudolf Steiner's spiritual research is documented. Supporting this approach, perhaps, is also the fact that we are dealing with a case of repeated earth lives that transpired well before the great wealth of karmic relationships which Steiner reveals in 1924, to which reference has already been made, i.e. when the resistance (amongst the membership of both the early Theosophical and the subsequent Anthroposophical Society) had subsided, as well as the defiant opposition to the divulgence of such spiritual realities amongst those spiritual entities who fought against Steiner's work in general and particularly against his core mission, which was finally overpowered: the 'demons [...] must now fall silent'.[11]

This chapter would not be complete without reference to something which, while having been made widely known as pure fact, appears to have attracted comparatively little written comment. Earlier in the book it was related how, during Marie Steiner's early life (1895), she was 'led' to Paris where, amongst all the cultural melting pot of Parisian life at the time she discovered Eduard Schuré and his work and recognized it as something of a spiritual lifeline. In 2002 a letter came to light that she had written to Schuré way back in 1907. The letter's contents related both to one of her, and to one of Rudolf Steiner's, previous incarnations but in very different measures. Others have detailed the connections that existed in this triangle of personalities (the two Steiners and Schuré), as already referred to. Here, I list briefly some key points:

- 1885 Marie von Sivers moves to Paris where she meets Schuré;
- 1900 Schuré makes von Sivers aware of the Theosophical Society;
- 1900/01 von Sivers first hears Steiner speak in Berlin;
- 1902 the lifelong collaboration between Steiner and von Sivers begins;
- 1902 von Sivers' realization of Steiner's previous incarnation. He reacts with *alarm* when she tells him;
- 1906 von Sivers mediates the first meeting between Steiner and Schuré in Paris;
- 1906 September, Steiner and von Sivers stay with Schuré as his guest at Barr;
- 1907 18 August, von Sivers' letter to Schuré and her hesitation ... resulting in the letter being unfinished and unposted;
- 1907 25 August, her continuation and completion of the letter, which discloses her own perception of the identity of Steiner's previous incarnation.

The above table of events is quoted here partly to chronicle some of the remarkable connection that existed between the three individualities, reaching into their past karmic relationships (though not overtly that of Schuré himself); and partly—and in this context slightly more importantly—to insert another phenomenon that has bearing on the incarnation sequence with which we are concerned. For in the letter of 18 August 1907 from von Sivers to Schuré, written during a visit to Rome, she refers to something that Annie Besant had communicated to her, gleaned from Besant's clairvoyant insight one assumes. As already mentioned and commented on, Besant had told her that 'when she was born into Christianity [i.e. in the years *following* the Mystery of Golgotha] it was only to fight against it ... and to be killed!' At some point after receiving the letter, it will also be recalled—one can only speculate as to whether it was an immediate revelatory recognition on his part, or whether the realisation filtered through after some time—Schuré wrote the word Hypatie (he spelt it as in French, his mother tongue), followed by a question mark. There is, of course, nothing that one can call conclusive about this in a strictly rational sense. Nevertheless, it seems to be an important tessera in the mosaic when one takes into consideration the three people concerned (four if one includes Annie Besant), their spiritual insight and in particular Schuré's key-link role in the direction which Marie Steiner-von Sivers took, which reached its turning point when she stepped from what would have proved to be an undoubtedly eminent career on the stage to the central contribution she made to the development of anthroposophy.

17
Summary and Conclusion

Libretto for the West

Rahel Kern & Brien Masters

Conspicuous by its absence in recent research from the Continent concerning the life and work of Marie Steiner-von Sivers has been her biography after Rudolf Steiner's death on 30 March 1925. The present authors do not feel it is within the scope of this book to go into the finer details of the personal difficulties that arose between Marie Steiner-von Sivers and her colleagues in Dornach and the ramifications of these which resulted in the rift which occurred between the British and Dutch Anthroposophical Societies and the Goetheanum. Firstly, we do not feel competent to assess the impact sufficiently, and secondly, it would be wise not to allow these difficulties to detract from the importance of her work.

Sadly, however, one does not have to look far to see signs that this would have appeared to have happened and it is one of the main aims of the present work to restore perceptions of Marie Steiner-von Sivers' achievements and her reputation, and thereby strengthen the impulses that she inaugurated in the performing arts. We therefore feel that it is incumbent upon us to ensure that her achievements after this date as part of her contribution central to the establishment of anthroposophy are not eclipsed. For it is abundantly clear that the tasks that she undertook in the last 22 years of her life were a focused, unswervingly dedicated and inspired continuation of the work which she and Rudolf Steiner together had inaugurated.

While their collaboration was continuous throughout the years, there clearly stand out moments in which the part played by their individualities was complementary in a way that was vital for both their missions. Let us therefore trace some of the more salient moments as if one were listening to the intervals formed by two notes of harmony.

Already very soon after they met in 1901, in an early conversation after one of Rudolf Steiner's lectures, *Christianity as Mystical Fact*, there is a very significant karmic moment in which Marie von Sivers asks him whether it would not be necessary to call into life a spiritual movement in Central Europe. This was the very question that, following spiritual laws, then allowed Rudolf Steiner to start formulating an answer—not the kind of answer that remains abstract on paper, but one that unravelled from that moment onwards in thought, word and deed. Clearly, the mutual interplay which lay deep in the foundations of their lives' work began. Whatever was latent in her soul must surely have been triggered by hearing Rudolf Steiner lecture on the theme of the Sun Spirit of Christ drawing near to his incarnation on earth and the need for the resurgence of that Spirit in present day culture. It was still to be a Jupiter rhythm of 12 years between her first formulating the question and her becoming a member of the *Vorstand* (Executive Council) of the newly formed Anthroposophical Society in 1913—and, significantly, a further Jupiter rhythm before she inherited the full responsibility of executor of Rudolf Steiner's literary estate after his death on 30 March 1925.

A few weeks after this decisive question, when Rudolf Steiner was asked to take on the responsibility of the General Secretary of the Theosophical Society, he accepted it, firstly, on the understanding that what he would contribute as a spiritual teacher would be entirely the result of his own inner research and, secondly, with the proviso that Marie von Sivers would be appointed the society's Secretary, which she then did. With this, the inner collaboration, which had already begun, takes its first outward step, a step which Rudolf Steiner refers to in his autobiography:

> Marie von Sivers and I soon became close friends. This friendship was the basis for an extensive working together in a wide and varied cultural sphere. Our lives soon centred on the task of cultivating anthroposophy as well as poetry and recitation. The spiritual life we cultivated could alone be the centre from which Anthroposophy could develop.[1]

This appointment and the eminence it gave to Rudolf Steiner amongst circles interested in spirituality would appear to have extended his lecturing activity beyond Berlin to centres that were interested in and inspired by his spiritual research. For her part, her position as Secretary entailed not only a tremendous amount of organizational and administrative work, but also included the planning of the journeys necessitated by his increased lecturing itinerary. Not only that, in accompanying him on these trips and encouraging him to visit art galleries with her, she frequently shared her insights regarding the works of art which they visited together across Europe. In referring to the importance of these experiences, Rudolf Steiner acknowledged the significant influence that this had on the way he was able to form anthroposophy for the West.

Returning to this theme in Dornach in the summer of 1923, he elaborated on the mission of the arts in six lectures. In her introduction to the lectures, Virginia Moore, one of the translators of the the first edition in the English language, summarizes some of his crucial points, referring to his assertion:

> That true architecture offers man the lines along which, when projected into the cosmos, the soul in life or death can expand; that true sculpture builds on the life-giving formative forces lying behind physical structure; that true painting relies on not spatial but colour-perspective, colour being an entire world in itself. That modern music, seeking depth in the single tone rather than in harmony or melody, begins, just begins, to find its way back to the spirit from which it descended; that poetry depends upon the relation between breath and pulse, nerve system and blood system; that eurythmy as 'expressive gesture' is linked with the invisible gesture-system which is language...

Significantly she concludes her introduction with connecting the content of the lectures with the perception:

> Perhaps such insights have a special significance for America [since] elsewhere Dr. Steiner has observed that, to achieve balance, Russia needs philosophy, America art.[2]

In June 1903, a further and long-lasting result of their collaboration is to be seen in the publication of the first number of the monthly publication *Luzifer* (later, *Luzifer Gnosis*). This was followed by the establishment of a publishing company which was later moved to Dornach and became what we now know as the Philosophical-Anthroposophical Publishing Company (Philosophisch-Anthroposophischer Verlag). As has been described elsewhere, she and Rudolf Steiner in the first instance acted as distributers of the journal. It was through her personal sacrifice and her literary expertise, as well as her own financial means, that the dissemination of Rudolf Steiner's research in the form of the printed word began. She became the sole executor of his literary estate, a responsibility she continued to effect with utmost faithfulness until the end of her life. Rudolf Steiner puts it in his will as early as 1904 and affirms on two later occasions that she should be the sole inheritor and executor.[3]

So much for her supportive role in the work undertaken by Rudolf Steiner. At the same time, we see from the beginning how her own unique relationship to speech and language became an increasingly significant and intrinsically complementary component in the 'answer' to the question of bringing into life a spiritual movement in the first place in Central Europe but with imperative repercussions for the West. For it was

Marie Steiner-von Sivers' rich inner gifts that enabled the words themselves to become invigorated in an artistic way. By the way she spoke, the etheric was quickened in every syllable and word. Rudolf Steiner, in encouraging this, incorporated recitations by her on public platforms such as the founding of the German Section of the Theosophical Society where she recited Goethe's *The Mysteries*. Moreover, there can be little doubt that the artistically saturated nature of Marie von Sivers' being was a significant factor in the releasing of Rudolf Steiner's own spiritually poetic wealth of language, which then streamed forth for the remainder of his life. This further step in their work becomes particularly apparent when Rudolf Steiner composes the well-known mantric verse *Behold the Sun at the Midnight Hour* which she recites in connection with a lecture he gave at Christmas 1906. It is evident from her description that this verse meant to her a major milestone in her life:

> The moment when, at Christmas, he gave me the first mantram that he had composed: 'Behold the sun at the midnight hour ...' belongs to the turning points, to the milestones of my life, and I had to find the strength within myself to encompass the fullness of this experience, to intone the sounds of each word and convey their impact that was as if carved into stone.[4]

A third step in the course that her gift in recitation took can be seen in the way it is linked with her own inner development, which the practice and performance of these poems seemed to support. It is clear that as an esoteric pupil of Rudolf Steiner she consciously undertook inner work from an early date, as we see from Rudolf Steiner's letter to her on 8 April 1904 in which he reassures her of her progress:

> Believe me, my dear Marie, you are making faster progress than you might notice yourself. I think of you with love ... To me you are the same priestess who faced me when I recognized your individuality. I respect you in the pureness of your soul and only that permits my fondness for you. We live together because we belong inwardly to one another, and we will always have the right to be to one another as we are, if we are aware that our personal relationship is immersed in the holy service of the evolution of the spirit. I know the moment must not come when this holiness might be disturbed, even in the slightest.[5]

Any pupil on an esoteric path of course will have inner questions about his or her inner progress. The reassurance within these warmly encouraging words from Rudolf Steiner must have spurred on her inner work. Substantiating this is the remarkable outcome, apparent in the selection of texts he gave to her to practise and perform, a prime example being Novalis' *Hymn to the Night*, which awoke a realization that the poet had been the painter Raphael in his previous incarnation. A few days later, Rudolf Steiner spoke for the first time about the connection between Novalis—Raffael—John the Baptist—Elijah.

Not only is this an example of her own inner awakening but it would also seem to indicate the way Rudolf Steiner was able to begin to carry out his own core mission of awakening a realization of karma. Although there was resistance to this in members of the Theosophical Society that prevented his being able to pursue this mission as part of his initial public work, he perceived where, in individual cases, it was appropriate for him to awaken awareness in those amongst his pupils who were 'ready'. What we know of this aspect of his work in individual circumstances, not surprisingly, varies enormously from individual to individual.

In the case of Marie Steiner-von Sivers it is known that, during their several visits to the theosophical branch in Cologne, at Rudolf Steiner's instigation the two of them called in at the church of St Andreas close to the railway station with the expressed purpose of visiting the sarcophagus of Albertus Magnus. Interestingly enough they were not always alone, and through this a conversation that took place on one of these occasions has been handed down. During the visit in question, as we have seen it was Helene Röchling who witnessed the brief exchange between Rudolf Steiner and Marie Steiner-von Sivers:

> After walking a few steps away from the sarcophagus of Albertus Magnus, Rudolf Steiner stopped and, standing with the other two, said to Marie von Sivers: 'Do you remember our work back then?' Marie von Sivers replied, 'Only very vaguely,' at which Rudolf Steiner responded: 'But at that time you were my teacher.'[6]

This raises an intriguing question. It is known that these visits, which by all accounts Rudolf Steiner was quite insistent about, evoked in her a degree of resistance. Her reply to Rudolf Steiner's question on the other hand would suggest that some stirring awareness of her karmic connection to Albertus Magnus must have been taking place in the depths of her soul. And possibly it was only because she was in the presence of Rudolf Steiner himself that enabled her to overcome whatever reluctance she may have had to respond in the affirmative way she did, however tentative.

Perhaps we may therefore presume that this was Rudolf Steiner's way of taking the first steps towards awakening in her her Orphic mission, through going backwards in time via the Albertus and Hypatia incarnations in order to strengthen the resolve that was part of her entelechy to carry that mission forwards into the future. After all it was only very recently that the first lecture of the course on *Occult History* had taken place in Stuttgart.

It was during these same years, 1910 to 1912/13, that the spiritual movement for Central Europe in which they were both intricately united was seeking a more permanent and worthy outer home. We have noted that in the first 12-year period of their collaboration, the inner foundations for that home had been thoroughly laid—Rudolf Steiner's unfolding of anthroposophical knowledge in his written and spoken word, Marie von Sivers' personal dedication to and perseverance with the arts of speech and eurythmy which were to play such a central part in the life of anthroposophy as experienced by those who were drawn to one extent or another towards the increasing momentum that it, as a spiritual movement, gained. The outer foundations too in that the Mystery Dramas had, by this time, been written and performed. The circumstances in which they had taken place led to the realization that the plays needed their own space, which then led to the plans for an outer home in the form of the Johannesbau being submitted to the authorities in Munich. In the event this submission was rejected—a disappointment naturally to all concerned, but nevertheless opening up the possibility of looking elsewhere. This eventually led to the gift of the land on the hill in Dornach by the Grosheintz family.

A thread that seldom stands out in the fabric of this development may be fittingly acknowledged here. It was largely through Marie von Sivers' attraction towards the writings of Eduard Schuré and their eventual meeting (a) that helped her identify her own artistic pathway amongst the dense and sudden undergrowth of materialistic realism that was springing up in Paris at the time she arrived there, after her departure from Moscow; and (b) that led to her introducing Rudolf Steiner to Schuré in 1904, to their collaborative work (Steiner's lecturing in Paris; Schuré's mystery drama *Eleusis* being performed at the Munich Theosophical Congress in 1907), to their visits to Schuré's country house in Barr, and on one of those occasions to the excursion to St Odile, the place nearby traditionally connected with the saint. During the visit, falling into silent contemplation, Rudolf Steiner appears to have realized that the spiritual connection with St Odile actually belonged to the district of Arlesheim and Dornach.

The being of Marie Steiner-von Sivers played another important role, closely bound up with the design of the first Goetheanum. In a letter she describes how she was required to sit silently at his side while he was modelling the building: 'I had to be an "Inspiratrice" as the Doctor called it, i.e. a silent figure beside him as he worked.'[7] Unfathomable though it is for ordinary consciousness, Marie Steiner-von Siver's role as inspiratrice for the building we refer to as the first Goetheanum was to make a vital contribution to what transpired. Normally, the essential partners in the generation of a building are the client and the architect. The former briefs the latter. The latter translates the briefing into bricks and mortar. Behind them both are, so to speak, spiritual archetypes. In the case of the first Goetheanum, we may ask: What was the voice of the client to which Rudolf Steiner as architect listened with his highly developed sense of hearing, his penetrating insight into human destiny and his spiritually informed aesthetic sensitivities? Though it is manifestly impossible to tell the whole story in detail, there must surely have been within the Orphic stature of his inspiratrice something that enabled the otherwise inaccessible archetypes to become transparent. For is it not the result of this inspirational process that is to be experienced in the architectural proportions of the cupolas, in the musical forms of the architraves and the other organic-sculptural elements of the building?

One thing is particularly pertinent here: although the clouds had not yet dispersed that prevented Rudolf Steiner from fully embarking on his core mission as far as conceptualizing it through the spoken and written word at the time when the first Goetheanum was 'opened', there can surely be no doubt that the building, both in its structural-visible features as well as in the anthroposophical activities for which it provided a home, embodied that core mission. This was particularly expressed in Rudolf Steiner's words when he emphasized that what was needed was 'an education for the awakening of karma'.[8] Witness the motifs painted in the large cupola which evoked images of mankind's vast evolutionary legacy; witness the very substance of the pillars made from woods that bore the imprint of planetary forces (Saturn-beech, Sun-ash, Moon-cherry, etc.) that sounded the same theme, the vista of Earth evolution; witness the 'musical' forms of the architraves sounding the intervals between Ancient Saturn, Ancient Sun and all the succeeding epochs. And enhancing these elements of the building that contributed to the awakening of individual karma into the realm of *the word*—like the strings resonated by the body of a violin or, still closer to home, the sounds of the vocal chords resonating in the cavities of the head, pharynx and chest—were the performing arts of recitation, drama and eurythmy, which took place in the small cupola. Accompanying this twofoldness of large and small cupolas, of visual and performing arts, were the windows' sunlight-through-coloured-glass images of the contemporary situation: man, in the twentieth century, poised crossing the threshold.

One of the most significant phenomena in humanity's crossing the threshold is the separation of the three soul forces of thinking, feeling and willing, a potential problem for the unprepared ego. In Rudolf Steiner's constant endeavour to unite those spheres of life which traditionally we refer to as science, art and religion, we may see on the broadest, global-cultural level what for the striving esotericist is a factor to reckon with on the inner path of human development. Leading from the inner to the outer we may also see the same phenomenon in the three stages of development of spiritual science, a yet further aspect of the incarnation of Anthroposophia.

In its first stage, Rudolf Steiner clothes the content of spiritual science in conceptual form through his writings and lectures, something, of course, which continues to flow from him throughout his life *but also something which he encouraged his esoteric pupils/colleagues/associates to become engaged in.*

In the second stage of this incarnation process, the arts begin their infiltrating into anthroposophical gatherings—the Theosophical Congress of 1907 is frequently acknowledged as that moment when the artistic impulse (both the visual and the performing) was brought by Rudolf Steiner as an integral component into the proceedings. The artistic work continues to flow through the life of the Anthroposophical Society, gathering momentum as it does so, and entering the public domain, through the eurythmy tours, for instance, not only as a partner alongside the lecture cycle or within a congressional meeting, but in its own right.

Thirdly, Rudolf Steiner is approached by those whose karma has been stirred to one extent or another and who, as a result, are seeking ways of informing the practical, vocational strand of their lives with the fruits of his spiritual research. As in former times religion had penetrated the practical activities in people's daily lives, moral impulses inspired by anthroposophy were now carried into the different professions. His abundant response is extant in the lecture courses spoken for Waldorf teachers, anthroposophical doctors, biodynamic farmers and others, each with their respective Section within the School for Spiritual Science. There is no need to further elaborate on this aspect of the incarnation of Anthroposophia, except in one respect, one that can easily be overlooked: Marie Steiner-von Sivers' position within this third stage, her unsurpassed role as *teacher*.

The part she played therefore in the overall founding of anthroposophy, however vital it was, becomes something of a background to her own personal mission in the arts. Right until the last month of Rudolf Steiner's lecturing activity (September 1924) she is centrally present in his disseminating the spiritual significance of the arts—the last course he was able to give being *Speech and Drama*—their mission and the direction towards which they pointed as informed by spiritual science, with seeds sown at the inception of this creatively inspiring approach for future practitioners to take up. At the second stage, there is no need to rehearse further her participation as performer, as solo reciter at the beginning of the collaborative work with Steiner—the source, like that of a mountain spring, being in the *spoken word*, which then attracted the mighty tributaries we meet in the Mystery Dramas and in eurythmy as visible speech. And at the third stage, she conveys, *as teacher*, that with which she was endowed as individual talent, albeit further developed with Rudolf Steiner's guiding insight, to those who performed in drama on the Goetheanum stage and those who followed in the footsteps of the first eurythmist Lory Smits. She takes centre-stage as teacher/director, tirelessly connecting speakers and eurythmists with their respective, newly born arts and that within their own creativity that could give etheric wing to word and gesture.

It is surely not for nothing that the House of the Word, the first Goetheanum, was not only an embodiment of all the arts—its very 'building stone' the spirit-fired essence of architecture, sculpture, colour in painting and glass, music, poetry, eurythmy and drama—but that, intended to stand at its focal point, was the Representative of Humanity. This was the towering wooden sculpture, with the figures of Lucifer and Ahriman on Christ's left- and right-hand side. He strides victoriously into the new world of Resurrection on Easter morning between those spiritual powers that would rob humanity of the benefits of His deed of Golgotha. The portrayal of the Risen One not only symbolizes the cosmic deed that brings new life to the earth, but also the healing forces that will carry humanity into the future. In that this event occurs at Easter, it evokes the image of Raphael passing on the healing impulse as Mercurial Intelligence from the heights.

Following the opening of the Goetheanum in 1920, it is known that it was Rudolf Steiner's intention to write a mystery drama that would bring what was represented in the carving, the Representative of Humanity— still being worked on at that time by himself and by Edith Maryon in the sculptor's atelier we know as the Schreinerei—into a dramatic dimension. In the event, the intention could not be carried out. Not yet standing in its intended position in the small cupola, the sculpture however remained. There also remained the Raphaelic 'remedies' accessible to humanity:

speech formation and eurythmic movement, which would be experienced by audiences in the Goeatheanum, performed in front of the statue.

It was two years after the opening of the first Goetheanum at Christmas 1922—just days before its tragic burning—that Rudolf Steiner gave the meditative verse to Marie Steiner-von Sivers 'Stars spake once to Man' (*Sterne sprachen einst zu Menschen*). Hearking back to the historic-cum-mythologic past, we are taken to the epoch when the song of Orpheus expressed what he heard as coming from the stars and his subsequent mourning at the fading of that language which led inexorably into human consciousness being immersed in the world of the senses. Hypatia's outstanding exposition of ancient Greek wisdom is like an echo—to what extent in her consciousness is unknown—of that stellar language. With Albertus we meet a consciousness already sensitive to the silence of the stars and painfully aware of wanting to reconnect to his own inner exertion. And travelling into the centuries that followed, the silence becomes deeper, the pain becomes more acute, the yearning for starry realms becomes more intense. Whilst the opposing powers increase their efforts, they succeed more and more in side-tracking consciousness away from any vestige of that inner process that would give wing to the soul, wracked by the pain of the silence which had befallen humanity, and yearning for a glimpse of the past or even the faintest echo of that stellar language which would affirm the existence of a spiritual world. Finally, in Marie Steiner-von Sivers' indefatigable and multi-layered work with 'the word'—'What man speaks to the stars' (*Was Menschen sprechen zu Sternen*, both what man speaks out loud and in his innermost silent being)—the way opens up for a gradual retracing of human consciousness, not in a backwards direction, but forwards to Spirit Man (*Geistesmensch*).

It would seem from very many contemporary accounts that on a well-nigh daily basis Rudolf Steiner *personally* connected with the work of his two main collaborators, mentioned above. Those who lived and worked in Dornach describe how he would walk from the Goetheanum to the clinic in Arlesheim, where Dr Ita Wegman had her practice, to discuss the medical work in general and the needs of the patients who came to the clinic in particular. Likewise, he was seen walking up the hill from Haus Hansi, the residence where he and Frau Dr Steiner lived, to where the one at the centre of our present study was involved in endless hours of rehearsal with the eurythmists, preparing for forthcoming performances.

The influence of the planet Mercury, the sphere of Raphaelic Intelligence, reflected, of course, in many ways of human life. Long tradition connects it with the trade of the merchant; and recent research has indicated how the surge in interest in the field of botany follows a

Mercurial rhythm. Moreover, giving our theme further resonance, the same planetary influence is evident in Gothic architecture.[9] Here, however, we are primarily concerned with those elements that flow from Raphaelic influence into, and affect, the inner nature of the human being, as a vital, healing complement to what is taking place in the Michaël Age of mankind's evolution.

The density of human bodies already in the nineteenth century meant that, despite the plethora of materialistic inventions and achievements, the incarnating human entelechy became obstructed, obliterated, to one degree or another in its effort to engender whatever counterforces would provide a balance to the descent of culture exclusively into the material.

In Steiner's and Wegman's co-authored *Fundamentals of Therapy* the resurgence of an understanding of the human constitution and of earthly substances in mineral, plant and animal kingdoms led to the 'extension of the art of healing' that has become widespread through the work of anthroposophical medical doctors. We may leave on one side the question of how much of human egotism is to a large extent the moving force behind the spread of an advance of anthroposophical medicine and simply remain with the gratitude that it is there, and that the illnesses which, for whatever reason, prevent us from making our bodies fit instruments for the reception and development of spiritual faculties can be overcome to whatever extent karma allows.

The other Raphaelic currency in modern life, however, is in rare supply by comparison. How does culture benefit from our inner work, from the insights we gain, from our application of them—particularly in the present context of the arts? It is, perhaps, a sobering thought that on the one hand an anthroposophical medical doctor, consultant or surgeon is able to command a worthy fee, and be engaged full-time in his or her profession while, by comparison, artists (be it in recitation, drama or eurythmy) mostly need to supplement their anthroposophical artistic activity economically by other means and are constantly appealing for financial support. The point need not be laboured, though its consequences have been disastrous for the arts. Here it is brought forth in order to highlight the difference between what Rudolf Steiner considered of top priority (take only his urging to the very end of his life the importance of public eurythmy performances as an example) and where that top priority now stands. This again serves to emphasize how inadequately Marie Steiner-von Sivers' work has been valued.

The encouragement of Rudolf Steiner's that Marie Steiner-von Sivers should pursue this aspect of their joint work reaches a point of poignant insistence from the extant correspondence dating from the New Year

1925. While she consistently writes of her concern for his health and well-being right until the very last, his concern is to insist on the continuation of the eurythmy tour that she was leading, in keeping with the way he was expressing again and again how much he values her commitment: 'I really cannot tell you *how much* I admire your devoted work and how thankful I am for all the things you do, that bring such blessing.'[10]

Might we not see in this importance that Rudolf Steiner attributed to the role that eurythmy has to play in creating a fertile ground into which the seeds of spiritual science, once sown, could germinate. The seeds, after all, were countless in number. In addition, the fertility of 'the ground' amongst the membership of the Anthroposophical Society had been cultivated time and time again. There remains the question: How could those fertile seeds which lay dormant in the souls of all the Michaël-inspired egos, incarnate already in 1925, be made fertile enough for the future?

Despite the Michaëlic letters, which Rudolf Steiner had been writing since having to give up lecturing, it must have been clear to him that the stream from the spirit world that flowed directly through him would have to continue through others and that Marie Steiner-von Sivers' unending support for this stream would be foremost in the several ways outlined in the foregoing chapters. Indeed, the delicate but emphatic way he formulates his perceptions would suggest that he saw her work not merely as being in a supporting role, but as synonymous with the stream itself.

Not that this implies that her own mission is not distinctive. Looking at this once more against the broad background of Marie Steiner-von Sivers' karma and karmic past, it is perhaps pertinent that already in the first lecture of *Occult History* Rudolf Steiner draws his hearers' attention right back to the significance of Orpheus and Euridice and interprets the story as symbolizing humanity's 'fall into the sense world'. This fall predates the gods' vouchsafing the cosmic intelligence, which was in their care, to man.[11] This means that, by some millennia, humanity had reached the stage of slowly becoming the new guardian for the cosmic intelligence—and did so *without* the supersensible consciousness informing this instreaming of intelligence. We may see how (with Aristotle and Aquinas in the background) one of Rudolf Steiner's first endeavours is to bring about the *redemption of thinking*. This, however, was to be made more effective in practice in the West through the healing streams of medicine and the arts. In the trinity of Rudolf Steiner, Marie Steiner-von Sivers and Ita Wegmann, we find the embodiment of those two healing streams on the one hand and on the other the igniting of the fiery spirit of the Michaëlic stream in Rudolf Steiner's representing the cosmic intelligence of the past in the form of spiritual science, atuned to the consciousness of the spiritual soul.

In the past as we, non-thinking humanity listened to the stars, we received the voice of cosmic intelligence. Arguably it was clairaudience rather than clairvoyance that informed the ancient cultures. This is surely a keynote as to where we stand today in the development of human consciousness but also the keynote to the mission of Marie Steiner-von Sivers. Through inner hearing, quickened by the renewal of the arts of movement and the word, as well as prompted and sustained by the mantric formulation of the words that Rudolf Steiner gave out in such abundance, we may approach that state of awareness encapsulated so succinctly yet all embracingly in the verse which Rudolf Steiner gave to Marie Steiner-von Sivers on Christmas Day 1922.

There can surely be no doubt, with Rudolf Steiner's insight into her long vista of past karma, together with his awareness of that within her own personal mission which was so central for the development of culture in the future, that he wished to enhance through this verse her own inner perception of this karmic journey—the past, the present, the future—in order to help strengthen her own resolves and work so that they would become a central factor in the development of the anthroposophical movement and all that it may crucially stand for at our present turning point in Earth evolution.

The Stars Spake Once to Man

Rudolf Steiner

Sterne sprachen einst zu Menschen,
Ihr Verstummen ist Weltenschicksal;
Des Verstummens Wahrnehmung
Kann Leid sein des Erdenmenschen;

In der stummen Stille aber reift,
Was Menschen sprechen zu Sternen;
Ihres Sprechens Wahrnehmung
Kann Kraft werden des Geistesmenschen.

The Stars spake once to Man.
It is World-destiny
That they are silent now.
To be aware of this silence
Can become pain for earthly Man.

But in the deepening silence
There grows and ripens
What Man speaks to the stars.
To be aware of this speaking
Can become strength for Spirit-Man.[1]

Sequence of Events

Pherecydes

BC
c. 600   *Pherecydes is born on the island of Syros*
c. 550   *Pherecydes dies*

Hypatia

AD
c. 370   *Hypatia is born in Alexandria*
c. 400   *Hypatia becomes head of the Platonist school at Alexandria*
415   *March, Hypatia is killed by Coptic monks*

Albertus Magnus

1194   Chartres Cathedral burnt down
1206   *Albertus Magnus born in Lauingen at the Danube*
1220   Chartres Cathedral rebuilt in Gothic style; reconsecrated 1260
1223   *Albertus Magnus joins the Dominican order in Padua*
1225/6   Thomas Aquinas born
1228–45   *Albertus Magnus commences teaching in German cities, chiefly at Cologne*
1240   *Albertus Magnus—Regent Master of Dominican School in Paris till 1248*
1245   *Albertus Magnus awarded his doctorate*
1245   *Albertus Magnus becomes teacher of Thomas Aquinas*
1245–8   *Albertus Magnus lives in Paris*
1248   Foundation stone laid of Cologne Cathedral
1248   *Albertus Magnus moves to Cologne with Thomas Aquinas*
1248   *Albertus Magnus appointed Regent Master of newly created Studium Generale in Cologne*
1252   Thomas Aquinas moves to Paris
1254–7   *Albertus Magnus fills the office of Provincial of his Order for Germany*
1260–2   *Albertus Magnus takes the position of Bishop of Regensburg*
1274   Thomas Aquinas dies
1277   *Albertus Magnus travels to Paris for the last time to defend the doctrines and memory of Thomas Aquinas*
1286   *15 November, Albertus Magnus dies in Cologne*

Maries Steiner-von Sivers

1867   *14 March: Marie born in Wlocławek, then part of Russia*
1875   *Moves with family to Riga, Latvia*
1877   *Moves with family to St Petersburg on her father's retirement Attends a private school*

SEQUENCE OF EVENTS 183

1879	Commencement of Michaël Age
1882	*Tours Switzerland, Germany and Austria with her mother*
	Attends a Russian Grammar School
	Graduates as a teacher
1885	*Goes to Paris*
	Attends sessions at the Sorbonne and the Conservatoire, studying with Favart
1888	*December: visits St Mark's Venice*
	Rudolf Steiner sees exhibition of paintings by Böcklin
1889	*Inspired by the Narodnik movement, goes with her brother to work amongst the disadvantaged*
	Schuré's The Great Initiates first published
1890	Schuré's *Sacred Drama of Eleusis* first published
1893	*Tours Italy, England and France with a cousin*
1895	*Goes to Paris*
1897	*Performs the title role in Schiller's* Maria Stuart *at her old school's Jubilee*
1898	*Studies Schuré's* The Great Initiates
1900	Schuré's *Children of Lucifer* first published
	Holidaying on the Latvian coast, reads Schuré's The Children of Lucifer
	Seeks Schuré's permission to translate The Children of Lucifer
	Schuré's letter in which he makes her aware of the Theosophical Society
	Is offered the title role in Schiller's The Maid of Orleans
	November 6: learns of Rudolf Steiner's lecture in newspaper and hears him speak
	Meets Rudolf Steiner in Berlin during winter
1901	*Summer: travels with mother to Estonia*
	Autumn: moves from Russia to Berlin
	17 November: asks Rudolf Steiner the 'significant' question
	Assists in founding the Italian Theosophical Society in Bologna
1902	May: Rudolf Steiner assumes leadership of the German Section of the Theosophical Society *on condition* that she become Secretary
	1 July: attends the Theosophical Congress with Rudolf Steiner on his first visit to London
	7 July: visits the National Gallery, London with Rudolf Steiner
	17 September: takes on Secretariat of Theosophical Society
	Her realization of Rudolf Steiner's previous incarnation and his 'alarm' at hearing of this
1903	June: first number of *Luzifer* published
1904	*Accompanies Steiner on lecture tours to Switzerland and Holland and twice to England*
	8 April: Rudolf Steiner's letter to her on her spiritual progress
	8–10 July attends Theosophical Society Convention in London with Rudolf Steiner
	Autumn: recites Goethe's The Mysteries *at the founding of the German Section of the Theosophical Society*

1905	9 January: Rudolf Steiner's letter to her containing the 'warning' from the masters
	17 April : receives letter from Steiner noting the deterioration of a feeling for form in sculpture
	28 April: receives letter in which Steiner makes her aware of the attack on culture building up
	25 November: letter from Steiner expressing the ideal that their work express form as an expression of the inner soul, without which culture will sink into abstraction
1906	6 January: Rudolf Steiner speaks for the first time about the karmic background of Raphael
	4 April: after the visit to Cologne, Rudolf Steiner's lecture to the members in Düsseldorf
	May: recites Hegel's Eleusis—*an Hölderlin*
	Mediates the first meeting between Schuré and Rudolf Steiner at the Theosophical Society Congress in Paris
	Rudolf Steiner's and her first visit to stay with Schuré at Barr
	Christmas: recites 'Behold the Sun at the Midnight Hour', Rudolf Steiner's first Ursprung Wort
1907	*18–25 August: writes—and sends a week later—her letter to Schuré concerning Steiner's previous incarnation*
	Schuré's *Sacred Drama of Eleusis* is performed at the Munich Congress of the Theosophical Society
1908	*26 October: recites Novalis'* Hymnen an die Nacht
	Founds the Theosophical Publishing Company
	Luzifer-Gnosis ceased being published
1910	Rudolf Steiner's Mystery Dramas performed at the Munich Congress of the Theosophical Society
	27 and 29 December: Lectures 1 and 3 of *Occult History*
1911	The visits to St Andreas church in Cologne begin
1912	*April: accompanies Rudolf Steiner to Helsingfors*
	24 September: names eurythmy, when the art was first evolved with Lory Maier Smits
1913	*February: appointed member of Vorstand of the newly created Anthroposophical Society*
	24 November: recites poems by Christian Morgenstern
1914	Outbreak of the First World War
	2 February: writes to Mieta Waller 'inspiratrice'
	30 March: Tatiana Kisseleff moves to Dornach initially at the behest of Marie von Sivers to direct eurythmy
	May: visits Chartres Cathedral with Rudolf Steiner and Schuré
	December: *Art in the Light of Mystery Wisdom* lectures commence
	31 December: is married to Rudolf Steiner
	She and Rudolf Steiner move from Berlin to Dornach

1915	18 March: Rudolf Steiner's final will is signed by both him and Marie Steiner-von Sivers
1916	30 March: Schuré's break with Rudolf Steiner
	July: third edition of Schuré's *The Great Initiates* published with Steiner's new Foreword—the painful irony being that it came just as the break with Schuré occurred
	Resigns from the Vorstand
1917	Samael's (Mars) sub-regency commences
1918	End of the First World War
1919	*24 February: first public performance of eurythmy in Zurich*
1920	*26 September: eurythmy rehearsal in small cupola, seven years since the laying of the foundation stone for the first Goetheanum—festive evening*
	Eurythmy School in Stuttgart established under the leadership of Alice Fels with the overall responsibility of Marie Steiner-von Sivers
	Rudolf Steiner's lectures on *Die Philosophie des Thomas von Aquino* (published in 1956 as *The Redemption of Thinking*)
	The Goetheanum is opened
1922	*13 April: in Stratford on Avon with Rudolf Steiner; sees three of Shakespeare's plays*
	October: 'French Course' of lectures attended by Schuré
	31 December: burning of first Goetheanum
1923	*August: at Penmaenmawr*
	Visits Macmillan in East End—a reminder of the poor estate of Russians
	First episode of Rudolf Steiner's *Autobiography* in 'Wochenschrift' *Das Goetheanum*
	November: moves Verlag to Dornach
1924	*Karmic Relationships* lectures
	Easter: Foundation Stone Meditation in eurythmy
	24 May: sets off for eurythmy tour in Ulm, Nürnberg, Eisenach, Erfurt, Naumburg, Hildesheim, Hannover, Halle, Breslau
	August: Rudolf Steiner's address at Torquay
1925	*February: departs for eurythmy tour*
	30 March: Rudolf Steiner's death
1927	*Her foreword published in English translation of Rudolf Steiner's lectures given in Torquay with the title, which Rudolf Steiner had himself given, changed*
	Her foreword published in English translation of Rudolf Steiner's lectures given in Penmaenmawr
	12 April: W.J. Stein writes to her referring to information he received that Hypatia was reincarnated as Albertus Magnus (no reply is known of)
1945	*12 March: refers to how she built up the Anthroposophical Society*
1947	27 December: her death in Beatenberg
1953	*Karmic Relationships Vol. 8* published in English
1956	*The Redemption of Thinking* published in English

1957	*Occult History* published in English
1967	Marie Savitch's biography, *Marie Steiner*, published in English
1969	A.H. Parker's revised translation of *True and False Paths in Spiritual Investigation* published in English
1988	*Documents and Correspondence: Rudolf Steiner and Marie Steiner-von Sivers* published in English
1989	Zachariel's (Jupiter) sub-regency commences
1993	Crispian Villeneuve's *Marie Steiner: Esoteric Studies,* a compilation of 'Forewords' she wrote for the publication of lectures by Rudolf Steiner, published in English
1994	Peter van Manen's *Marie Steiner* published in English
1997	Andrew Welburn's *The Mysteries* published with references to Pherecydes of Syros
1998	Wilfried Hammacher's *Marie Steiner* in which the link between Hypatia and Albertus Magnus is first made public (published in German)
2010	T.H. Meyer's *Rudolf Steiner's Core Mission* published in English

Notes

1 Proem

1. Hanbury, Frederick J., 'The Rock Garden at Brockhurst', in *The Garden*, 16 February 1924, pp. 82–6.
2. At the time of writing (2010), at least five prominent 'anthroposophical activities' in England alone had gone through a bleak time in their history.
3. In the following August there followed continued cooperation in an anthroposophical conference with a lecture and workshop on the same subject.
4. Meyer, T.H., 1992, *D.N. Dunlop: A Man of our Time*, pp. 451–6.
5. Blaxland-de Lange, Simon, 2006, *Owen Barfield: Romanticism Comes of Age— A Biography*.
6. Kiersch, Johannes, 2006, *A History of the School of Spiritual Science*, Chapter 5.
7. Steiner, Rudolf, 1927, *True and False Paths in Spiritual Investigation*, Lecture 9.

2 Introduction

1. Steiner, Rudolf, 1957, *Karmic Relationships*, vol. 4, lecture given on 7 September 1924, p. 23.
2. Steiner, Rudolf, 1957, *Occult History*, pp. 19f.
3. Ibid. p. 54.
4. Ibid. p. 22.
5. Steiner, Rudolf, 1927, *True and False Paths in Spiritual Investigation*.
6. Hammacher, Wilfried, 1998, *Marie Steiner: Lebensspuren einer Individualität*, pp. 137f.

Orpheus with his Lute

1. This 'Song', which appears in *Henry VIII*, Act III scene (ii), is sung by one of Queen Catherine of Aragon's women, at her request: 'Take thy lute wench: my soul grows sad with troubles;/Sing and disperse 'em, if thou canst.' The choice, left ostensibly to the 'wench', is as far as it goes well suited to disperse the Queen's apprehension about her future. Were the song to continue, however, it would enter the subsequent fate of Orpheus and thus is an ill omen of what follows in the play in which her 'troubles' are only too well-founded.

3 Marie Steiner-von Sivers I

1. Steiner, Rudolf, 1968, pp. 97ff.
2. Leino Pirkko's research, published in 1991 as *Kieleen mieltä—hyvää suomea*, discovered no fewer than 19 dialects/languages that are interrelated extending east to the Ural mountains and south past the Carpathians into Hungary.

3. Masters, Brien, 2009, 'On the Sands with Printless Foot', in *Keynotes in Life and Work*, p. 262.
4. Savitch, M., 1967, *Marie Steiner-von Sivers*, p. 19.
5. Steiner, Rudolf, 1987, *Conferences with the Teachers at the Waldorf School Stuttgart 1921–1922*, vol. 2, p. 64.
6. Steiner, Rudolf, 1989, *Conferences with the Teachers at the Waldorf School Stuttgart 1923–1924*, vol. 4, pp. 58f.

4 Marie Steiner-von Sivers II

1. Savitch, M., 1967, *Marie Steiner-von Sivers: Fellow Worker with Rudolf Steiner*, Chapter 2.
2. Masters, B., 2009, 'On the Sands with Printless Foot', in *Keynotes in Life and Work*, p. 266.
3. See Charpentier, Louis, 1980, *The Mysteries of Chartres Cathedral*, p. 28, for a diagram showing the relative geographical location of these cathedrals.
4. Savitch, M., 1967, *Marie Steiner-von Sivers*, p. 38.
5. Ibid.
6. Their order goes in the opposite stream of time to the days of the week; Sunday, Moon-day, Mars-day, etc. Through his 18-year-long research into the lesser planetary rhythms (of 72 years), observed by the Babylonian astronomers in ancient times, Dr Emil Páleš, a Slovak mathematician, has shed immense light on the qualities brought through these archangelic influences in cultural life across the world in all spheres of society. These flow in the order of Jupiter (to take as a starting point where we now stand, the period commencing in 1989) preceded by Mars (1917–89), preceded by Sun, preceded by Venus, preceded by Mercury, preceded by Moon, preceded by Saturn, which takes us back to the earlier Jupiter period. See Páleš, Emil, 2009, *Seven Archangels: Rhythms of Inspiration in the History of Culture and Nature*, passim.
7. pp. 117ff.
8. See Páleš, Emil., 2009, *Seven Archangels: Rhythms of Inspiration in the History of Culture and Nature*, pp. 25–33; and chronograms on pp. 128f showing dates of peaks of natural science discoveries, atomism and the foremost materialistic philosophers.
9. Steiner, Rudolf, 1999, *Autobiography: Chapters in the Course of my Life 1861–1907*, n. 593, p. 399.
10. Ibid. p. 274.
11. Hammacher, Wilfried, 1998, *Marie Steiner: Lebensspuren einer Individualität*, p. 35.
12. Lectures given between October 1916 and February 1917, not published in English.
13. Steiner, 1999, *Autobiography*, p. 283, my emphasis.
14. Steiner, Rudolf, 1985, *Self-Education*, p. 40.

15. Steiner, Rudolf, 1999, *Autobiography*, p. 284.
16. Ibid.
17. Steiner, Rudolf and Steiner-von Sivers, Marie, 1988, *Correspondence and Documents 1901–1925*, Rudolf Steiner Press, London, p. 35.
18. Savitch, M., 1967, *Marie Steiner-von Sivers*, p. 45.
19. See note 2, Chapter 17.
20. Steiner, Rudolf, 1957, *Karmic Relationships*, vol. 3, lecture 7.
21. Steiner, Rudolf, 1957, *Karmic Relationships*, vol. 4, pp. 153f.
22. Meyer, T.H., 2010, *Rudolf Steiner's Core Mission*, p. 96.
23. Steiner, Rudolf and Steiner-von Sivers, Marie, 1988, *Correspondence and Documents*, p. 47.
24. Meyer, T.H., 2010, op. cit.
25. Ibid.
26. Regarding all the above, the reader will recall how Rudolf Steiner advised tactful caution when referring to matters of karma. See Chapter 2 where W.J. Stein had suggested he speak about the karmic background of Alexander the Great.
27. Meyer, T.H., 2010, op. cit., p. 94. In Chapter 8 it will become clear that Hypatia does, in fact, *not* 'fight against' Christianity. This does not make Besant's possible insight into the Hypatia–Albertus connection invalid.

Hypatie

1. This speech from Leconte de Lisle's dramatic poem *Hypatie* was recited by Marie Steiner as an example of the Alexandrine. In it she refuses to recant and by doing so escape the brutal death which Bishop Cyril points out awaits her; and she strongly affirms her adherence to the wisdom that derives from the ancient esoteric sources, the wisdom for which she is so famed in Alexandria. Translation by V.E.W.

5 Marie Steiner-von Sivers III

1. Steiner, Rudolf, 1970, *Art in the Light of Mystery Wisdom*, Lecture 1.
2. Masters, Brien, 2006, *Mozart: His Musical Style and his Role in the Development of Human Consciousness*, pp. 77, 82–4.
3. The example of music has been used rather than drawing examples from these three professions, partly because of what follows but also partly so that music is not left out of the picture—alongside the art of eurythmy as *visible speech*, her sister art, eurythmy as *visible sound*, was also being developed.
4. This reached a point of culmination when she spoke the first '*Wahrspruchwort*' that Rudolf Steiner composed, which one may safely assume was in great part due to her influence and exceptional gift. Her remark on that occasion sheds special light on their collaborative work: 'I count among the turning points, among the momentous events of my life, the hour when, at Christmas time, Rudolf Steiner gave me the first of his "*Wahrspruchworte*" to

be written in poetic form' (quoted in Savitch, M., 1967, *Marie Steiner-von Sivers: Fellow Worker with Rudolf Steiner*, p. 62).
5. See Steiner, Rudolf and Steiner-von Sivers, Marie, 1981, *Poetry and the Art of Speech*.
6. Savitch, M., 1967, *Marie Steiner-von Sivers*.
7. Ibid. p. 61.
8. This took place on 8 September 1924. Before reciting the passage, Marie Steiner-von Sivers gives a few words of introduction. If taken with an audience unfamiliar with the poem and its also being in a foreign language, her words would appear to be a straightforward exposition of what is about to be heard. Bearing in mind, however, the karmic context of the incident, they are truly remarkable. She interpolates, 'The example I am giving is taken from a dramatic poem by Leconte de Lisle: *Hypatie*. The cultivated young adherent of ancient wisdom, who will shortly be torn in pieces by the infuriated mob in the streets of Alexandria, is admonished by Bishop Cyril to be converted and so escape violent death. She on her part points to the everlasting disputes that go on within the Church, a Church that has become not only terribly dogmatic, but brutally savage, and affirms her unswerving adherence to the ancient esoteric wisdom.'
9. Savitch, M., op. cit., Chapter VII.
10. Steiner, Rudolf, 1970, *Art in the Light of Mystery Wisdom*, pp. 23f.
11. See lecture given by Rudolf Steiner on 11 February 1911.
12. Rudolf Steiner did not elaborate what this seventh art would be.
13. Cf. his enormous editorial input into both the Kirschner edition and the complete Goethe edition being prepared in the Weimar archives.
14. Savitch, M., op. cit., p. 38.

6 Orpheus

1. Steiner, Rudolf, 1968, *Background to the Gospel of St Mark*, p. 107.
2. 770 BC–AD 1413.
3. How Rudolf Steiner frequently refers to the Mystery of Golgotha.
4. Anderson, W., 1980, 'Muses' in *The New Grove Dictionary of Music and Musicians*, vol. 12, p. 795.
5. *Metamorphoses* XI, 15–19.
6. Steiner makes further reference to this in Chapters 7 and 15 of *Background to the Gospel of St Mark*.
7. Ibid. p. 108.

Metamorphoses

1. In this passage from the *Metamorphoses* Book XI, Ovid describes nature's sorrow following the destruction of Orpheus by the fierce Maenads. Translation by Frank Justus Miller.

7 Pherecydes of Syros

1. In *Heptamychos*, his work that is extant in fragments only.
2. Steiner, Rudolf, 1973, *The Riddles of Philosophy*, Anthroposophic Press, Spring Valley, p. 13.
3. Aristotle, 1935, *The Metaphysics*, Harvard University Press, vol. II, Book XIV, p. 287.
4. The early Presocratics were influenced by his thought, especially by the eternal nature of his first principles, the self-creation of the cosmos, and thereby his denial of *ex nihilo* creation.
5. Steiner, Rudolf, 1957, *Occult History*, Anthroposophical Publishing Company, London, pp. 19–20.

8 Hypatia of Alexandria

1. Alexandria, founded 331 BC by Alexander around a small Pharaonic town, it remained the capital of Egypt for nearly a thousand years.
2. Alexander III of Macedon, 356–323 BC, commonly known in the West as Alexander the Great.
3. Rudolf, Steiner, 1957, *Occult History*, Anthroposophical Publishing Company, London, p. 22.
4. Rev. 12:7–9.
5. Aristotle, 1928, *The Works of Aristotle*, Clarendon Press, Oxford, vol. 1, Chapter 4, pp. 6–7.
6. See Steiner, Rudolf, 1968, *The Easter Festival in the Evolution of the Mysteries*, Rudolf Steiner Press, London, Lecture 4.
7. Ptolemy I, *c.* 367–*c.* 283 BC, a boyhood friend of Alexander at Pella, later a general under Alexander, then ruler of Egypt 323–283 BC. He took the title of Pharaoh in 305/4 BC.
8. Theon of Alexandria, *c.* AD 335–*c.* 405.
9. In Hypatia's time, some parts of the library's collection had already been destroyed. It was seriously damaged by various military campaigns such as the siege by Emperor Aurelian in AD 270 and eventually became completely destroyed by the Arab conquest of AD 642.
10. Plotinus, AD 205–70. Today he is officially considered the founder of Neoplatonism.
11. Synesius Cyrene, *c.* 373–*c.* 414, Greek bishop of Ptolemais from 410.
12. Apollonius of Perga, *c.* BC 262–*c.* 190.
13. Astronomer, mathematician and geographer *c.* 100–180 AD.
14. Euclid, Greek mathematician *c.* 300 BC.
15. The Tolerance Edict was issued by Emperor Constantine in AD 313 and stated that followers of all religions have the same rights.
16. Synesius of Cyrene, Letter 16 and 10 respectively (both were written approximately 397/396), in: *The Letters of Synesius*, Oxford University Press, 1926, p. 99 and p. 95.

17. Synesius Cyrene, 1930, *The Essays and Hymns of Synesius of Cyrene*, Oxford University Press, London, vol. II, p. 328.
18. Synesius of Cyrene, Letter 137, written in approximately 412, in: *The Letters of Synesius*, Oxford University Press, 1926, pp. 229–30.
19. Socrates Scholasticus, *The Ecclesiastical History of Socrates*, Book VII, Chapter 15, pp. 348–9.
20. Ancient historian, *c.* 460–399/396 BC.
21. Socrates Scholasticus, *The Ecclesiastical History of Socrates*, Book VII, Chapter 13, p. 345.
22. John Bishop of Nikiu, *The Chronicle of John Bishop of Nikiu*, LXXXIV, 87–8, 100–1.
23. The Greek word *ostrakois* is literally translated as 'oyster shells' but is also the word used for roof tiles made of clay.
24. See *Suda Lexicon*, pp. 644–6.
25. In Damascius, *Life of Isidore*, reproduced in the *Suda Encyclopaedia*.
26. The ones most worthy of mention are Hierocles, Ammonius, John Philoponus and Olympiodorus.
27. Russell, Bertrand, 1961, *History of Western Philosophy*, Routledge, London, p. 365.
28. Steiner, Rudolf, 1968, *The Easter Festival in the Evolution of the Mysteries*, Rudolf Steiner Press, London, p. 77.

Epigram

1. The contemporary tribute by the Alexandrian poet Palladas speaks of his passionate love for Hypatia and her wisdom which has made her almost divine. Palladas, *Greek Anthology (XI 400)*. Translation by Rahel Kern.

9 Albertus Magnus I

1. For an account of his two-day visit, see Meyer, T.H., 2010, *Rudolf Steiner's Core Mission*, Temple Lodge, London, pp. 114–18.

10 Albertus Magnus II

1. Steiner, Rudolf, 1957, *Occult History*, Anthroposophical Publishing Company, London, p. 54.
2. Jordan of Saxony (*c.* 1190–1237), one of the first leaders of the Dominican order.
3. Dionysius the Areopagite, mentioned in the Acts of the Apostles (Acts 17:34). Nowadays, it has been determined that his books must have been written down several centuries later than the time of Dionysius the Areopagite and are therefore referred to as 'pseudo-Dionysius the Areopagite'.
4. Attributed to Magister Heinrich von Würzburg (until 1265), German poet, who probably knew Albertus from the time 1264–66 when Albertus was

staying in Würzburger at the Dominican monastery. In, Streit, Jakob, *Albertus Magnus: Am Wendekreis des abendländischen Denkens*, p. 43, translation by Rahel Kern.
5. Ulrich Engelbert von Strassburg (1225–77) joined the Dominican order at the age of 20 and became later one of the order's leaders.
6. *The Catholic Encyclopedia*, 1912, Laxton Publishing Company, London, vol. 14, p. 664.
7. Ibid. p. 667.
8. The polyptych was painted by Carlo Crivelli in 1476 to sit on the high altar of the church of San Domenico in Ascoli Piceno, eastern central Italy. It is composed of a central panel and eight smaller panels with saints, also in the National Gallery. Interestingly, the same altar piece also has panels showing St Catherine of Alexandria and St Dominic, both of which are also to be seen in the gallery.
9. Proverbs 9:1–6.
10. Flavius Magnus Aurelius Cassiodorus Senator, (*c.* 480–*c.* 575), commonly known as Cassiodorus, Roman senator, writer and monk.
11. Alcuin (*c.* 735–804), scholar, theologian, churchman, poet and teacher from York, England.
12. For more on the theme of metamorphosis, see Steiner, Rudolf, *The Bridge between Cosmic Spirituality and the Physical Constitution of Humans.*
13. Albertus Magnus, 1999, *On Animals*, John Hopkins University Press, London, p. 528.
14. *The Catholic Encyclopedia*, 1912, vol. 14, p. 264.

Theology as a Science

1. For Albertus Magnus theology is a branch of systematic knowledge and, indeed, the highest of all sciences. The science that deals with pure reason, which is in God, is the surest and most noble of sciences. Prologue to his *Summa Theologiae*, contained in Tomes XVII and XVIII of the *Opera Omnia*.

11 Albertus Magnus III

1. *C.* 624 BC–*c.* 546 BC.
2. Russell, Bertrand, 1945, *The History of Western Philosophy*, Routledge, London 1961, p. 25.
3. Born in Athens 427 BC.
4. Steiner, Rudolf, 1929, *Philosophy and Anthroposophy*, Anthroposophical Publishing Company, London, p. 16.
5. Steiner, Rudolf, *Mysterienwahrheiten und Weihnachtsimpulse—Alte Mythen und ihre Bedeutung.* Translation by Rahel Kern.
6. Steiner, Rudolf, *Die Stellung der Anthroposophie zur Philosophie*, translation by Rahel Kern.
7. Avicenna (Pur Sina), 980–1037, Persian polymath and Islamic philosopher

during the Islamic Golden Age. He wrote nearly 450 treatises on numerous subjects, and is known for his doctrine of illumination, a Muslim Aristotelian theory of knowledge.
8. Averroes (Ibn Rushd), 1126–98, Andalusian Muslim polymath, marks the climax of Muslim Aristotelianism. Often simply referred to as 'the commentator', he was among the foremost commentators on Aristiotle's work in Arabic.
9. Albertus' breadth of learning earned him a place in Dante's *Divine Comedy*, where Thomas Aquinas introduces him to Dante:

> My brother and master, of Cologne,
> neighbours me on the right: Albert his name,
> and Thomas, called Aquinas, is my own.

In, Alighieri, Dante, 1981, *The Divine Comedy*, Basil Blackwell, Oxford, *Paradiso*, X, 97–9, p. 589.
10. See Aristotle's *The Metaphysics*, VII-IX.
11. Steiner, Rudolf, *The Philosophy of Freedom*.
12. Steiner, Rudolf, *Knowledge of the Higher Worlds. How is it achieved?*
13. Albertus Magnus, *Summa* I, tr. 3, q. 15, c. 3, a. 3 (Ed Colon printed 1978, vol. 34), p. 81.
14. Aquinas, Thomas, 1912, *The Summa Theologica of St. Thomas Aquinas*, R & T Washbourne, London, first number, I question 1, article 1, reply 2, p. 3.
15. Ibid. first number, I q. 1.9ad2, p. 13.
16. Steiner, Rudolf, *Über Philosophie*, translation by Rahel Kern.
17. Steiner, Rudolf, 1929, *Philosophy and Anthroposophy*, Anthroposophial Publishing Company, London, p. 21.
18. Immanuel Kant (1724–1804), German philosopher and central figure in modern philosophy significantly influencing fields of philosophy until today.
19. Kant, Immanuel, 1887, *The Critique of Pure Reason*, George Bell and Sons, London, p. 6.
20. Steiner, Rudolf, 1929, *Philosophy and Anthroposophy*, Anthroposophical Publishing Company, London, p. 25.
21. Steiner, Rudolf, 1993, *Knowledge of the Higher Worlds, How is it Achieved?*, Rudolf Steiner Press, Bristol.
22. Steiner, Rudolf, 1964, *The Philosophy of Freedom*, Rudolf Steiner Press, London, pp. 92–3.

12 What was the Point of Gothic?

1. Steiner, Rudolf, 1947, *How does Mankind find the Christ again?* Lectures given in December 1918, p. 33.
2. Ibid.
3. See the reference to Carnuntum in Julius Caesar's *Gallic Wars*.
4. Querido, René, 1987, *The Golden Age of Chartres: The Teachings of a Mystery School and the Eternal Feminine*, Introduction *et passim*.

5. To refer only to 'soul and spirit' in this process is not intended to exclude any effect that also may have occurred in the etheric body.
6. The frequency of the *orantes* gesture in the images on the sarcophagi is highly suggestive of the spiritual awareness of those Christians who met together in the catacombs. See Heidenreich, Alfred, 1931, *passim*.
7. Steiner, Rudolf, 1956, *The Redemption of Thinking: A study in the philosophy of Thomas Aquinas*, translated and edited with an Introduction and Epilogue by A.P. Shepherd and Mildred Robertson Nicoll.

13   The Mission of Drama

1. Steiner, Rudolf, 1976, pp. 114–33.
2. Commencing 1413.
3. See Stevens, John, 'Medieval Drama' in, *The New Grove Dictionary of Music and Musicians*, vol. 12, pp. 21–58, Macmillan Publishers Limited, London 1980.
4. See Smodden, W.H., 'Liturgical Drama' in *New Oxford History of Music*, vol. 2, pp. 175–219, Oxford University Press, London 1984.
5. See Happe, Peter (Editor), 1975, *English Mystery Plays*, Penguin Books, London, pp. 9–35.
6. The new style of music pioneered by the Florentine Camerata, principally between 1577 and 1582.
7. His opera was first performed in Vienna on 5 October 1762.
8. Principally at the court of Louis XIV.
9. In the case of oratorio, the performing of popular works such as Handel's *Messiah, Israel in Egypt*, etc., Haydn's *Creation*, Mendelssohn's *Elijah* and Elgar's *The Dream of Gerontius*, by large choral societies, is a unique example of entertainment that enters popular culture not simply through people's *spectator consciousness*, as in theatre, film or 'Wimbledon', but through actual participation.
10. The example with which we started out on the present line of thought was the inception of conscience in Greek drama. This is a faculty which is deeply bound up with the ego. Despite their closer external link with Greek via Latin, it has been pointed out that modern Romance languages differentiate less between consciousness and conscience than those of Germanic origin. This, of course, is a philological point and is not necessarily reflected in the psyche of people who speak their respective language and their ability to feel the 'inward-biting' of conscience.
11. Though worthy, in other contexts, of more than a footnote, this is a pertinent place to mention Alexander Scriabin's concept for his last (planned) orchestral work, *Prometheus* (1910), which included in the score a 'clavier lumières', the part being written in ordinary musical notation with each note bringing into play a corresponding colour which should flood the audience. The work was designed for full symphony orchestra, piano, organ, choir and the colour keyboard. This *Gesamtkunstwerk* Scriabin thought of as a composition which would, through combining 'dancing, music, poetry, colours

and scents [...], induce a "supreme, final ecstasy" [in which] the physical plane of our consciousness would disappear and a world cataclysm would begin'. See Abraham, Gerald, 'The Apogee and Decline of Romanticism' in, *The New Oxford History of Music*, vol. X, p. 35.

15   Redemption of the Senses

1. Goethe, Johann Wolfgang von, 'On Natural Science in General' (Vol. 34, p. 1), in, *Readings in Goethean Science*, Biodynamic Literature, Wyoming, Rhode Island 1978, pp. 12–13.
2. Steiner, Rudolf, 1986, *The Gospel of St Mark*, Rudolf Steiner Press, London, p. 138.
3. Steiner, Rudolf, lecture of 31 December 1921, in, *Occult History*, Anthroposophical Publishing Company, London 1957, p. 82.
4. Steiner, Rudolf, lecture of 27 December 1910, in, *Occult History*, Anthroposophical Publishing Company, London 1957, p. 22.
5. Written by Thomas Aquinas around 1264 after a request for a new Mass of Corpus Christi.
6. Steiner, Rudolf, 1950, *The Spiritual Guidance of Man*, Anthroposophic Press Inc., p. 47.
7. Steiner, Rudolf, lecture of 31 December 1911, in, *Occult History*, Anthroposophical Publishing Company, London 1957, pp. 92–3.
8. Sease, Virginia, 'The Future Task of the English Language and The Mission of the English Speaking People', inserted into the *Anthroposophic Newsletter* 2011.
9. Barfield, Owen, 1928, *Speakers Meaning*, Faber and Faber, London, pp. 57–67.
10. Steiner-von Sivers, Marie, in her foreword to the first edition of Rudolf Steiner's *Speech Formation and Dramatic Art*, Dornach 1926, in, *Marie Steiner Esoteric Studies—The Flaming Word*, Temple Lodge, London 1993, p. 27.
11. Ibid. p. 24.
12. Ibid. p. 43.
13. Steiner, Rudolf, lecture of 9 November 1988, *Goethe as Founder of a New Science of Aesthetics*, Rudolf Steiner Publishing Company, London, no date, p. 47.
14. Steiner, Rudolf, 1975, *A Road to Self Knowledge*, Rudolf Steiner Press, London.
15. Steiner, Rudolf, 1975, *Anthroposophical Leading Thoughts*, Rudolf Steiner Press, London, p. 13.

16   The Karmic Background of Marie Steiner-von Sivers

1. See Welburn, Andrew, 1997, *The Mysteries: Rudolf Steiner's Writings on Spiritual Initiation*, p. 167 n. 29. 'Steiner was highly unusual in attributing to [Pherecydes of Syros] an important role in the emergence of thought, but

opinion has increasingly given him prominence. See the recent remarks of Schibli, H.S., *Pherecydes of Syros*, Oxford 1990.'
2. See Steiner, Rudolf, 1957, *Occult History*, p. 55. A fuller quote is given in Chapter 11.
3. Steiner, Rudolf, 1956, *The Redemption of Thinking: A study in the philosophy of Thomas Aquinas*, translated and edited with an Introduction and Epilogue by A.P. Shepherd and Mildred Robertson Nicoll.
4. 1998 Verlag Freies Geistesleben.
5. English translation 1994.
6. Tautz, Johannes, 1990, *W.J. Stein: A Biography*, p. 169.
7. Meyer, Thomas, 1994, *Ludwig Polzer-Hoditz: Ein Europäer*, Chapter 29.
8. See the biography written by his son, Zeylmans, Emanuel, *Willem Zeylmans van Emmichoven: An Inspiration for Anthroposophy*, p. 51.
9. See Kirchner-Bockholt, Margarete & Kirchner-Bockholt, Erich, 1977, *Rudolf Steiner's Mission and Ita Wegman*, p. 14 *et passim*.
10. See Hammacher, Wilfried, 1998, *Marie Steiner: Lebensspuren einer Individualität*, n. 24.
11. See Meyer, T.H., 2010, *Rudolf Steiner's Core Mission: the birth and development of spiritual-scientific karma research*, p. 135.

17 Summary and Conclusion

1. Rudolf Steiner, *An Autobiography*, Rudolf Steiner Publication, Blauvelt, New York, 1977, 1988, p. 360.
2. See Virginia Moore's 'Introduction' in, Steiner, Rudolf, 1964, *The Arts and Their Mission*, Anthroposophic Press, New York. From the context in which she writes, it is clear that with 'America' she is implying the Anglo-Saxon West: the USA and the UK.
3. Rudolf, Steiner, 1988, *Correspondence and Documents 1901–1925*, Rudolf Steiner Press, London, pp. 44–5.
4. See Weisberger, Hella, 1989, *Marie Steiner-von Sivers—Ein Leben für die Anthroposophie*, Rudolf Steiner Studien Band 1, Rudolf Steiner Verlag Dornach/Schweiz, p. 233. This foreword was included in the 1st edition of *Anthroposophical Leading Thoughts* and did not, in fact, appear in German until 1935.
5. Rudolf, Steiner, 1988, *Correspondence and Documents 1901–1925*, pp. 35–6.
6. Meyer, T.H., 2010, Temple Lodge Publishing Company, Forest Row, pp. 119f, quoted from: *Mathilde Scholl und die Geburt der Anthroposophischen Gesellschaft 1912/13*, Ekkehard Meffert, Philosophisch-Anthroposophischer Verlag am Goetheanum, p. 122.
7. Selg, Peter, 2006, Verlag am Goetheanum, *Marie Steiner-von Sivers*, p. 106, letter of 2 February 1914.
8. Steiner, Rudolf, 1956, *Karmic Relationships*, vol. 2, Anthroposophic Publishing Company, London, p. 86. Lecture of 27 April 1924.

9. See Páleš, Emil, 2009, *Seven Archangels: Rhythms of Inspiration in the History of Culture and Nature*, Sophia, Bratislava, p. 171.
10. Steiner, Rudolf and Steiner-von Sivers, Marie, *Correspondence and Documents 1901–1925*, p. 263.
11. See Steiner, Rudolf, 1953, *Cosmic Christianity and the Impulse of Michaël*, Anthroposophical Publishing Company, London, pp. 34–40. Lecture of 21 August 1924.

The Stars Spake Once to Man

1. Steiner, Rudolf, 1961, *Verses and Meditations*, Anthroposophical Publishing Company, London, p. 97.

Bibliography

Abraham, Gerald, 'The Apogee and Decline of Romanticism', in *The New Oxford History of Music,* London 1974

Albertus Magnus, *On Animals,* translated by K.F. Kitchell and I.M. Resnik, John Hopkins University Press, London 1999

Alighieri, Dante, *The Divine Comedy,* Translated by G.L. Bickersteth, Basil Blackwell, Oxford 1981

Anderson, W., 'Muses', in *The New Grove Dictionary of Music and Musicians,* Macmillan Publishers Limited, London 1980

Aquinas, Thomas, *The Summa Theologica of St. Thomas Aquinas,* R&T Washbourne, London 1912, first number QQ I–XXVI

Aquinas, Thomas, *The Summa Theologica of St. Thomas Aquinas,* R&T Washbourne, London 1912, second number QQ XXVII–LXXIV

Aristotle, *The Works of Aristotle,* translated under the editorship of W.D. Ross, Oxford Clarendon Press, 1928

Aristotle, *The Metaphysics,* translated by H. Tredennick, Harvard University Press, 1935

Barfield, Owen, *Speakers Meaning,* Faber and Faber, London 1928

Bishop of Nikiu, John, *The Chronicle of John Bishop of Nikiu,* translated by R.H. Charles, Oxford University Press. 1916

Blaxland-de Lange, Simon, *Owen Barfield: Romanticism comes of Age—A Biography,* Temple Lodge Publishing, Forest Row 2006

Bock, Emil, *The Life and Times of Rudolf Steiner,* Floris Books, Edinburgh 2008

Charpentier, Louis, *The Mysteries of Chartres Cathedral,* Robert Laffont, Paris 1980

Chesterton, G.K., *St Thomas Aquinas,* Hodder and Stoughton, London 1943

Goethe, Johann Wolfgang von, *On Natural Science in General,* in *Readings in Goethean Science,* complied by Herbert H. Koepf and Linda S. Jolly, BioDynamic Literature, Wyoming Rhode Island 1978

Grosse, Erdmuth Johannes, *Das Rätsel des Urvorstandes,* Verlag am Goetheanum, 2008

Hammacher, Wilfried, *Marie Steiner—Lebensspuren einer Individualität,* Verlag Freies Geistesleben, 1998

Hanbury, Frederick J., 'The Rock Garden at Brockhurst' *The Garden,* 16 February 1924

Heidenreich, Alfred, *The Catacombs,* The Christian Community Press, London 1931

Kant, Immanuel, *The Critique of Pure Reason,* translated by J.M.D. Meiklejohn, George Bell and Sons, London 1887

Kiersch, Johannes, *A History of the School of Spiritual Science,* Temple Lodge Publishing, Forest Row 2006

Kirchner-Bockholt, Margarete and Erich, *Rudolf Steiner's Mission and Ita Wegman,* Rudolf Steiner Press, London 1977

Masters, Brien, *Mozart: His Musical Style and his Role in the Development of Human Consciousness,* Temple Lodge Publications, Forest Row 2006

Masters, Brien, 'On the Sands with Printless Foot', in *Keynotes in Life and Work,* Perevale Publications, Forest Row 2009

Meyer, T.H., *D.N. Dunlop: A Man of our Time,* Temple Lodge Publishing, London 1992

Meyer, Thomas, *Ludwig Polzer-Hoditz: Ein Europäer,* Perseus Verlag, Basel 1994

Meyer, T.H., *Rudolf Steiner's Core Mission: The Birth and Development of Spiritual-Scientific Karma Research,* Temple Lodge Publishing, Forest Row 2010

Ovid, *Metamorphoses,* Harvard University Press, Cambridge Massachusetts 1984

Páleš, Emil, *Seven Archangels: Rhythms of Inspiration in the History of Culture and Nature,* Sophia, Bratislava 2009

Pieper, Josef, *Scholastik—Gestalten und Probleme der mittelalterlichen Philosophie,* St Benno Verlag GmbH, Leipzig 1960

Poeppig, Fred, *Marie Steiner—Ein Leben im Dienst der Wiedergeburt des Wortes,* R.G. Zbinden & Co. Verlag, Basel 1949

Querido, René, *The Golden Age of Chartes: The Teachings of a Mystery School and the Eternal Feminine,* Floris Books, Edinburgh 1987

Russell, Bertrand, *History of Western Philosophy,* Routledge, London 1961

Savitch, Marie, *Marie Steiner-von Sivers: Fellow Worker with Rudolf Steiner,* Rudolf Steiner Press, London 1967

Scheeben, Heribert Christian, *Albertus Magnus,* Bonner Buchgemeinde, 1955

Sease, Virginia, 'The Future Task of the English Language and The Mission of the English Speaking People', *Anthroposophic Newsletter,* 2011

Selg, Peter, *Marie Steiner-von Sivers—Aufbau und Zukunft des Werkes von Rudolf Steiner,* Verlag am Goetheanum, 2006

Socrates Scholasticus, *The Ecclesiastical History of Socrates—Comprising a History of the Church in Seven Books,* translated by Valesius, George Bells and Sons, London 1884

Steiner, Marie, *Esoteric Studies: The Flaming Word,* complied and translated by Crispian Villeneuve, Temple Lodge Publishing, London 1993

Steiner, Rudolf, *A Road to Self Knowledge,* Rudolf Steiner Press, London 1975, GA 16

Steiner, Rudolf, *Art in the Light of Mystery Wisdom,* Rudolf Steiner Press, London 1970, GA 275

Steiner, Rudolf, *Anthroposophical Leading Thoughts,* Rudolf Steiner Press, London 1975, GA 26

Steiner, Rudolf, *Background to the Gospel of St Mark,* Rudolf Steiner Press, London 1968, GA 124

Steiner, Rudolf, *Conferences with the Teachers at the Waldorf School Stuttgart 1921–1922,* Steiner Schools Fellowship Publications, Forest Row 1987, GA 300a

Steiner, Rudolf, *Conferences with the Teachers at the Waldorf School Stuttgart 1923–1924,* Steiner Schools Fellowship Publications, Forest Row 1989, GA 300c

Steiner Rudolf, *Cosmic Christianity and the Impulse of Michaël*, Anthroposophical Publishing Company, 1953, GA 242

Steiner, Rudolf, 'Die Stellung der Anthroposophie zur Philosophie', in *Die Beantwortung von Welt-und Lebensfragen durch Anthroposophie*, not fully translated into English, GA 108

Steiner, Rudolf, *Goethe as Founder of a New Science of Aesthetics*, Rudolf Steiner Publishing Company, London, no date, GA 30

Steiner, Rudolf, *How can Mankind find the Christ again?*, Anthroposophic Press Inc., New York 1947, GA 187

Steiner, Rudolf, *Karmic Relationships*, Vol. 3 Anthroposophical Publishing Company, London 1957, GA 237

Steiner, Rudolf, *Knowledge of the Higher Worlds, How is it Achieved?*, Rudolf Steiner Press, Bristol 1993, GA 10

Steiner, Rudolf, *Mysterienwahrheiten und Weihnachtsimpulse—Alte Mythen und ihre Bedeutung*, not fully translated into English, GA 180

Steiner, Rudolf, *Occult History*, Anthroposophical Publishing Company, London 1957, GA 126

Steiner, Rudolf, *Philosophy and Anthroprosophy*, Anthroposophical Publishing Company, London 1929, GA 35

Steiner, Rudolf, *Philosophy of Freedom*, Rudolf Steiner Press, London 1964, GA 4

Steiner, Rudolf, *Redemption of Thinking*, Hodder and Stoughton, London 1956, GA 74

Steiner, Rudolf, *Riddles of Philosophy*, Anthroposophic Press, Spring Valley 1973, GA 18

Steiner, Rudolf, *Rosicrucian Esotericism*, Anthroposophic Press, New York, 1978 GA 109

Steiner, Rudolf, *Self-Education: Autobiographical Reflections, 1861–1893*, Mercury Press, Spring Valley, NY 1985

Steiner, Rudolf, *Speech and Drama,* Anthroposophical Publishing Company, London 1960, GA 282

Steiner, Rudolf, *The Bridge between Cosmic Spirituality and the Physical Constitution of Humans*, Anthroprosophic Press, 1958, GA 202

Steiner, Rudolf, *The Easter Festival in the Evolution of the Mysteries*, Rudolf Steiner Press, London 1988, GA 233a

Steiner, Rudolf, *The Gospel of St Mark*, Rudolf Steiner Press, London 1986, GA 139.

Steiner, Rudolf, *The Spiritual Guidance of Man*, Anthroprosophic Press Inc., 1950, GA 15

Steiner, Rudolf, *The Story of my Life*, Anthroposophic Press, New York 1999, GA 28

Steiner, Rudolf, *True and False Paths in Spiritual Investigation*, Anthroposophical Publishing Company, London 1927 GA 243

Steiner, Rudolf, *Über Philosophie*, not fully translated into English, GA 108

Steiner, Rudolf, *Verses and Meditations,* Anthroposophical Publishing Company, London 1953

Steiner, Rudolf and Steiner-von Sivers, Marie, *Correspondence and Documents 1901–1925*, Rudolf Steiner Press, London 1988, GA 262

Steiner, Rudolf and Steiner-von Sivers, Marie, *Poetry and the Art of Speech,* The London School of Speech Formation in association with Rudolf Steiner Press, London 1981, GA 281

Streit, Jakob, *Albertus Magnus: Am Wendekreis des abendländischen Denkens*, Verlag Freies Geistesleben, Stuttgart 1982

Stevens, John, 'Medieval Drama', in *The New Grove Dictionary of Music and Musicians,* Macmillan Publishers Limited, London 1980

Synesius Cyrene, *The Letters of Synesius*, translated by A. Fitzgerald, Oxford University Press, 1926

Synesius Cyrene, *The Essays and Hymns of Synesius of Cyrene*, Oxford University Press, London 1930

Tautz, Johannes, *Walter Johannes Stein: A Biography*, Temple Lodge Publishing, London 1990

The Catholic Encyclopedia, in 15 Volumes, Laxton Publishing Company, London 1912

Turgeniev, Assya, *Reminiscences of Rudolf Steiner and the Work on the First Goetheanum*, Temple Lodge Publishing, London 2003

Unattributed, *Gedenkblatt für Marie Steiner*, Marie Steiner Verlag, 2004

Van Manen, Hans Peter, *Marie Steiner: Her Place in World Karma*, Temple Lodge Publishing, London 1995

Welburn, Andrew, *The Beginnings of Christianity: Essene Mystery, Gnostic Revelation and the Christian Vision*, Floris Books, Edinburgh 1991

Welburn, Andrew, *The Mysteries,* Floris Books, Edinburgh 1997

Weisberger, Hella, *Marie Steiner von Sivers—Ein Leben für die Anthroposophie*, Rudolf Steiner Studien Band 1, Rudolf Steiner Verlag, Dornach/Schweiz 1989

Woloschin, Margarita, *The Green Snake: Life Memories*, Floris Books, Edinburgh 2010

Villeneuve, Crispin, *Rudolf Steiner in Br...*, Volume I, 19... ...ne II, *1922–1925*, Temple Lodge Press, 2004

Zeylmans, Emanuel, *Willem Zeylmans van Emmichoven: An Inspiration for Anthroposophy*, Temple Lodge Publishing, Forest Row 2002